SEEING EVIL

JASON PARENT

Unlocking New Worlds

ISBN-13: 978-1-940215-49-5
ISBN-10: 1940215498

Red Adept Publishing, LLC
104 Bugenfield Court
Garner, NC 27529
http://RedAdeptPublishing.com/

Cover and Formatting: Streetlight Graphics

CHAPTER 1

"**W**HAT'S THAT KID STILL DOING here?" Samantha asked. She wasn't a mother and had no desire to be, but she couldn't believe anyone, and particularly not her officers, would leave a child surrounded by blood and death. A crime scene was no place for a three-year-old. And since it was her crime scene, the boy was her responsibility.

"When we tried to move him, he screamed so loud," Officer Ronald Tagliamonte said. He and his partner had been the first responding officers, and they had locked the small apartment down tightly. Samantha appreciated that, but they should have done something with the kid.

"I thought my eardrums were going to burst," he continued. "I just touched his shoulder. It was awful, a high-pitched whine, the kind that can break glass. Anyway, we thought he was special needs with the way he's been rocking and all, so we figured DCF would know what to do with him. A social worker should be here soon."

"Let me get this straight. You two idiots can take down armed assailants, handcuff all sorts of scumbags and murderers, but you were too scared to move a screaming kid away from a crime scene?"

Since her promotion to the Fall River Police Department's Major Crimes Division last April, Samantha had already seen a few homicides. Before that, while working narcotics, she had been called to hundreds more crime scenes. As an officer before that, she'd seen thousands. Never once had she left a toddler sitting next to a dead body.

To make matters worse, the corpse wasn't just any old dead body. That particular individual had gone violently, his brain splattering the wall and ceiling behind him. The nickel-sized hole in the ceiling was lined with what looked a little like raspberry yogurt. Samantha glanced at the child. She was a cop, not a babysitter. The boy, with baby-fat arms and stubby fingers, sat hunched over his crossed legs next to the headboard of a queen-sized bed, facing the far wall. One body was splayed out on the carpet not more than a few feet behind the boy, near the bedroom's entrance. Another two lay in the bed to his left. The intimate and brutal affairs of the dead surrounded him.

Samantha wondered if the boy understood murder or even death. She stared at him sadly, thankful he had tuned out. She hoped that wherever his thoughts were, they brought him happiness.

Poor kid. He's going to need a ton of counseling. Then, switching off her emotions as easily as turning a dial, Samantha became Detective Reilly: detached, confident, and prepared. But she still realized some emotions couldn't be shut off forever.

"Someone get that kid a helmet before he cracks his head against the wall," she shouted at no one in particular.

She turned her attention to the bodies. Reconstructing the past few hours in that room fell far short of a challenge. Her analytical mind opened and closed the case in a matter of seconds. A man and woman slumped naked in bed, blemished by an excessive number of bullet holes. Another man, fully clothed, formed a crumpled mess near the base of the bed. A single shot had exited the back of his skull. His face was still intact, no entry wound evident. The bullet could only have gone in through his mouth.

"Husband?" Samantha asked, pointing at the man on the floor, whose brain matter was staining the carpet. She was sure she already knew the answer.

"Yes," Officer Tagliamonte responded. "Mark Florentine, age thirty-six. According to the neighbor who called in the gunshots, Florentine and his wife, Alice, were separated," he said, extending a pen toward the woman in bed.

"And the other man?"

"James Whittaker. We don't know much about him yet other than the information obtained from his license. We found that in his wallet, which was in a pocket of those pants on the floor beside the end table."

"Well, you don't need me for this one." Samantha removed her latex gloves and stuffed them into her pockets. She buttoned up her long overcoat. "Florentine shot his wife and her lover before turning the gun on himself. Classic murder-suicide. The motive is obvious. Given the number of bullets he plugged into those two, Florentine must have come here with one purpose only. That or he suspected they would be here together and he caught them in the act. He even reloaded to shoot them some more before turning the gun on himself."

"Ouch," Tagliamonte said. "The barrel must have been scalding."

"The least of his worries," Samantha said dispassionately. She had all but closed the case, yet a nagging thought kept her from leaving. "Where's the gun?"

"We haven't found it yet."

"It can't be far. It probably just slid under the bed. When you find it, bag it for fingerprints. We can't leave any question concerning Florentine's guilt, even on a case as clear-cut as this. Write up the report when you get back to the station, and I'll approve it."

Samantha stepped away from the officer. She'd chosen to be a warrior against the depravity of humankind, but that didn't mean she enjoyed witnessing its imbalanced illustrations. Her past had led to her present, for better or for worse.

"What about the kid?" Tagliamonte asked.

Samantha had already forgotten the boy. Once she switched into detective mode, he had become inconsequential. He simply wasn't critical to her analysis of the crime. Samantha tried not to glance in his direction, knowing that to do so would be a mistake, but she couldn't stop herself. From where she stood, she could make out much of the left side of his face and body. Pity surged through her.

The boy rocked rhythmically in front of the wall as if he were a pendulum, never wavering. She squinted, straining to see what he stared at so intently, but saw only a blank wall, off-white paint lined with cracks. He never blinked, never broke his rhythm. Samantha could no longer leave his present care to the tardy Massachusetts Department of Children and Families, if DCF was better qualified to deal with the boy's obviously fragile psyche.

"What's his name?" she asked.

"Michael Florentine."

Samantha approached the boy. "Michael?" If he heard, he didn't react. Samantha walked over to the spot on the wall upon which he seemed fixated. She wondered what could be going through the toddler's undeveloped mind and whether she really wanted to distract Michael from it. She half expected to see Jesus's face etched in the wall's cracks, or some kind of optical illusion. Instead, she just saw faded paint.

"Is he autistic?" she asked.

"Don't know."

Samantha turned around to face the boy. She crouched beside him and waved her hand in front of his face. The boy straightened.

"Oh my God! Tagliamonte, you fool. He's got blood all over his hands and between his legs. Get an EMT in here now, for fuck's sake."

Stepping back so as not to alarm the child, Samantha scanned Michael for wounds, but she couldn't find the source of the blood. She hoped it wasn't Michael's, but she saw no evidence, no tracks or prints, that suggested Michael had been anywhere near the bodies. *Then again, shouldn't he be in a crib or something? What's he doing in here? There's no part of this that he should have been forced to witness.*

Samantha moved in for a closer look. His hands rested on his thighs, the blood on them dry and cracking on his skin. Something protruded from beneath them, something dark and metallic.

Samantha gasped. "Michael, don't move, okay?"

Michael seemed oblivious to her presence, swaying to a beat only he could hear. It was as though she wasn't part of the world he was seeing. Slowly, she reached for the object with the caution of one taking a bone from a snarling dog. Only Michael wasn't snarling. He seemed uninterested in her, still rocking and staring blankly through her, unblinking and locked on that same focal point.

Maybe he's in shock. Maybe he does understand what happened here. His unresponsiveness was certainly beyond mere willful ignorance. Samantha didn't think he would notice if she lit a firecracker in front of him. He seemed out of touch with reality. For the moment, Samantha preferred him that way.

With a hand as steady as a surgeon's, Samantha reached for the pistol Michael was huddled over like a bear protecting her cub. She avoided contact with him, fearful of what would happen if she disturbed his trancelike state. Her fingers treaded over the barrel, searching for its grip.

She pulled the handgun, a black Smith & Wesson M&P 9mm, from beneath Michael. The barrel brushed against his thigh. With cold, empty eyes bulging open like those of the drowning, Michael gazed into Samantha's. She felt exposed, as if with only a look, the child could delve into the recesses of her mind, revealing her every secret. The thought terrified her. So did Michael.

With reflexes beyond one of his age, Michael grabbed the gun with both hands. Samantha quickly pulled it away. Unnerved as she was, she still had Michael's safety at the forefront of her mind. She removed the weapon from the boy's reach, at all times conscious of its threat. When she found the safety smeared in blood, she clicked it on and breathed a sigh of relief. As she'd expected, there had been a bullet in the chamber. She dropped the gun into an open evidence bag held by Tagliamonte.

Michael's eyes remained on her. They were blue and cloudy like the sky before a rainbow, a fire as bright as the sun burning behind them. His mouth creaked open as though tiny gears controlled its laborious motion. When his chin dropped so low it nearly rested on his throat, a sound, low and indistinguishable at first, emitted from somewhere deep within the boy. As it amplified, its sharp clamor made Samantha's blood ice within her veins.

At once, Samantha knew that not only did Michael comprehend what had happened to his parents, but also that he felt it in the worst sort of way. His wail was ghostly and ghastly, the cry of one seized by agony. Samantha was afraid, both for him and of him, and of what such trauma might cause him to become. Backing away, not knowing how to comfort the lost child, Samantha knew it would not be the last she would see of Michael.

CHAPTER 2

Eleven years later.

HER ORANGE SODA GLIDED OVER the tabletop and onto her lap. Tessa had tried to catch the plastic cup as soon as it tipped, but she was too late. Most of the liquid in the nearly full cup made its way free, cascading across the table's smooth wooden surface as she fumbled.

Tessa's blue jeans were soaked. The soda dripped onto her chair, but so far, the tile floor had been spared. She wondered if it would be any consolation. As she stared at the mess in her lap, Tessa's horror grew. Her breathing quickened, and her heart pounded behind her breasts. Her knee bounced, banging against the table leg and rattling their empty plates. She stiffened her leg, willing it to stop, but it refused to obey. Silverware tinkled as if exposed to a tiny earthquake, vibrating in time with Tessa's every cell. Wisps of her strawberry-blond hair clung to the sweat on her forehead.

Fear assailed her, unrelenting. Her mind submitted to it. She was too scared to move, fearing that she might spread the mess to the floor. But she couldn't sit still either, knowing her inaction would only provoke further hostility. Tessa couldn't guess how he thought she should act, but whatever she did was sure to be wrong.

Most of all, Tessa feared making eye contact with him. Those eyes gave no hint of the mechanisms operating behind them. Her inability to read them made her suspect the worst, but he usually showed her that the worst she could imagine was a great deal better than what he had in store.

A proper lady would never have spilled the soda in the first place, Father would say. As she sat and did nothing, the soda continued to drip onto her pants. It seeped through the fabric, the syrupy fizz chilling her thighs and wetting her underwear. Those would have to be cleaned, too. Oh God, what a mess!

I am not a proper lady. Her body trembled more violently. She buried her face in her hands.

"Well," Father said, his voice emotionless yet firm. His was a tone she had long ago learned to dread. "What do you have to say for yourself?"

"I'm sorry," Tessa blurted, and she meant it. She was sorry for the response her negligence would provoke. "I—"

"You're sorry? That's it? That's all you have to say? Does 'I'm sorry' excuse all the soda you've wasted or the mess you've made? Does being sorry clean it up? And look at yourself, Tessa." He *tsk*ed then glared at her, his eyes daring her to respond. She knew better.

"You're soaked. It's disgraceful." Father said the words with disdain.

She wondered why he hated her so much. She obeyed every rule, followed every command, even those she knew to be wrong. And having lived alone with him for half of her fifteen years, she had seen plenty wrong. Her life was like walking on a tightrope through a hurricane. Always demanding perfection, Father set her up to fail. And when she did, a spark lit behind his deadpan eyes. Tessa wondered if it was pleasure.

She raised her head, hopeful she would not see that spark, but there it was.

"Well, I suppose we need to get you cleaned up," he said.

"No, Father, please." Tessa started to sob. She knew begging was useless, but that didn't stop her from trying. Maybe this time would be different. She had to hope it would be. Fooling herself gave her strength. Imagining the alternative was far more terrifying. "I'll clean it up. I'll buy us more soda."

Father seemed to think it over, and for a moment, Tessa's hope became real. But the moment was as fleeting as Father's mercy.

He leaped from his chair like a man possessed. "Come here."

Tessa cringed. She tucked her elbows into her sides and shrank behind her forearms, shielding herself from Father's anger. But her arms wouldn't stop him. Nothing ever did.

Father grabbed her wrist and wrenched her from her chair. He dragged her into the hall, Tessa only partly on her feet. The heels of her sneakers scraped along the carpet until one caught and freed itself from her foot. She envied that sneaker. It had escaped where she would not, no matter how much she tried.

And yet she tried. She had to. Her fingers found the doorframe as Father pulled her into the bathroom. Her nails dug into the wood, and she held on with all the power in her small frame. But Father easily yanked her free, and she stumbled backward into the room. She screamed as two of her fingernails stayed behind.

Father threw her to the floor, her head just missing a collision with the porcelain toilet. He stepped around her and slammed the door shut. He returned swiftly, and before Tessa could react, his hands were around her neck, lifting her off the floor. He swung her to his left, toward the bathtub. The side of her calf hit the rim of the tub with a thud. Her momentum carried her upper body forward. She ricocheted off the far wall and collapsed into the tub, banging her head and hip against the cold fiberglass as she fell. Catching beneath her, the shower curtain tore from some of its rings, hanging like overalls attached at one suspender.

Seated in the bath, Tessa pulled her knees up against her breasts. The cold soda dampened her T-shirt, and to her further humiliation, her nipples hardened. Her face warmed, and she buried her head between her wobbly knees. Blood from her fingers streaked her jeans. She cried, wishing she was bigger and stronger, or simply any place but there. With him.

The room fell silent. Maybe he had finished punishing her and Tessa would get off easy this time. She reached for the side of the tub. Her head rang and her hip throbbed, and she winced as she started to rise. Looking up, she saw Father glaring at her.

"Sit down," Father commanded.

Tessa did as she was told. She knew enough not to hesitate or question. To disobey meant a punishment far worse than whatever Father had planned.

Father closed the drain and turned on the water. He didn't seem to care that Tessa was fully clothed. Furiously, he turned the hot water until he couldn't turn it any farther. He never touched the knob for the cold water.

Realizing his intentions, Tessa retreated as far as she could against the back of the tub, tucking her heels against her butt. The tub quickly began to fill. Steam rose from the water as it flowed from the faucet.

Even through the denim fabric, Tessa's bottom began to burn. She tucked one sneakered foot beneath the other, but soon the hot water crept in through the leather. The searing steadily crept up her legs and torso with the rising water. She bore it for as long as she could.

"It's too hot! Please, Father. It's too hot!"

She tried to stand, but Father grabbed a handful of her hair and drove her back down. Her rubber soles slipped along the tub floor, and she slid down into the water. It turned her exposed skin a deep red.

The tub continued to fill. Tessa continued to scream.

CHAPTER 3

MICHAEL TURCOTTE UNBUCKLED HIS BELT, unbuttoned his jeans, and let them drop around his ankles. He glanced behind him at the seat, hoping it was clean. He saw no streaks or nasty liquids. Normally, he would paper it three times over, but he had no time for daintiness. His cheeks were clenched tighter than a nun's legs. He hastily pulled down his boxers and lowered himself onto the toilet seat.

School was the last place a small fish like Michael wanted to let loose. The bigger fish were always circling, targeting the weak and the helpless. He couldn't think of another place where he felt so vulnerable, so exposed. But sometimes, it just couldn't be helped, so it was best to do it as quickly and as silently as possible.

The restroom had been empty except for one boy, another freshman named Jimmy Rafferty. Jimmy had made eye contact with Michael as he entered, nodded, and let out a sigh of relief when he had seen that Michael wasn't a threat. From the entrance, the urinals were on the right, the sinks on the left, and the stalls along the back wall. Jimmy had hurried to finish his business at a urinal—Michael assumed for the same reasons he was in a hurry—and had headed across Michael's path to wash his hands as he shuffled toward a stall.

Michael squirmed on the throne, waiting for Jimmy to exit the restroom. He feared that if he let his bowels loosen, he would release a booming burst of wind as last night's supper exited his colon. As a high school freshman in an unfamiliar school, he was only beginning to develop his identity within his class. The last thing he needed was to be known as the loud farter or something equally stupid. So he clenched his cheeks a bit longer, hoping Jimmy would hurry.

The restroom door creaked open. Assuming it was Jimmy leaving, Michael started to relax. He listened for that wonderful sound of the door closing, leaving him in blissful solitude.

"Excuse me, Glenn," Jimmy said, his voice trembling.

Not Glenn. Michael leaned forward and checked the lock to the stall. All that stood between him and the worst bully Carnegie High School had to offer was a cylindrical metal latch secured in a flimsy rusted casing. He lifted his legs, hoping to make himself invisible to anyone peeking under the door. Then, he closed his eyes and prayed.

Please, God. Not now. Not when I'm like this.

Michael hadn't yet fallen victim to Glenn's cruelty, but he'd seen it go unpunished nearly every day at lunch. He knew his time would come sooner or later, but he would have given anything for that time to be anytime other than the present.

"That's Mr. Rodrigues to you, shit for brains."

Ugh. Michael recognized that burly voice. Glenn was bad enough alone, but with his posse, he gave new meaning to the term "mean-spirited." And Robbie Wilkins, the voice's owner, put might behind Glenn's malevolence. A sophomore whose growth spurt had hit early and never stopped, Robbie was all brawn and no brains, easily manipulated muscle. His size alone made him ripe for enlistment as one of Glenn's henchmen. His unquestioning loyalty made him a vicious puppet.

"I got this, Robbie," Glenn said. "You just stick to what you do best."

"So what's the plan for this punk? Make him lick the toilet? Eat a pube? They don't call those things urinal cakes for nothing. Who doesn't like cake? You like cake, don't you, you little motherfucker?"

And there's the third. With Glenn and Robbie, Ryan Taylor was never far behind. Like Glenn, Ryan was a junior but much smaller, 105 pounds fully clothed and after Thanksgiving dinner. Without his partners in crime, Ryan wasn't much of a threat—all bark, no bite. Michael never understood how Ryan had made it into Glenn's gang; his wickedness was his only noticeable contribution.

"This freshman's taller than you, Ry," Robbie said.

"Yeah? What's your point, meathead?" Ryan asked.

"I'm a meathead? Your mother gives my meat good head."

"Okay, okay, settle down, boys," Glenn said. "You're scaring our new friend here. You don't have to be scared of us, kid. We were just teasing. What's your name?"

Glenn's friendly act wasn't fooling Michael. He doubted it was fooling Jimmy. His classmate was in some serious trouble. He had broken a cardinal rule: always call Glenn "Mr. Rodrigues" or "sir." Freshmen learned that even before they learned who their teachers would be.

Michael wondered how Jimmy could have messed up so badly. His heart bled for his fellow freshman. He put his feet down and started to rise when he noticed he was shaking. Ashamed, he sat back down. Jimmy was on his own.

Without Glenn, the gang was a snake without its head, no better than a band of mindless thugs. Glenn was the real threat. He was smart and could have had a bright future had he not wasted his intelligence on developing ways to torment those weaker than him. A delinquent with a soul blacker than night and a conscience empty enough to turn a blind eye to his every evil inclination, Glenn was the bane of all underclassmen. With shifty eyes and a sinister grin lined by sporadic stubble, he would dole out punishment indiscriminately.

And it was Jimmy Rafferty's turn to be punished.

Frail and nerdy and a ginger kid to boot, Jimmy had taken enough abuse from his own classmates, the usual high school hazing. But the hazing Glenn applied was never of the usual variety. Jimmy was defenseless against the brutes who harassed him in the bathroom. Michael wanted desperately to help him, to muster all his courage and rush to his classmate's aid, to face might with might without consideration of the consequences.

But there were always consequences, and Michael couldn't ignore them. He was scared. Any help he offered would only redirect Glenn's wrath toward him. Right or wrong, Michael wasn't prepared to face that wrath. Feeling low, he sat quietly and did nothing, hating himself for it.

"Well?" Glenn prodded. Some of the pleasantness had retreated from his voice. "I asked you a question, kid."

"J-Jimmy... sir. Mr. Rodrigues, sir."

"Well, Jimmy," Glenn said loudly. "Nice to meet ya." He laughed, the kind of laugh that seemed touched by insanity. Michael didn't know if it was genuine or if Glenn was merely being theatrical. Either way, the sound sent shivers down his spine.

"Now, J-J-J-Jimmy," Glenn continued. "You do know that it is polite to address your elders as 'sir,' don't you?"

"I'm sorry, Mr. Rodrigues, sir," Jimmy said, his voice breaking. Michael could almost feel his trembling. "It won't happen again, sir."

"That's right. It won't." Glenn's easy tone was misleading, the calm before the storm. "Robbie, put him in the urinal."

"Sure thing," Robbie answered. "Sorry, kid. This ain't your lucky day."

Michael couldn't see much. His vision of the happenings outside his stall was limited to vertical slivers where the door was hinged to the stall's left wall and at the opposite side of the door, where it latched into the stall's right wall. Through this latter crack, Michael saw Jimmy backing toward the sinks. He looked ready to wet himself. Michael almost laughed when the thought crossed his mind that at least Jimmy was in the right place for it. Guilt immediately followed.

Robbie came into view, his face void of emotion. Jimmy shrank between two sinks.

"No." He held his hands up in front of him.

Robbie grabbed Jimmy's shirt at the shoulder, stretching out the collar. Jimmy sank deeper between the sinks. The oversized brute was too big to squeeze in after him, so he crouched and reached underneath the sinks for Jimmy's legs. Jimmy kicked but only succeeded in making his leg easier for Robbie to grab. Robbie dragged him by his ankle across the filthy floor. The vultures circled.

Fight them, you idiot. Stand up for yourself. Michael wanted to believe the world was ideal, that if Jimmy proved himself brave and virtuous, some karma god would see justice done. But Jimmy didn't even try to flee, much less fight back. He seemed resigned to his fate.

Robbie stood over Jimmy. He bent over and jabbed his meaty hands into Jimmy's armpits, then scooped up the smaller boy as if he were as light as a doll. He turned and carried him beyond Michael's view out of the door crack but reappeared a second later through the hinge crack on Michael's left, still carrying Jimmy toward the urinals. Repulsed, Michael watched as Robbie pressed Jimmy's back into a urinal. Ryan ran over to them and flushed the urinal repeatedly, sending waterfall after waterfall down the back of Jimmy's shirt. Glenn watched, never so much as getting a finger dirty.

Jimmy looked sheepish, defeated. Michael hoped the kid wasn't about to cry. Crying would make things worse for him. Robbie remained quiet, robotic, while Glenn and Ryan laughed hysterically.

"Enjoy the rest of your day, freshman," Glenn said. "And remember, if you tell anyone who did this to you, you're dead."

Robbie released Jimmy, who bolted for the door. His sneakers squeaked and squished with every step. Michael heard a muffled thump, followed by a yelp from Jimmy and more laughter from Ryan. Michael guessed the bastard had kicked Jimmy on his way out.

"Jerks," Michael muttered. He slapped a hand over his mouth. *Stupid.*

The bathroom went eerily silent. Michael's anxiety caused his bowels to loosen. He could no longer hold in what needed to come out. His fecal matter hit the water with a plop and a muted splash. A few footsteps approached the stall. Michael froze more solid than a glacier. Silence returned, and for a moment, he tried to believe he was safe.

With a violent crash, the stall door swung open. It slammed into his knee, and Michael winced as sharp pain shot through his leg. When he looked up, Glenn was glaring at him. The smile on Glenn's face spoke volumes. More pain would come.

"What do we have here?" Glenn asked. "Another victim?"

Michael's rage boiled over. "Screw you!"

"So, the dog bares his teeth," Glenn said, his smile widening into a thin curl. "But does he have any bite?"

Robbie loomed behind him, blocking the light and the exit. Michael couldn't see Ryan, but he knew he was there somewhere, waiting for his turn to strike.

The evil thoughts forming in Glenn's brain played out upon his face. Cornered and half-naked, Michael had nowhere to go. He reached for his jeans' waistband, but Glenn got to it first. He yanked Michael off the seat. Michael flailed his arms as he was dragged partly out of the stall. His fingers slid along the walls, grasping for anything to hold on to but finding nothing. His tailbone hit against the hard tile floor, the pain sending nausea into his gut.

"Robbie, help me lift him," Glenn said.

Before he could so much as kick in protest, Michael was hanging upside down, his head hovering over the bowl. His own shit and piss stared back at him. He squirmed with Robbie's arms wrapped tightly around one of his knees and Glenn's arms secured around the other.

Ryan crouched and put his mouth so close to Michael's ear that his breath stirred the hairs behind it. Michael swung his head sideways, trying to head-butt him, but he only managed to graze Ryan. Still, Ryan fell against the stall, a minor but not insignificant success. Michael could at least say he tried to fight, even if it did him no good.

Ryan returned, and he looked pissed. The slap he gave Michael's cheek stung, but it hurt his pride more than anything. *I bet that's the best he's got.*

Robbie let go of Michael's leg with one hand and reached for the toilet lever. Michael's level remained steady; Robbie needed only one arm to support his weight with ease.

"Leave it," Glenn said. "This one needs to be taught a lesson."

Robbie's hand lingered on the lever for a moment. Perhaps even a mindless deviant could show some compassion. Glenn was going too far. His lackey had to know it. Michael couldn't imagine anyone else being as vile as Glenn. But if Robbie had internally debated the action, Glenn's command won out. His hand returned to Michael's leg. The toilet remained unflushed.

"You shouldn't have done that to Ryan," Glenn said. "You may have only ended up with some wet hair. Now, we need to make sure you understand your place at this school, freshman."

Michael stretched out his right hand, reaching for the handle, but it was just out of reach. If only his arms were a little longer, he could save himself a ton of humiliation.

"Ryan, lift the seat," Glenn said.

"I'm going to enjoy this," Ryan said.

Glenn and Robbie raised Michael over the back of the toilet, clutching his knees with powerful grips. Without warning, Ryan backhanded Michael, temporarily stunning him. When his mind settled, the toilet seat was up and his head hovered inches above the water. No longer able to see the lever, his hands searched for it blindly. But Michael was disoriented. He had missed his opportunity to flush.

"Dunk him," Glenn said.

"Are you sure?" Robbie asked. "It's kind of—"

"Dunk him," Glenn commanded.

Michael clamped his hands around the rim in a vise grip. In a sort of assisted handstand, his body weight bore down on his wrists as Glenn and Robbie loosened their holds.

"How long do you think he can hold himself up?" Ryan asked. He obviously found amusement in Michael's struggles. The thought filled Michael with hostility, and with it came greater strength.

"Three more seconds," Glenn said, chuckling.

Michael's muscles were already straining. The athletic pose was not one to which he was accustomed. He managed to hold it for another ten seconds before his arms started to shake. He'd outlasted his own expectations, and he didn't want to give up, but his body no longer wanted to cooperate. Slowly, he descended. His hair dipped into the foul water. Then his forehead went under. He closed his eyes, defeated and full of hate.

When his nostrils were submerged, Michael couldn't keep the putrid filth out of them long. Soon, they filled, and unwilling to open his mouth, he couldn't breathe. Doing so would only have offered him minimal relief, since his mouth soon followed the rest of his head into the depths. His heart raced faster than a car in the Indianapolis 500. Panic made it harder to hold his breath. He wanted to scream. He wanted to be free. He even wanted to kill.

When he heard the toilet flush, Michael thought that at least his horrible circumstances would soon come to an end. The water swirled and rose around him. But the water stopped rising somewhere near the bottom of his neck, and it didn't recede.

A clog? The thought sent Michael spiraling toward hysteria. He needed oxygen desperately. If they didn't release him soon, he would pass out, or worse, suffocate and die. And he would die before he swallowed what was in that bowl. Like a worm dangling from a hook, Michael wiggled frantically.

Something inside him snapped. Like a film reel spinning absently after the credits, Michael's mind went blank. He was swallowed by emptiness, a great big expanse of nothing, a cold, dark place where bad things hid. A flicker of light like a candle's flame burning faintly in the distance beckoned him out of the dark. The light filled him with peace and warmth as it grew bigger, brighter. Then it was too big, too bright, like wildfire raging toward him. It barraged his senses: tastes, sounds, smells—all foreign. A world painted itself into existence around him.

Somehow, he had been transported away from Glenn and that godforsaken toilet. He wondered if maybe he had drowned. He was surprised the thought didn't bother him all that much. Any place was better than that bathroom. Even death was preferable.

As if from far away, he heard a door slam against a wall.

"Put him down!" someone shouted.

Michael felt his body being lowered, Glenn's hands tight around his ankle, yet he saw himself standing somewhere else, his surroundings vaguely familiar. The rank water was already becoming a distant memory.

"You scumbags." The second voice—so faint, then gone—had sounded like Jimmy Rafferty's.

Michael no longer cared about the people of the real world. His mind had traveled far away from that abysmal bowl. His body seized. Cold and wet, he twitched on the bathroom floor. For better or worse, his mind embraced the detailed canvas of his thoughts.

CHAPTER 4

MICHAEL STARES BLANKLY AT THE back of an open locker. An Avenged Sevenfold poster gazes back at him. He stands in a corridor lined by rusty aluminum lockers, their barricade broken by the occasional classroom door. He knows the corridor well—the west wing of Carnegie High School.

The locker before him is his. The poster is a remnant from a previous occupant. He likes the rock band, so he decided to keep it. The bottom half of the poster is hidden, blocked by books and notebooks piled in no discernible order. A few extra pens and a box of granola bars sit alongside the stack of books.

He glances at the digital display on his iPod: 12:54 p.m., October 14. His lunch period is almost over. Michael has six minutes to reach his algebra class on the opposite side of the school. He grabs his math and history textbooks, their corresponding notebooks, and a granola bar and throws them into his backpack. Slinging the bag over his shoulder, Michael shuts his locker and mentally prepares himself for another dull afternoon of class.

As he heads toward what will undoubtedly be another round of Ms. McCormick's overzealous selling of the applications of the Pythagorean Theorem to everyday life, his backpack seems unnaturally light on his shoulder. No, Michael himself seems lighter, as if gravity has decided to give up its normally relentless bullying. He thinks he could float to class if he *wished, his feet making no sound as they move into the hallway traffic. But his own lightness somehow seems to make the atmosphere heavy.*

He has taken only a few steps when Nancy Pettigrew shimmies by, offering him a smile. Nancy is "chubby" in the eyes of most boys. In Michael's eyes, she is perfect. With hair as fine as silk, tan capris, and a fuzzy blue sweater that accentuates her curves, Nancy's mere presence is enough to quicken the beat of his heart. Her unexpected attention makes him blush. He turns up the collar of his black polo shirt to hide his face, knowing his goofy smile must make him look just that. Better to look shy than stupid.

When he wipes off his smirk and summons the courage to raise his head, he sees Jimmy Rafferty coming his way. He waves at Jimmy and calls out to him, but Jimmy shoves forward through the herd, seemingly without noticing him.

Jimmy's face is pale, sickly even. Dark purple circles his eyes, thick as a raccoon's mask. His auburn hair is a tangled, greasy mess; his clothes are disheveled, a frumpy and oversized hooded sweatshirt hanging halfway to his knees over wrinkled jeans. Michael wonders if he's been sleeping in those clothes or if he's even been sleeping at all. It doesn't take significant powers of observation to see that Jimmy is distressed.

Michael can't blame him. Glenn and Robbie are back from their suspensions today. Unwritten social policy dictates that they will have to seek revenge for Jimmy's going to the principal's office after the bathroom incident. At Carnegie High School, people earn many labels and are unjustly awarded several others on a daily basis. Few are worse than being branded a rat. As if they are preparing for prison life, the juvenile delinquents of Fall River always make examples of those who spill the beans on their criminal exploits. In their fractured minds, the weak are supposed to accept their abuse.

Jimmy must have known this cardinal rule when he decided to break it, and in doing so, he possibly saved Michael's life. The act, whether selfless or vengeful, had gained Jimmy a mountain of student scorn... and Michael's friendship. They spent a lot of time together the past week, in and out of school. By the week's end, however, Jimmy had become increasingly distant.

Jimmy's actions have made him a target, not just of Glenn and Robbie but of every bully in the school. Their contempt for Jimmy is seen in their scowls and heard in their scoffs as Jimmy walks by them. Still, like attack dogs held at bay, they leave Jimmy alone. Michael can only assume they're saving him for Glenn.

Revenge would come. It didn't need to be said, but that didn't stop Ryan from saying it. Occasionally, Michael had been present when Ryan purposely bumped into Jimmy or made threats, toothless without Glenn's backing. Ryan's suspension had been for only one day, since he technically didn't physically participate in Michael's dunking. Glenn and Robbie got three days to think about their actions and their futures at Carnegie, which Michael doubts are pressing concerns to them. And now, the week is over.

"Jimmy?" Michael calls.

Jimmy keeps on walking, his hands buried inside the front pocket of his sweatshirt. The pocket hangs low over his crotch, looking as heavy as the burden on his shoulders.

Concerned, Michael follows him, even though he knows doing so will make him late for class. "Jimmy?" he calls again, this time more loudly.

Jimmy either doesn't hear him or refuses to acknowledge him. Instead, he continues down the hallway, his every step forming a march with purpose. His path leads him directly to Glenn Rodrigues.

"Well, well," Glenn says as Jimmy stops a foot or two in front of him. "Look who we have here." Glenn is rummaging in his locker. No henchmen are nearby to offer support, but his solitude seems to have little impact on his bravado.

Michael lingers a few steps away, not knowing what he should do, afraid for Jimmy and for himself. A moment passes before he considers that maybe Glenn is the one who should be afraid.

Jimmy doesn't say a word. He doesn't even blink as he stares into Glenn's eyes with only an arm's length between them. Michael admires his guts, but those guts are going to get him killed. To survive high school, Jimmy needs more cunning. He wonders if his new friend is masochistic. He wonders what else he doesn't know about Jimmy.

The hallway is crowded, so the threat of danger is minimal. Surely, Glenn will not openly defy school policies with so many witnesses and so soon after his suspension. Even Glenn has to be concerned by the possibility of expulsion.

Glenn's thin, wry smile spreads across his face, the same smile Michael saw before he was plunged headfirst into a toilet. Michael looks around for teachers but sees none. Students crowd around the two, their number growing as if a giant magnet is drawing them.

"Don't you students have classes to attend?" Mr. Wilfork asks, parting the crowd like the Red Sea.

Michael breathes a sigh of relief. Michael doesn't know the history teacher that well, but he is immensely glad to see him. He and Jimmy would live to see another day.

"Come on, Jimmy," Michael says, tugging on his arm.

The crowd begins to disperse, and Mr. Wilfork returns to his classroom, obviously thinking he has resolved the tension. If Michael can just lead Jimmy out of here, he's sure everything will go back to normal, at least until the next break.

Still pulling Jimmy along, Michael can feel his friend's triceps flex with tension. Jimmy's hands are balled into fists. His whole body seems to stand at attention, ready to act. Glancing over his shoulder, Michael sees Glenn leaning against his locker with arms crossed and a smug, sideways grin.

"Run away, little rat," Glenn says. "It won't be long before you're exterminated."

Jimmy stops dead in his tracks, his face redder than a candy apple. His eyes are wide, practically bulging from their sockets. Like a shaken champagne bottle, Jimmy is ready to pop.

Michael can sense an explosion coming. He tries to shuffle Jimmy along more quickly, but his friend will not budge. The pressure is doing its damage internally. One look at Jimmy, and Michael knows it's too late. Jimmy has broken. And now, he'll surely burst.

Growling like an animal, the sound low at first but quickly mounting to a lion's ferocity, Jimmy jerks his arm from Michael's grip. He whips around to face Glenn, who is still smiling, not the least bit intimidated. But Glenn's smile fades quickly when Jimmy pulls a gun from his pocket.

"What the fuck?" Glenn shrieks, staggering back into the row of lockers.

Even in a hallway full of students, he has nowhere to hide. Mixed within the chaotic confusion welling inside him, Michael can't help but feel a modicum of joy at the terror on the bully's face. He wears the same look he has inspired in so many others.

But frightening Glenn is one thing. Michael doubts Jimmy will stop there. Jimmy has gone too far. Once the gun has been drawn, there's no turning back.

Two shots are fired, both hitting their mark. Glenn falls. A girl screams. Some students run, but whether in fear or in search of help, Michael doesn't know. Everything has happened so fast, he can't fully process it. His mouth hangs open in disbelief.

Jimmy stares into space, his eyes fixed on the spot where Glenn once stood. His hand, still clutching the gun, lowers robotically to his side. The gun slides from his hand. It hits the floor a second before Jimmy is tackled by Mr. Wilfork.

The fingernails on Michael's right hand were chewed down to the quicks, some trickling blood. His stomach turned over and over. His foot wouldn't stop tapping. He squirmed in his seat, unable to get comfortable. He hadn't slept more than an hour or two the last few nights. Tomorrow was the day. Tomorrow, it would happen. No one would stop it. No one believed him.

Michael had seen it all as clearly as if he'd lived it. With the blood rushing into his head, shit and piss circling him as he drowned in shallow water, he remembered begging for an escape. As if playing some cruel joke, his mind had transported him from one horror to another.

Nearly a week had passed since his dunking. As he relayed what he'd seen to Sam over an iced coffee, his voice hushed so the other patrons wouldn't hear him and think him crazy, Michael knew she wouldn't believe him, either. He had called her out to that diner for nothing. Knowing all the crap he'd gotten into better than anyone else, Sam probably already thought he was bat-shit crazy.

For as long as he could remember, Sam had been the one constant in his life. A sort of surrogate mother who kept an eye on him mostly from a distance, she came to his rescue whenever he needed it—but not without a lecture in morality. She'd been there for him through it all, bailing him out each time he got into trouble while living with so many different foster parents that Michael had lost count.

During one of those hard times, Michael had asked her why she came to clean up his messes. Most of the time, he hadn't been living anywhere near Fall River, which was her jurisdiction, yet no matter the distance, there she would be. Sam said it had something to do with his parents—not Helen and Greg, his foster parents at that time—but his biological parents, whom he didn't remember. Samantha would never explain it further no matter how much he nagged. He always assumed she had been a friend to them.

Still, Michael appreciated everything Sam did for him, though he would never admit it out loud. Having a detective old enough to be his mother as his only real friend was kind of embarrassing, particularly when she always seemed to catch him at his worst. Even when he could bullshit his way out of trouble with others, Michael couldn't bullshit Samantha. She had eyes that could see right through him. He'd learned long ago that he couldn't lie to her, so he never bothered to try.

But turning to her for help for someone else's mess, one that might or might not have been a product of his imagination? Michael couldn't guess how she would respond. He hadn't lied to her in years. He wondered if she thought he was lying about what he had seen. She had to help him. There was no one else who would listen. Michael needed to convince her—and he knew it *sounded* crazy—to stop something that hadn't happened yet, the only evidence of its inevitability being a dream he'd had while his head was submerged in crap.

Michael saw nothing but pity in her eyes, the same look she had given him after he'd let off a stink bomb at his last school or when he'd painted a neighbor's poodle fluorescent green. She didn't believe him. *Pity's a start, though. What did I expect? Maybe I can guilt her into action.*

"At least frisk him and check his locker," he said. He twisted a straw wrapper around his pinkie and stared at the coffee rings staining the table. He raised his eyes, letting her detect whatever lies she could find in them. "I'm not making this up. I swear it. I know what I saw, and it was as real as the conversation we're having right now, and it's sure as shit gonna happen."

Sam rapped her fingernails against the table then tucked her hair behind her ears. "I know you're not making it up, Michael. That's what makes this all the more upsetting. What that Rodrigues boy did to you was terrible. You were probably in shock or having some sort of hallucination. I've heard that some people can imagine alternate realities, even create fictional second lives, as a means to escape the real world. It usually happens to those who need to cope with painful or traumatic experiences like what you went through. And sometimes, when they escape to these fictional constructs, they don't come back."

Her coolheaded way of thinking made Michael regret coming to her for help. *Yep, she thinks I'm insane.* He became certain he was wasting his time. Frowning, he watched Sam without responding until her own gravity seemed to lighten.

"Or," she said, "you were probably unconscious and had a nightmare."

"It wasn't a dream. Why does everyone keep saying that?"

"Who else have you told about your… incident?"

"Principal Alves, Greg, and Helen. They all said the same thing. 'It was just a dream. It was just a dream.' You're all freakin' clones of one another," Michael scoffed. "Helen even laughed at me. She said, 'Only God knows our fates.' I don't know my fate, and I sure as hell don't know Helen's, but I know Glenn's. He's gonna be dead real soon if people don't start taking me a little more seriously."

Sam sighed. "Have you told Jimmy?"

Michael shrugged. "No. I was afraid to tell him in case—"

"In case you were dreaming?"

His plastic coffee cup crinkled in his fist. He felt the heat of his anger burning beneath his collar. "It was *not* a dream."

Sam offered no reaction to his tantrum. "You didn't want to accuse him of plotting an awful crime that he might never have been plotting in the first place?"

"Something like that." Michael hung his head, briefly succumbing to her logic, all based on science and medicine. Science and medicine couldn't explain everything. No, he *knew* what he saw was going to happen. He couldn't explain why or how he knew. He just did. "I've had so many dreams. This wasn't anything like them. This was different. I lived it, I felt it, and I experienced it just like any other day in my life. It was real."

"How could it have been real if it hasn't happened yet?"

Sam's skepticism was becoming infuriating. He sat on his hands to keep them still. "I didn't say any of this made sense. But if I had knowledge of a crime before it was going to happen, you would want me to tell you so you could stop it, right?"

"Of course. Why?" Sam leaned toward him, her stare piercing. "Did Jimmy tell you he was going to do this?"

Michael felt small beneath her penetrating gaze. *Why am I the bad guy for trying to do the right thing?* "Haven't you been listening to me? No, Jimmy knows nothing about this beyond whatever is going on in his head right now. Let's pretend he told me what he was going to do, though, and that he told me exactly when and where he was going to do it. What would you do?"

"Stake him out. If your tip led to proof, we'd arrest him. It's rare we get an opportunity to stop a crime before it happens. Most of our police work by its very nature comes after the fact, when it's too late for somebody."

"So do that, Sam. Stake him out. Please."

Sam smiled, a rare occurrence. She was a beautiful, athletic woman in her forties with stark features made cold and unapproachable by years of investigating the worst humanity had to offer. The detective had a way of scoping out secrets with her emerald-green eyes, a splash of color against her milky skin and dark hair and clothing. Her years and experiences had hardened her like cement, and not just on the inside. Michael was worried her smile would cause her normally stoic face to crack and crumble into ruin.

For certain, Sam did little smiling, but when she did, it was usually directed toward him. For some reason, he seemed to be her only soft spot. But her uncharacteristic smile wouldn't make Michael soft. Rather, he found it off-putting. Right or wrong, he inferred condescension from it. Michael was fairly convinced a boy's life was in danger, a circumstance he was unwilling to ignore. A large part of him understood why Sam doubted him. Still, he wasn't just some random kid crying wolf. He was her friend, and his concerns were worthy of her attention.

He crossed his arms. "What's so amusing?"

"Nothing. I'm sorry." Her mouth returned to its usual flat line. "It's just that, well, you're the only one who calls me that."

"What? Sam? That's your name, isn't it?"

"I suppose it is."

"Can we get back to the kid who's gonna get shot tomorrow?"

"There's little I can do based solely on a dream… or a vision. If he said something to you, anything at all, say so, and I'll be all over Rafferty like flies on... poop."

Michael rolled his eyes. "Believe me, I've heard people say 'shit' before. Hell, I just said it a minute ago." He shook his head. "Anyway, if I say now that he did tell me something, will that make a difference?"

"No, because I would know that you were lying. I'm sorry, Michael. Believe it or not, even might-be killers have rights that can't be circumvented. You can find comfort in the fact that every entrance to Carnegie High School has security posted and metal detectors in place to stop guns from getting in. Rafferty won't be able to sneak a gun by them. Plus, if it will make you feel better, the school will conduct a *random* locker search tomorrow morning, just in case. I'll make sure Rafferty's locker makes the list."

Michael huffed. "Those metal detectors aren't worth a damn. Every kid knows a half-dozen ways to sneak into and out of Carnegie. How do you think kids play hooky so much? They can't walk through walls."

"It's the best I can do and a heck of a lot more than I legally should. Your friend Jimmy has constitutional rights, you know? Next time you have to read the Bill of Rights for a class, check out the Fourth Amendment. It's a real pain in the ass for law enforcement."

Michael shrugged. He slumped back against the booth. "Well, I guess it's better than nothing. But what if he has the gun on him? You won't find it in his locker then."

"Look for him tomorrow. If you see anything suspicious, anything that would lend credence to your vision, give me a call right away. You have my cell. I'll have my phone with me all day. But if nothing happens, please promise me you'll try to relax, be a normal teenager, and stay the hell away from Glenn Rodrigues."

Michael nodded. The results weren't ideal, but at least contacting Sam hadn't been a complete waste. He was thinking of ways to provoke a more serious response from her when she stood to leave.

"I have to get back to work," she said. "I'll talk to you later." She took out her wallet and dropped a ten on the table. She stepped from the booth and rested her hand on Michael's shoulder in an awkward display of affection, even rarer than her smile. "Take care of yourself, Michael."

The battle was over before he could take his last shot. Michael didn't want anyone's death on his conscience, not even that good-for-nothing toad, Glenn Rodrigues. He grumbled quietly, steaming in his frustration. He felt a lot like the Trojan princess, Cassandra, he had read about in school last year, with her disbelieved prophecies of doom. Michael had liked the story then, not so much at that moment.

His frustration hit its boiling point after she had already exited the diner. "Fine!" he shouted, jumping to his feet. "But don't you ever say I didn't try to warn you."

She apparently didn't hear him through the glass door because she continued out into the parking lot. He watched through the window as she got into her car and drove off, then he noticed several customers staring at him.

He plopped back into his seat. "If you won't help me, I'll stop him myself."

CHAPTER 5

THE WHITE BUTTON-DOWN BLOUSE FIT tightly across her budding breasts. A khaki sash, filled with pins that didn't belong to her, twisted over her shoulder and across her body. Flashes of metal had been placed strategically to draw the eye. Pulled back into a ponytail, her strawberry-blond hair was neat and flat against her head. Two bobby pins, each set just beyond the corners of her forehead, wove her long bangs into the rest of her hair. Every inch of Tessa, from her subtle makeup to her pressed knee-length skirt and recently polished flats, was perfect, arranged with more care than a floral masterpiece. Such delicate care for indelicate business.

All dolled up, Tessa felt as though she were made of glass, her inside empty and exposed, her outside fragile and revealing. She wondered if her shirt was made from that see-through white material or the solid kind. Maybe it would blend with her milky skin. She hoped so; she didn't want anyone to see her scars.

Dressed like that, she was out of her element, an actress on a stage when she only wanted to be locked inside her room writing poems to the loves she would never have—those lean, dreamy boys, far too cool for the likes of her. Boys like Jacob Dorsey didn't notice Plain Janes like her, especially when she scurried through school like a mouse, trying not to be seen. *Maybe he would notice me if I dressed like this.*

Tessa bit into her lower lip. She almost smiled, considering the possibility that she might be pretty. She knew she was supposed to look it. She wished, just for a moment, she could feel it.

No guy wants a girl with small boobs, buckteeth, blah-blond hair, and not one but two *pimples!* She was far too old to believe in Prince Charming coming to save her from her wicked stepfather. Fairy tales were for idiots who thought life could be like their dreams. Her life was a nightmare. *Never kissing a boy is the least of my problems.*

With what Father would often make her go through, Tessa wondered if she had ever truly been in her element, whatever that was. Her world had always belonged to him. She couldn't even imagine what "normal" might feel like. She had no friends, no family, no one… except him. On the rare occasions she'd tried to talk to a classmate, she always said the wrong things and came across as creepy. She was the "weird girl." She heard it in their whispers, felt it in their stares. After a while, she just gave up, figuring it hurt less to be lonely than it did to be ridiculed.

She felt ridiculous as she stood on that doorstep. Her push-up bra pinched her skin. Her nylons bunched in all the wrong places. She just wanted to be home wearing a T-shirt and jeans, writing notes to Jacob she would never share, while staying clear out of Father's way.

But there she was, helping him instead. *But helping him do what? Sell some cookies?* Father had never asked her to help before. He was taking things to the next level. Whether she wanted to help never seemed to matter.

One thing was certain: Tessa did not want to ring the doorbell. No good would come from it. The engine of Father's Chrysler Crossfire purred quietly on the street, set back a bit from the front walkway in the late-afternoon shade of a great oak. As she glanced back at the windshield, she couldn't see Father through the tinted glass, but she knew he was watching her. He was always watching her. And every second she delayed, she risked provoking his wrath.

The Crossfire's headlights flashed, a sure sign that his patience was already waning. She exhaled for what seemed an eternity and turned to face the door. The house was like any other, a raised ranch on the suburban street, which resembled hundreds of other streets. Nothing special. Nothing to be afraid of. Yet Tessa was terrified all the same.

She stared at the doorbell, her finger hovering. She traced the gold-colored metal around the white button and dared to wonder what would happen if she refused to push it. Her imagination played out gruesome consequences she was not prepared to face. But to ring the doorbell meant to shift those consequences to another.

If it works. Why would this guy want me? Why would anyone?

Before she could decide, the inner door swung open. Startled, Tessa clutched her shirt just below her neck. Her eyes opened wide, taking in the sight of the guy who stood there. Only the thin pane of glass constituting the storm door separated her from an enormous, hairy beast of a man clothed in a stained wife-beater and ragged sweatpants that disappeared under a bulbous belly. Crumbs of unidentifiable food on his triple chin and shirt told Tessa he was exactly the type of guy who would appreciate the goods she was selling. Father had planned wisely.

The man opened the storm door about seven inches, which allowed only his massive head to peek through the crack. The glass fogged up, preventing any view in or out of the house.

"Yes?" the man asked through the opening.

"Hi," Tessa began, just as she rehearsed. "My name is April, and I'm selling Girl Scout cookies for my local troop. May I come in and show you the delicious cookies I have for sale?"

"Do you have any of those caramel ones?"

"I certainly do," Tessa said, flashing a flirtatious smile. She pushed her shoulders back to accentuate her breasts just as Father had told her to do. She twisted side to side, which had not been planned, her nervousness getting the better of her.

The man's eyes followed the sway of her cleavage, his tongue apparently incapable of staying inside his mouth. "Aren't you a little old to be a Girl Scout?"

Tessa knew she had him. Father had told her what to look for, taught her how to reel him in. She wanted to shy away. The thought of that man ogling her, putting his meaty hands on her, made her tremble. Then she thought about Father touching her.

"I'm mature for my age," she said, giggling as if she hadn't a care in the world. But she did. The gross pig in front of her disgusted her, but he didn't deserve what was coming.

"Come on in," he said, his own smile perverted, devious.

His eyes wandered down her body as he opened the storm door slowly, allowing Tessa to pick up her tote bag full of cookies and step out of the way of its swing. He filled the doorway as he gestured her in with a nod. Tessa had barely enough room to squeeze by him, not enough to make it through without rubbing against his belly. A stale odor, like old sweat mixed with mold, filled her nostrils, and she turned away from it. She wanted to push him back, sure he stood in her way on purpose. His leering almost made her forget to feel sorry for him. Almost.

The strap of her tote bag snagged on the doorknob, and Tessa waited to see if the man would unhook it for her. He seemed content to hold the door open so she could get it herself. Her face heated from a mix of anger and humiliation, but she was fortunate enough to gather her bag without further contact.

The door opened into a living room. A brown recliner sat in its center, sprinkled with broken potato chips and looking worn and tired. The wall it faced was home to a massive flat-screen TV. An unmatched sofa with plastic covering its hideous floral pattern hugged the near wall. A paw swiped out from beneath it, crinkling the potato chip bag its owner had stolen. Tessa smiled at the cat, but she struggled to keep her cheeks from falling, thinking about her kitten, Smokey, that she had loved so much, back when Mom...

Back when "pets" wasn't just a four-letter word. She sniffled, but only once, then straightened. "Where to?"

Beyond the living room, a large dining room was partly filled by a massive oak table and matching chairs. The man pointed toward it. With her bag tucked under her arm, Tessa moved toward the dining room table. He followed her like a puppy. The storm door swung nearly shut, not quite latching. She glanced over her shoulder to make sure the house door remained open.

It had. Her shoulder drooped. She plodded forward to finish the act.

Tessa poured the cookies onto the table. She rummaged through several boxes of mint and peanut butter cookies, looking for the caramel variety the man had requested. "Looks like I only have two left," she said, holding up two boxes. When she put them back on the table, she slid them toward the man, leaning forward to give him a better view of her cleavage while squeezing her arms against her breasts.

"I'll take them both," the man replied, and at that moment, Tessa despised herself. Worse still, she couldn't tell if he meant he wanted both boxes or both breasts. She watched his hand fumble in his right pocket, his breathing heavy.

"How much are they per box?"

"Five dollars each."

"Damn, they keep getting more and more expensive, don't they?" Suddenly energized, he yanked his wallet from his pocket as if the cookies wouldn't wait for him.

He pulled out a stack of ones and counted ten of them, no doubt ensuring some unfortunate stripper would be getting fewer tips later. He clutched the bills between two sausage fingers and returned the wallet to his pocket.

The door creaked behind them. The act was over. Tessa could no longer pretend to be the pretty schoolgirl when everything about her felt ugly.

The man must have heard the door open, too. He turned and faced Father, who at five-eight stood nearly a foot shorter than the pervert, not to mention the two-hundred-pound difference in weight.

Father was small but solid, like an Olympic gymnast. His hair was squarely combed, each brown hair cut short and placed along a part, as meticulously cared for as the greens at Augusta. Black horn-rimmed glasses with a horizontal line splitting the lenses made him look a little like a character from *Mad Men*. With handsome features made awkward by his long-outdated style, he might as well have been a puritan in his white shirt and black slacks. He and the fat man stared at each other for a moment, sizing each other up like two boxers just before the bell.

Tessa retreated around the table and cowered in a corner. She slid down against the wall until her knees touched her chest. She wanted to bury her head between them, but she couldn't look away. Father wouldn't like that.

"Who are you? Her father?" the man asked, obviously oblivious to the meat mallet protruding from Father's grip. "We're almost done here."

The sound the mallet made as it ricocheted off the man's skull, bone cracking like tires over glass, echoed into Tessa's ears. The sight of that first hit replayed over and over again in her mind. She knew more hits would come. Her stomach turned, but she swallowed against her gag reflex. Father wouldn't like her vomiting, either.

The man fell to his knees. His eyelids fluttered as if they were trying to rip themselves free of his face. The stunning blow caused his body to reel like a Weeble toy—he rocked back and forth, but he wouldn't go down.

With another swing of the mallet landing against a blubbery cheek, the man's lower jaw twisted. Dislocated, it hung open at a grisly angle. The man reached below his chin and tried to hold his jaw in place, losing his shaky balance in the process. He fell onto his side, blood gushing from his mouth.

Through slurred, gurgling speech that must have required considerable effort, he managed to ask, "Why?"

"You are undisciplined."

Father's response was simple, and he didn't seem to feel the need to elaborate. The three words came out cold, deliberate, and absent of any indication that he recognized the heinousness of his conduct. Emotionless, Father's expression complemented his words, as icy and indifferent as his face had been every moment since her mother's death. Not even sleep seemed to bring him peace. Tessa would stare at him for hours as he slept, waiting for that moment when Father's strain would break. But even then, he wore that chiseled, somber face. She wondered if it was the only face he had left.

"Rules were made to be enforced," Father said, directing his voice toward Tessa.

It was her lesson to learn. She gasped, wanted to cry, but held it back. *He does this for me, so that I learn to follow the rules. This man... Oh God, for me. Because of me.* She had learned all his lessons a long time ago, but every so often, Father seemed to feel they needed reinforcing. As if to drive his point home, Father swung the mallet repeatedly into the man's head. Once, twice, three times. Fresh blood, thick and dark, poured from new wounds. The man's eyes rolled back into his head.

"Rule breakers were meant to be broken." With a final bludgeon to the man's forehead dead center, Father recoiled. Blood had spurted in an arc that stained his face and the front of his shirt. He scrubbed his glasses with a clean spot.

Between some chair legs, Tessa had seen every vicious stroke. The whites of the dying man's eyes were aimed her way, but she doubted he could see anything through them. She watched as the blood flow diminished from waterfall to trickle. The cyclic rise and fall of the man's chest became slower. Eventually, he stopped breathing.

Why? Father had always tried to make her understand, often forcefully, but his idea of justice always seemed unjust. *What was this man's crime? What could he have done to deserve such harsh punishment? Parked in a handicap spot? Farted in an elevator?* Tessa didn't know what the man had done to offend Father, but she could be certain that whatever it was, he did not deserve to die for it. If he had broken the law, then the law should punish him. What made Father's justice better? She wouldn't dare ask. Was it enough that people like this poor fat bastard who lay dying on his rug would never commit their crimes again?

Father glared at her, his features a tad more icy. Blood dripped off his mallet like raindrops from a gutter. Had he sensed her doubt? Could he feel her disapproval?

"We must teach them proper etiquette, darling," he said, his tone only slightly warmer. "We must teach them discipline."

How can he learn discipline if he's dead? Tessa couldn't stop the thought from forming, but once it had, she quickly tried to expel it. *Do as he says. Do as he says, and don't say a word.* She'd been taught enough discipline of her own.

She stood and used her hands to flatten the wrinkles in her blouse and skirt. Her terror stayed beneath the surface. She couldn't let Father know how horrified she was by his actions or how guilty she already felt for her part in them. Her insides were in turmoil, but her exterior was all Father could see.

Before moving, Tessa inhaled deeply, then she parted her lips only enough to release the air and, with it, a fraction of her anxiety. Collected and faking confidence, she stepped toward Father. Opening the tote bag on the table, she began to gather the boxes of cookies into it.

"No," Father said, gripping her arm with a bloodied hand. His fingers dug into her, imprinting her blouse with their red-stained grooves and fissures. "Leave two boxes. He paid for them. Pick up the money, and let's go."

Tessa didn't immediately understand what he wanted her to do. When it registered, she placed the two boxes of caramel cookies on the table. They were her favorite, though Father would never let her have them.

Father headed for the door, taking his improperly used tool with him. Tessa knew he wouldn't tolerate waiting long for her.

Ten one-dollar bills jutted from the dead man's left hand. Even in his eternal slumber, he clenched those bills tightly, perhaps thinking he could carry them with him into the afterlife. He had suffered whack after whack from Father's mallet, yet somehow, he never released those greenbacks. Maybe he could have protected himself better if he'd just tossed aside the cash and made use of his free hand. Amazed, Tessa wondered if money really was the root of all evil.

Her amazement quickly turned to fear when she realized she would have to pull the money from the hand of a corpse. Since she had discovered her mother's body lying limp and naked in their bathtub, blood from her carved wrists turning the water into cherry Kool-Aid, Tessa panicked at the thought of being near a dead body. The nightmares she'd had after her mother's death were dark and sinister. She would dream of her mother's corpse trying to drag her into the earth, down to hell. In her dreams, her mother blamed Tessa for her death.

Ever since then, Tessa crossed to the opposite side of the road every time she walked past a cemetery or funeral parlor. Standing beside a body, being forced to look at it, nearly made her skin crawl off her bones.

Maybe I could use my own money and tell Father I got it from him. No. Father would know. He always knows when I disobey, and the punishment would be far worse than this. She shuddered.

Tessa tiptoed over to the hand, which was curled into a fist around the cash. She avoided the spattered blood wherever possible, the bigger pools clustering near the man's head. Closing her eyes and bending over, she dug her fingers between the man's and wrenched his sausage-like appendages back one by one. She snagged the bills. *That wasn't so bad. At least he doesn't need change.* Hysterical laughter burbled in her throat.

She let out a shrill scream as a hand wrapped around her ankle and squeezed. She looked down to see the man's eyes wide open, outlined in blood and staring up at her. Her knees went weak, and she nearly collapsed. She leaned against the back of a chair and tried to step away. When he wouldn't let go, she let out another yell.

She kicked at the man's wrist with her free heel until he released her. A saliva bubble formed around his mouth then was popped by a wheeze and a gurgle. His eyes closed, and his body went limp. She couldn't help but hope he stayed dead this time.

Father rushed into the house. Tessa stood shaking, her fear of Father compounding her anxiety. She wanted to explain what had happened, that there was good reason for her screaming, but she feared she would just be increasing the punishment to come.

Father's eyes darted back and forth between Tessa and the fat, and now presumably dead, man. He signaled Tessa to move back, then he crouched beside the body. Holding the man's wrist, he felt for a pulse.

Tessa sidestepped around them and slowly crept closer to the door. Selfishly, she thought only of how the man's death had impacted her and how every slight deviation, real or imagined, that Father saw her make in his well-crafted plan would lead to more brutality—against her. She couldn't be a part of it anymore. She had neither asked nor wanted to be a part of it. But Father would never let her stop. She'd tried once before. The scars on her back proved it.

Still, no one stood between her and the door. *All I have to do is run.* She had a million opportunities to run, but for some reason, she couldn't accept even one of them.

As if by its own volition, her hand groped her hair. She tore out one of her bobby pins and dropped it to the floor.

Seeming satisfied that the man was dead, Father stood and said, "Go out to the car. I'll be right behind you."

As she walked toward the car, she again imagined herself running. Then, she imagined Father catching her and all the horrible things he would do after he did. She opened the door and got into the passenger seat. Someone else would have to save her. She would leave as many bread crumbs as she could to help that someone find her.

Father exited the house and hurried toward the car. He looked angry. Father never lost his temper, even if he had lost his mind. The rage in him brought out the panic in her.

She hugged the door as he got in behind the wheel. By the time he sat down, his usual disinterested expression had reappeared. The only signs of his anger were his silence and his hands balled up so tightly the knuckles flashed white.

"You left this behind," he said in his deadpan voice. He held up the bobby pin.

Oh God. She gasped, then she clamped her mouth shut. Nothing she could say would help her.

"Looks like someone needs to be taught some discipline," Father said, his mouth twitching as though it had tried to smile.

Tessa covered her face with her hands and cried silently. Praying for mercy or at least a quick recovery, Tessa trembled the whole way home. *Maybe he'll kill me this time.* The prospect was scary at first but bittersweet, tinged by a euphoric suggestion of release. The only problem was how much pain she would have to endure before death came.

CHAPTER 6

THE ALARM CLOCK BLARED INCESSANTLY, shouting in its mind-splitting, rage-invoking voice for Michael to get out of bed. His fingertips fumbled along its buttons, searching for the off switch. Finding it felt like a major victory. The noise stopped, but the alarm clock had the last laugh. Michael was awake. And he had to get ready for school.

He plucked a few crusties from the corners of his eyes as anxiety flooded in. Thoughts of Jimmy and Glenn had kept him awake most of the night. His sheets were tangled around his legs like a boa constrictor. He must have fallen asleep at some point, but he couldn't remember when.

Maybe Sam's right. Maybe it was only a dream.

But he didn't believe it. He knew what he'd seen, what he'd experienced, wasn't a dream. Glenn was going to die today, and nobody seemed interested in stopping it but him.

His rational side fought back. *If it wasn't a dream, then what was it? A premonition? A vision of the future?* Michael didn't subscribe to that psychic crap. He'd never had psychic abilities before. He wasn't special. He hadn't felt any different when he'd woken up that morning than he had a lifetime of mornings prior.

After crawling out of bed, he stood in front of his mirrored closet doors. The person he saw was still Michael Turcotte, plain and ordinary and inconsequential. And if he didn't move, he was going to be late for school.

He was scared as hell, but despite his fear, a small part of him wanted to go. He needed to know whether what he had seen was real or not, if it would really happen. *Curiosity never gets you anything but trouble.* He sighed. By the end of the day, he would at least have answers. Whether they were the answers he wanted, he figured he would have to wait and see.

He flexed to admire his pecs in the mirror. He checked for chest hair, but his skin was as smooth as a baby's butt. Though he was only five-eight, his weight was reasonably proportional to his height. It made no difference that he ate often and as much junk as he could get his hands on.

He mock-combed his short hair by running his palm over the top from back to forehead, smoothing it against his scalp. Not bothering to shower, he pulled a black polo over his head and paired it with some dark jeans. After donning mismatched socks—both were white, he justified—and his black Airwalks, Michael left the comparable comfort of his foster home for the cold, damp morning.

During the mile walk to school—he didn't care for the classmate interaction that taking the bus often entailed—he kept an eye out for Jimmy, but he didn't spot him. He waited by one of the entrances as long as he could, hoping he would catch Jimmy on his way in. Eventually, he was forced to follow the rest of the cattle to roll call.

As soon as the bell signaled the end of homeroom, he hustled back into the hallway. No Jimmy. He was beginning to wonder if his friend had skipped school.

His morning classes came and went. Michael spent every free moment searching for his friend. He checked Jimmy's usual classes and anywhere he thought Jimmy could be hiding: the locker room by the track, the library, the audio-visual room. He was becoming more certain that Jimmy had decided to take the day off. Perhaps there would be no Columbine reenactment after all. Michael prayed he was right, even if it did mean his "vision" was nothing more than a hallucination.

I still have lunch to find him. No one skips lunch. Even killers have to eat.

Lunch passed without Jimmy making an appearance. *He has to be out today. If he were here, I would have seen him by now.* Relaxing a little, he wolfed down his three-dollar cheeseburger and tater tots and guzzled two cartons of milk. He snuck out of the cafeteria before his lunch hour was over so he could rush back to the west corridor. If anything were going to happen, it would happen there. Michael would be ready. He would stop Jimmy from making the worst mistake of his life and perhaps begrudgingly save Glenn in the process. He wondered if it would buy him a pass from future abuse.

The west corridor was silent, upperclassmen somberly attending classes in session around him, lowerclassmen still at lunch. Michael spun the dial of his combination lock as though someone's life depended on his haste. He grabbed the books he needed for the afternoon and shoved them into his backpack. Before shutting the locker, he caught a glimpse of himself in a small mirror inside the door. His lack of sleep showed in the dark half circles under his eyes. He suddenly realized that in his absentminded preparation for school, he had put on the same shirt he'd been wearing in his vision.

He cursed himself for the oversight, as if changing shirts could have changed what was to come. Slamming his locker shut in disgust, Michael turned to face a still empty, quiet hallway. He glanced at his watch: 12:49 p.m. His solitude was coming to an end.

Less than a minute later, an obnoxious fire alarm-like bell rang, signaling the end of the classes that had begun at noon. The hallway filled with hurried footsteps and hundreds of voices, each one competing to be heard over the others. Their simultaneous existences made them one, producing an indistinguishable, constant murmur that resembled static. To Michael, it was like a blanket, easy to get lost in and easy to hide under. Too many fishes crowded into a small pond, easy for a small fish like him to go unnoticed, the way he usually liked it.

But not today. Today, he needed to be noticed, if not by Jimmy, then by Glenn. Finding Jimmy was obviously preferable. But spotting Glenn was considerably less difficult.

Upperclassmen shuffled out of their classrooms like zombies, their high school lectures apparently sucking the vigor from their muscles and the consciousness from their minds. Glenn was first out of the classroom nearest Michael, a startling revelation he made sure to ingrain into memory. Glenn continued down the hallway, thankfully without noticing him, and stopped near a water fountain to speak to a girl Michael didn't know. Glenn then walked with the girl to the sixth or seventh locker past the fountain, where they talked for a moment. When the girl left, Michael hoped Glenn would follow her.

But Glenn stayed and opened his locker. He turned the lock one click at a time, seemingly without a care in the world. The seconds passed painfully slow for Michael as he watched Glenn maneuver books and fix his hair in a mirror. He supposed he should pardon Glenn's loitering. The senior scumbag couldn't know what Michael knew: that Glenn had only a few minutes left to live.

Should I warn him? Michael wanted to, but he wasn't too proud to admit he was afraid of Glenn. Jimmy would be appearing soon. If Michael could stop his friend before he even got close to his prey, Glenn would never be the wiser. He leaned his back against his locker and waited, unable to keep his foot from tapping as he watched for Jimmy.

The next five minutes were almost unbearable. He glanced at his watch incessantly, the time ticking by as though it had lost interest in its immortality. Finally, after Michael had checked his watch a twenty-fourth or twenty-fifth time, it read, "12:56 p.m."

Like a sign of the apocalypse, Nancy Pettigrew strolled toward him. As she passed, she flashed him a smile, just as she had done in his vision. *And she's wearing the same fuzzy blue sweater.* He was too distracted by the fact it proved his vision was true to appreciate the way Nancy looked in it.

Unlike in his vision, Michael didn't blush. Nancy was the last person he wanted to see or, perhaps, the second to last. Given how her face contorted into a look of disgust, she must have seen the revulsion that festered within him at the sight of her. She huffed and hustled by more quickly than he'd envisioned. He had no time to explain that his queasiness had nothing to do with her. If his vision was accurate, and he no longer had any reason to doubt it, Jimmy was near.

I'm not prepared for this. He began to panic. He paced and turned, paced and turned. *What am I going to do? What am I going to do? How could I have been so stupid?* He had no plan, no idea how he would stop Jimmy from doing the unthinkable. And the gun? What was he supposed to do about the gun?

Bullying was one thing, but Jimmy must have felt the fear of something worse to bring a gun to school. He didn't strike Michael as crazy. *No, he'll listen. He has to.* He started to believe he could convince Jimmy not to shoot Glenn. If he couldn't, he would have to overpower Jimmy. Every scenario that crossed Michael's mind ended with one or more people being shot. Glenn no longer seemed worth the risk. He reminded himself that Glenn wasn't the one he was really trying to save.

Through the mass of students cluttering the hallway, he caught a glimpse of Jimmy's messy auburn hair coming toward him. As Jimmy neared, Michael could make out his clothing. Jimmy wore the same frumpy sweatshirt and wrinkled jeans from Michael's vision. Likewise, Jimmy's hands were buried in the sweatshirt's giant front pocket. Michael didn't have to guess what was in there with them.

"Jimmy?" Michael called. His voice squeaked even though he was trying to sound normal. "Can I talk to you for a second?"

Jimmy passed within two feet of him but never averted his gaze or acknowledged him. He pressed forward, a blank-faced and tunnel-visioned killer, his mind clearly on the task he had set for himself.

Michael stepped into his friend's path. "Jimmy?"

Jimmy gave no sign of slowing.

Michael began backpedaling at a pace equal to Jimmy's. "Don't do it, Jimmy," he said, skipping the small talk.

Jimmy grunted. His eyes were fixed somewhere past Michael, no doubt homing in on his target. Walking backward in front of a boy hell-bent on murder, Michael supposed he should have been happy Jimmy paid him little attention. But it got him nowhere in his efforts to stop the crime. Still, a grunt was better than nothing.

"Jimmy!" he shouted loud enough to make heads turn.

Jimmy's trance was broken. Finally, his charge halted, and he gazed at Michael with hate-filled eyes.

Most of the eavesdropping busybodies quickly returned to their own conversations, his outburst deemed less important than the latest clique gossip that generally didn't pertain to him. Michael avoided the social class structure of high school. In fact, he avoided high school and its students wherever possible. In doing so, he ironically placed himself in the "invisible" grouping, a sometimes lonely place to be. At least he wasn't an outcast. People had to notice someone for that, and once they did, school got a whole lot tougher. Being lonely was better than being bullied.

Yet for some reason, he was going way out of his way for a bully and his victim, the latter vying for a role reversal. The disdain oozing from Jimmy made Michael want to shrink inside himself. Again, he felt like a villain for trying to play the hero, a part he'd never wanted but that was thrust upon him by foresight.

"Hey, Mike," Jimmy said, his voice low and menacing. "I can't talk right now. I'm going to be late for class."

Michael glanced around, scanning for prying ears. The hallway traffic flowed around them as if they were rocks jutting out of a river. No one seemed to care about them or their conversation.

Michael leaned close to Jimmy. "I know what's in your pocket."

"What? How?" Jimmy's expression revealed his nervousness at having been discovered, but it quickly transformed into one of anger. It wasn't the fleeting kind, either; Jimmy looked pissed, his rage continuing to mount. His scowl resembled a snarling dog's.

I'm making things worse. I've got to calm him down, or the janitors will be mopping up two dead bodies at the end of the school day.

"Get out of my way," Jimmy said through clenched teeth.

He grabbed Jimmy by his left arm. "I can't let you do it."

Jimmy tore his arm free while pulling his other hand from his pocket. He pointed a gun at Michael's forehead.

Don't piss yourself. Die with dignity. Maybe you'll get a nice memorial in the yearbook.

Michael heard the gasps of astonished students, then dead silence. He was surprised by what he didn't hear: screams and the sound of running feet. Unable to tear his gaze from the dark circular cavern where the bringer of his oblivion dwelled, Michael couldn't see a thing happening around him. Jimmy's finger rested on the trigger.

This was not my best idea. Michael's body began to ache, yearning for a release from its frozen posture. He was afraid, but not nearly as afraid as he thought he should have been. After all, his life was in the hands of a boy he'd already witnessed murder another student, even if it was all just some sick, unavoidable prophecy. Michael knew what Jimmy was capable of, and with that gun pointed in his face, there wasn't a damn thing he could do. Having drawn the gun, Jimmy wouldn't be stopped. There was no going back.

Jimmy drew back his arm and batted Michael against the ear with the side of his pistol. Michael heard a crunch, the sound of cartilage breaking, and the hallway blurred. Michael fell, half from the impact and half from the loss of balance caused by the ringing in his ear.

By the time Michael shook off his daze and stood, Jimmy was approaching Glenn with his gun raised high. *Why weren't they all running? Why wouldn't anyone help?* The thought crossed his mind that it was all just some twisted form of entertainment to them. Students filled the hallway, watching like gawkers at a car crash. No one did anything to stop Jimmy, not even Glenn. The stupid bully didn't even have enough sense to get the hell out of there.

Seeing the gun coming toward them made the students at least get out of the line of fire. They pressed against the lockers on each side of the hall. The pistol cut its way to Glenn like a transport cart inside a crowded airport as Jimmy zeroed in on his prey.

"You don't have the—" Glenn was interrupted when his face exploded.

He fell to the floor. A mass of blood and torn flesh remained where his right eye and nose had once been.

As Mr. Wilfork tackled Jimmy, Michael stared at Glenn's lifeless body. All emotion left him, shock and disbelief succumbing to emptiness. *I tried to tell them.* That small consolation was all he had. At least he could say he told them so.

CHAPTER 7

FOR THE NEXT FEW DAYS, Michael spent most of his time locked inside his bedroom. He had no desire to see anyone, least of all his foster parents. They hadn't tried to console him or even to understand him. Instead, they treated him like a visitor who overstayed his welcome. Every time he walked by them, they would stand as still as portraits in a haunted house, their beady eyes following him wherever he went.

"We should call Father Preston again," Helen had said after Michael climbed the stairs to his bedroom the evening after the shooting. She obviously thought him out of earshot.

"Honey," Greg replied, "the priest already told us what to look for. We took that boy in, gave him a home. He's our responsibility now. We can't just give him back."

"But Greg, that Rodrigues boy... he died. Michael knew that would happen. What if he caused it? What if he's dangerous?"

What if I'm dangerous? Michael had heard enough. It made his stomach turn how Helen and Greg didn't fear the bully or the shooter but their own ward. For a second, he had wondered how they could think so little of him, but the moment passed quickly. After all, they weren't his first foster parents, and they certainly weren't his *real* parents. He'd retreated to his room and come out only to eat.

School had been cancelled for the remainder of the week. He was thankful for the time away from Carnegie High and the reporters swarming around it.

People were shot once every other month in Fall River. Some died, and some didn't. Unless the victim was a cop, a politician, a kid, or someone with a ton of money, the crime received little press.

But a school shooting was front-page news that expanded well beyond city boundaries. Parents were already lobbying local government for stricter security at the public schools. School Committee members were investigating programs to prevent hazing and to warn of the dangers of firearms, as if high school students didn't already know that firing a gun into another's face was harmful. City Councilors blamed rap music and the latest edition of *Grand Theft Auto*. Liberals blamed the NRA and called for gun control. Conservatives blamed gun control and argued for armed guards in every school.

Everyone pointed fingers, but Michael blamed them all. He had told representatives of each faction—school, police, and parents—what was going to happen. Each had chosen to ignore him. Glenn's blood dripped from the fingers that pointed; those pointing them were just too blind or ignorant to see it.

Despite all the hysteria going on in the city, and his rather accurate prediction, no one wanted to speak to Michael. Even after a week, his foster parents kept their distance. They were staunch Catholics and probably still thought he was some sort of demon or accomplice. Though they occupied the same house, he barely saw them.

His first friend in his new surroundings, Jimmy Rafferty, was taken away to where only God, and law enforcement brass, knew. Michael doubted he would ever see him again. His other friends, few that they were and scattered across the state where he'd lived in foster homes in the past, had made no effort to reach out to him. In the age of social media, where Michael had hundreds of "friends" on Facebook, their silence gave him a deeply rooted feeling of abandonment, one to which he was no stranger.

When he received a wall post on his Facebook page from a dummy account, he began to understand the reason for his isolation. He had finally become an outcast. One word, "freak," told him all he needed to know. Someone had talked. Someone had shared his vision with the public at large. Among his fellow students, gossip traveled fast. Apparently, they weren't receptive to his "gift."

Damn Helen and Greg and their big mouths. They probably think I'm that kid from The Omen. He collapsed onto his twin bed in a room still decorated for a real son who had died fighting in Afghanistan or some other desert. Everywhere he went, in every suburban Massachusetts town the powers that be shipped him off to, Michael felt like an outsider. Even back in the city of his birth, he didn't seem to belong. *Why should I have expected Carnegie High School to be any different?*

"Fuck!" He strangled his pillow then whipped it at the wall. "Punished once again for doing what was right." He let out a deep, heavy sigh. No one was there to console him. He was alone. He'd always been alone. Except for Sam, he'd never had anyone he could really talk to. But even she had let him down.

His cellphone rang. Michael ignored it until the noise became annoying. Aggravated, he snatched up the phone, intending to send the caller to voicemail. But he decided to pick up when he saw Sam's name.

"Hello?"

"Hi, Michael. How are you holding up?"

"I'm okay, I guess. I'm not really sure what to make of it yet. I get the sense that everyone knows about my vision. They think I'm a freak."

"How would anyone have found out? Did you tell other people?" Sam sounded concerned, which made Michael feel a bit better.

"Not sure. I only told Helen, Greg, Principal Alves, and you."

"Michael, I hope you know I would never put you in a situation like that."

"Yeah, I know." There was something else that needed to be said. He didn't know how to broach the topic.

The silence became awkward. Perhaps she was having difficulty, too.

Then, Sam blurted, "I wish I had listened to you, Michael."

"It's okay," he lied.

"If I had just listened to you, you wouldn't be going through all this now, and Glenn Rodrigues wouldn't be dead. I'm so sorry."

"It's not your fault. If I were you, I doubt I would have believed me either. What's important is that you believe me now, right?"

After a moment, she replied, "I don't know what to think. I believe that *you* believe it."

Michael could almost hear her brain calculating through the phone. She was taking her time, choosing her words with caution. He wished she would speak her mind and be done with it. She'd never held back before. *She doesn't think Jimmy confided his plans to me ahead of time, does she?*

As if sensing his thoughts, Sam added, "I don't think you had anything to do with this. I'm on your side here. But people are going to have a lot of questions about how you knew what you knew. I'll try to protect you as much as I can. You're not to blame here. *We* are. We should have listened to you."

Yes, you should have. He found it hard to bite his tongue. *That's exactly what you should have done.* He wanted to shout out his agreement, to ream her for not trusting him. "What's done is done."

"Yes," Samantha replied. He wondered if she could sense his frustration. She certainly wasn't trying to provoke it. "Well, I'll let you go. If you need me, I'm here for you."

"Thanks, Sam." Michael hung up the phone without saying goodbye. He appreciated her show of concern, but if she'd just listened to him in the first place, her call wouldn't have been necessary.

He tossed his phone onto the dresser, grabbed his pillow off the floor, and let his head sink deep into it. The stress and worry had worn him down. His eyelids were like windows that refused to stay open— each time he lifted them, they slowly slid closed again. If sleep insisted on coming, he hoped it would last the month. He would have settled for Tuesday, as if delaying his first day back after the shooting would somehow mitigate its difficulty. He closed his eyes and let his dreams take him where they would.

When Monday morning came, Michael was unable to think of any good reason to stay home. Sooner or later, he would have to face that awful first day back as the freak who had foreseen Glenn's death, so he might as well just get it over with.

All morning long, he kept his head down. He could feel the other students watching him, though, condemning him. But no one spoke to him. *I may get through this day yet.*

Class after class passed uneventfully. Lunch came, and he ordered his usual cheeseburger and tater tots. He sat at the end of a table that was nearly full except for the seats adjacent to and across from him. He was alone but not conspicuously so, just as he intended.

The chatter of six hundred voices, none of which seemed interested in him, made Michael feel nonexistent. It was a good feeling. The noise drowned out his thoughts. He appreciated the chance to let his mind go blank. He huddled over his food, content to be undisturbed.

Silence had a way of unsettling the calmest nerves, particularly when it came unexpectedly. In a crowded cafeteria, silence had no rightful place. Michael wondered how long it had been before he noticed the stationary mouths, voices turning into whispers or quieting altogether. Someone or something had caught the attention of a cafeteria full of students, but Michael kept himself ignorant, eyes on his meal.

Footsteps came close to his table. He tried to think nothing of them, guessing they would soon pass him by, but a feeling in his gut told him to beware. The footsteps grew louder. Then, the owner stopped right beside Michael. A shadow loomed over him, a very big shadow. Reluctantly, Michael raised his head.

Robbie. Fuck. He was the last person Michael wanted to see. *Does he blame me for Glenn's death? Does he want revenge? What else could he possibly want from me?* With a gulp and a quick prayer, Michael looked away. He didn't want to see the pain coming.

"I heard what you did," Robbie said. He didn't sound angry. "You tried to save him, even though he... no, *we* were jerks to you."

Michael was speechless. *Why am I not dead yet? Is he actually apologizing?* He couldn't believe he was hearing Robbie correctly. He wondered when Robbie would get to the punchline and how painful or humiliating it would be. *Or maybe he's worried I might try to shoot him.*

"Anyway," Robbie continued, "I'm sorry for what we did to you. I was against taking it that far, but that doesn't excuse my part in it. It wasn't right."

Flushing with anger, Michael met Robbie's eyes. "Tell that to Jimmy," he blurted then immediately regretted the outburst. Robbie could snuff him out as easy as extinguishing a cigarette. Michael leaned away as far as he could, fully expecting a beatdown to ensue.

But Robbie just shrugged. "I wish I could. I owe him more than that. I owe you, too. Anyway, if you ever need anything…"

Michael could see Robbie meant it. He wondered if the big, scary monster had a heart after all. His anger and fear retreated. Without a word, he returned to his food, dismissing Robbie's presence as though the boy weren't worthy of his time. Robbie left, probably going back to whatever group of post-growth-spurt mongoloids he hung out with at lunch.

The rest of the day went smoothly. Michael held his head a little higher with each passing hour. When the final bell rang, he even had the slightest skip to his step as he exited the building.

"Michael," someone called from near the exit.

He looked up and saw Sam standing by her Toyota Camry, her personal and professional vehicle, not the typical American-made car most cops were required to use. If there was one thing Michael knew for sure about Sam, it was that she was never really off duty. He walked over to greet her.

"Spying on me?" he asked, only half joking.

"Not at all." Sam smiled back. "I did want to check in on you, though. How's everything going?'

"Could be worse, I suppose."

"I've got someplace I've gotta go. Can you come with me? There's someone I would like you to meet. I'll take you home afterward."

Michael considered his options: go home and be bored, or go with Sam and probably be bored. He opted for the latter. Jumping into the Camry, he slouched back into the seat, feeling a mixture of pride and relief and hoping tomorrow would be easier.

CHAPTER 8

GLORIA DIDN'T KNOW WHAT TO make of Robbie Wilkins. In all her years as a guidance counselor, she had never met a bully who seemed to be genuinely sorry for what he had done, and not just because whatever infraction he had committed had landed him in detention or jail. She wouldn't feel sorry for him, though, not until she was certain he had learned his lesson. "Give me something, Robbie. Help me to understand why someone as big as you needs to terrorize the younger kids by stuffing them in toilets?"

"I don't really like talking about this stuff, Ms. Jackson." Robbie averted his eyes, slid down low in his chair, and shoved his hands in his pockets. "I mean, what we did to those freshmen was wrong. I know that. I knew it when we did it, too."

"You don't seem like a bad kid, Robbie." Gloria folded her hands together and leaned forward, resting her elbows on her desk. "If you knew better, why did you do it?"

Robbie shrugged. "I don't know."

"I'm going to ask you something, and remember that whatever you say in here is one hundred percent confidential—do you regret what you did?"

"To which one?"

"Both."

Robbie's eyes began to shimmer, and his lower lip trembled. He cleared his throat. "Yes."

Gloria smiled softly. It was a smile she wore often to pacify those who came to see her, to let them know she was a friend. And although the smile was contrived, the sentiment behind it wasn't the least bit phony. She knew what kids like Robbie generally thought of high school guidance counselors. Yet he had come to see her without prompting. "There's hope for you yet, Mr. Wilkins."

Gloria stood. "What you did was wrong, and I don't have to tell you how much harm your actions have caused. The important thing is that you realize your mistake, and you learn from it. You did a bad thing, but you can still be a good person."

Robbie nodded. As he walked out of Gloria's office, she asked him to send in her next appointment.

Two girls entered, one pushing past the other and charging up to Gloria's desk while the other girl, quiet as a mouse, hung just inside the door.

"Veronica—" Gloria managed to say before the over-made-up Barbie doll cut her off.

"Ms. Jackson, we need to talk about Jocelyn. She keeps running cheer practice like she's Hitler and we're her slaves. I mean, I'm way better than her. She can't even do a split all the way down. How she got to be captain is beyond me." Veronica threw a thumb back at the girl at the door as she chomped down on a massive wad of gum. "This one would make a better captain than that slut Jocelyn. What do ya say, Tessa? Feel like trading your church wear for a short skirt and spandex? Maybe let the boys see what you got hiding under there?"

Gloria slammed a hand on her desk. "Veronica!" The bubbly cheerleader jumped, and Gloria pointed at the door. "I have an appointment with Ms. Masterson. Please, wait outside, and I will be with you when we are through here."

Veronica smirked. "You have an appointment with Tessa? I know freshman boys who are more interesting than her. I'm not even sure she speaks. At least I won't have to wait very long." She stuck out her tongue at Tessa and skipped out the door.

"Veronica?" Gloria called.

"Yes?"

"Shut the door."

When the room was finally theirs alone, Gloria scrutinized the skinny sophomore standing in her office, hugging herself tightly. If there were any bruises or scars on the girl, they were in places well hidden. Tessa's turtleneck and pants covered all the usual locations where physical abuse manifested itself on the human body. But from her face, Gloria's trained eye could read volumes. Tessa had no black eye, split lip, or other smoking-gun indicators of a problematic personal life. But her inability to even fake comfort, her nervousness that far exceeded that of a normal self-conscious teen, called out to Gloria. It cried, "Help me," even if Tessa didn't realize it herself. But without proof of physical abuse, Gloria would have to poke and prod for another type of scar, the emotional kind.

Tessa stood behind a chair, one of two mismatched, upholstered monstrosities the school had probably picked up from yard sales. Shaking like an addict in withdrawal, the teen seemed as if she were only half there, her mind a prison to fear. To call her introverted would have been an understatement. One look at Tessa, and Gloria knew the girl was a recluse. At her age, Tessa had two choices: accept and insert herself into a superficial and often cruel high school social class structure or retreat from it. Gloria didn't need her files to tell her which Tessa had chosen.

Her gaze cast downward, Tessa fidgeted with her hair, awaiting her instructions. Gloria could see she didn't want to be there. None of them ever did. How could Gloria explain to the poor child that she had taken the job as one of Carnegie High School's four guidance counselors— four to guide more than two thousand—to help girls like Tessa, girls who thought there was no way out of the hell that surrounded them. They never asked for her help, but she gave it all the same. She helped as many as she could and took comfort in the fact that they were usually grateful after they received her help. *Usually.*

"Sorry about Veronica. She can be a real pain in the you-know-what." Gloria hoped the jab at Veronica would endear her to Tessa, but the girl didn't show any sign that she had even heard it, never mind a smile. "Please, have a seat." She watched closely as Tessa pulled back the chair with slow precision, as though any noise it made against the carpet would shatter the fragile balance existing in the air, opening the world to chaos.

After stepping in front of the chair, the girl scooted it forward and beneath her with the same caution. She sat with her back straight and her legs crossed. Still, she avoided Gloria's eyes.

"Hello, Tessa," Gloria said gently. She needed Tessa to see that she was a friend, someone she could not only trust but also confide in. But trust came only with time, if it ever came at all. And for those whose trust had already been betrayed, it rarely did.

Tessa's mouth moved, but no sound came out.

Gloria took it as a responsive greeting. *Small talk won't likely be fruitful with this one.* She decided to delve right into the business at hand. "Your teachers have come to me with concerns about you. Let me say first that you are not in trouble. We are worried about your well-being. That's it. We want to help."

She paused. Tessa didn't look at her, nor did she respond. Getting through to the girl wasn't going to be easy. But the toughest cases usually required Gloria's interference the most.

"Your teachers say you don't talk to anyone, you have no friends, and you're having trouble fitting in. They say some of the other girls have been picking on you."

"I get along with everyone just fine," Tessa said softly but with a hint of defensiveness. Her head tilted slightly, and Gloria thought she might make eye contact, but it didn't happen. "And my grades are good," she added.

"You're not in trouble here, Tessa. This has nothing to do with your grades, which are excellent. You could have a bright future... if other issues don't hold you back. You're even in the running for valedictorian, though from what I'm gleaning from you, I doubt you would like that very much."

Tessa shuffled her feet.

Gloria sighed. *What can I say or do to connect with this child?* But she wasn't defeated. She wouldn't stop trying. She would never stop trying. "I want to help you, Tessa. If anything were wrong, anything at all, not just here but outside of school as well... at home, maybe... you could tell me. You know that, right? Anything you say here would never leave the confines of this office."

Gloria knew she was required by law to report any abuse disclosed to her. She hated lying to Tessa, particularly when she was asking the girl to trust her, but finding out the truth took priority. Extracting a child from an abusive home had to be her primary goal.

Her lie didn't matter; Tessa wasn't talking. She would have to ask better questions, pry a bit deeper. The smart kids were always harder to crack.

"You started here as a freshman, but before that, you went to school in Denver. So you're no stranger to big-city public schools. Still, that had to be quite a change. Fall River probably seems small to you. But it's still big enough to get lost in the crowd, isn't it? What was school like in Denver?"

Tessa didn't say a word, just picked at her fingernails.

Gloria wondered if the girl was even listening. *Perhaps I should try a more sensitive topic. If I get lucky, she'll open up or at least lower her guard.*

"I've read your file." Gloria pulled a manila folder from a desk drawer and hunched over it as though it contained Tessa's most precious secrets. In reality, only report cards, sparse details pertaining to the girl's educational history, and Gloria's notes were kept inside the folder. The rest, she had learned from Google.

She pretended to rifle through the folder. "It's been almost two years since your mother died." Gloria paused to observe the child's reaction.

Tessa stopped fidgeting and frowned, her lower lip quivering. She looked up briefly, her cold stare saying more than all the words she had managed to utter since she entered the office. Fury raged behind the ice, and Gloria thought Tessa might leap out of her seat and attack her, but the anger seemed to pass quickly.

The wound is still fresh. Maybe the child wasn't a victim of abuse after all. Maybe Tessa couldn't cope with losing her mother. Dealing with a hurt in the past was a whole lot easier than dealing with a hurt that was repetitive in nature. Gloria wasn't naive enough to believe that time healed all wounds, but Tessa was young and impressionable. She had a lot of time to try to heal.

"On top of her passing, you had to move from Denver and give up your old life, all your old friends. It's not easy making friends in a new school. Unless you put in the effort, you're not likely to make any."

Tessa let out one of those long-suffering sighs that only a teenager could produce. Gloria knew she was losing her, if she'd ever been gaining her to begin with. The girl appeared annoyed, likely wondering how much longer their meeting would take.

As long as it needs to. "I can see that you don't want to talk to me, and that's fine. I understand. I'm a stranger. But if you give me just an ounce of your trust, I think you'll find me deserving of it. Anyway, you have to talk to somebody. It's obvious something's going on inside that head of yours. Carrying around the burden isn't healthy. And you don't have to carry it alone. If you don't want to talk to me, maybe I can arrange a meeting with your father, and he and I can discuss—"

"No!" Tessa leaped from her seat.

Surprised by the outburst, Gloria leaned back in her chair. But just as quickly as Tessa had jumped to her feet, she settled back into her chair, acting as if her reaction had been normal.

Tessa cleared her throat. "I mean... um, we shouldn't bother Father with this. He's had a hard time with the loss of Mother, too."

Bingo! She's scared of her father. I bet she's hiding bruises beneath all that clothing, unless it's purely psychological. I doubt it, though. The poor kid skulks like a dog with its tail between its legs. Though Gloria was now certain Tessa was a victim of child abuse, she still lacked evidence. "Are you sure?" she asked. "In the right setting, talking with your father may help you cope with the feelings you keep locked up inside you."

"Please, Ms. Jackson." Tessa finally looked at her. She tried to appear cool and collected, but the way her eyes trembled in their sockets gave her away.

Gloria saw through her act as if it were the box around a mime. Little signs and subtle movements—the clenching of her teeth, the brushing back of her hair around an ear—revealed much to those who understood their impetus. Together with her hollow words, they painted a portrait with dark colors. Tessa was broken.

She leaned forward a little. "I'll make new friends. I promise. I'm just a little shy."

It's worse than I thought. Gloria felt tears welling up in her eyes. At that moment, she would have sacrificed everything to give the girl a chance at happiness. She stifled her heartache to be strong for the both of them. "Okay. We'll see how things go for now. If you need anything, though, you come and see me. Okay?"

"Yes, Ms. Jackson. I will." Tessa flashed her a smile. It didn't seem forced, probably due to the relief she felt from Gloria's reprieve. "May I go now?"

"Yes."

Tessa left in a hurry, a stark contrast to the speed with which she had arrived. Gloria, however, had no intention of leaving the matter at that. Tessa didn't need to know her suspicions. Too many times, Gloria had seen victims protect their abusers. She would not let Tessa be her own worst enemy.

She picked up her telephone and dialed a familiar number. The call was answered on the second ring. "Department of Children and Families. Janet speaking. How may I help you?"

"Hi, Janet. It's Gloria over at Carnegie. I think I have another one for you." *And I hope this time, we're not too late.*

CHAPTER 9

"**W**HERE ARE WE GOING?" MICHAEL didn't like surprises. He'd experienced enough of them in the past two weeks to last a lifetime.

"I told you. I want you to meet someone," Sam answered.

"Who?"

"Just someone. Don't worry so much. How's school going? Is everyone treating you all right?"

"I guess. Everyone's treating me the same as before the shooting. Nobody talks to me. Except... well, Robbie Wilkins came up to me the other day."

"Really? What did that son of a bitch have to say for himself?"

"He apologized."

She raised her eyebrows. "That's surprising. Still, I would keep clear of him. What he did to you is beyond normal teenage delinquency. He should be in jail, or at least in juvenile hall, if only you hadn't refused to testify."

"You know that would have only made things ten times worse for me at school. Besides, I would hardly want what happened to me published in the newspaper. Everyone probably knows anyway, but at least now they aren't making fun of me for it."

"Do you have any other friends besides Jimmy?"

"I barely know Jimmy, and he's the closest friend I have around here... unless *you* count."

Sam gave him one of her awkward smiles. "Have you thought about playing a sport? It would be a great way to meet new people and stay busy."

"Like what? Football? I would get killed. Cross country? Soccer? Both seem like a ton of running to me. Anyway, the season is half over. Maybe I'll try out for basketball in the winter."

"I played point guard, you know," Sam said enthusiastically.

"Oh yeah? When was that? 1965?"

"Oh, you're a funny one. Anyway, we're here." Sam pulled up in front of a duplex on Rock Street. The house was old, probably built sometime in the 1940s. Its light-blue paint was worn and peeling. A shutter hung at a slant from one of the upstairs windows.

Michael glanced at the houses beside it. They looked pretty much the same, not necessarily run-down but aged and weathered. The only difference was their colors, one a freshly painted white and the other a horrid shade of yellow. *It looks like Helen and Greg's place. Hell, it looks like every duplex in Fall River. What are we doing here?*

Sam leaned in close to him. "The guy who lives here is John Crotty. His wife has gone missing. I have to ask him a few questions. It'll only take a couple of minutes. He says his wife ran off with another guy, but I don't know."

"Okay." He shrugged. "So why am I here exactly?"

"No reason," Sam replied matter-of-factly. "I thought I could use an unbiased second opinion. Let me know what you think of him. Obviously, you aren't supposed to be here, so let's keep this between you and me. Afterward, we can get some dinner. How's Flapper Jack's sound?"

"Are you buying?"

"Of course."

"Then it sounds good to me."

They got out of the car and strolled up the walkway to the front steps. Sam rang the doorbell.

Almost immediately, the door was opened by a man who looked a little older than Greg. His expression was unfriendly, as though he was agitated by their presence. He donned a grin as phony as nondairy creamer.

Sam put on a phony smile of her own. "Mr. Crotty, do you have a minute to talk?"

"Sure," Crotty said. "I didn't expect to see you again so soon, Detective. Any news of my wife?"

"Unfortunately, there have been no new developments. I just had a few more questions."

"Well, come in." Crotty stepped back. "It's getting too cold to be outside." He nodded at Michael. "Who's this?"

"My nephew," Sam replied. "We're about to grab an early dinner. This won't take long."

"Nice to meet you," Michael said, extending his hand in an attempt to be polite.

Still holding the door open, Crotty offered only a grunt. Sam frowned, and Michael wondered if he'd done something wrong. He let his hand fall and proceeded through the doorway. *Jerk.*

Crotty closed the door and directed them over to a couch not far from the entrance. "Can I get you and your sidekick something to drink, Detective?"

"No, thank you. We've got to be going soon. I just wanted to ask if you could think of anything else about the man your wife was seeing."

"Nope. Nothing more than I've already told you. Sorry. They're probably in Hawaii by now, having the time of their lives while maxing out our credit cards. Is it wrong for me to hope that they both get eaten by sharks out there?" He chuckled.

"It happens," Michael said. "I always watch Shark Week on the Discovery Channel and you should see—"

Sam put a hand on his knee. "Michael…"

Crotty barked out a laugh. "I like this kid."

Michael was glad he could act as comic relief, though he had no clue what he had said that was so funny. He nodded. "Good. Then I'll take that drink you offered. Soda, if you have it."

Slapping his palms on his legs, Crotty stood and disappeared into the kitchen. A minute later, he returned with a glass half-filled with a dark bubbling liquid. "I hope Diet Coke is okay." He held the glass out to Michael.

"Yes, it's fine. Thank you." Michael reached for the glass. As he wrapped his fingers around it, the side of his index finger rubbed against the tip of Crotty's pinky finger.

Michael's body seized. He felt himself falling back against the couch, but instead of stopping against it, he seemed to sink right through it. He heard echoes of Sam's voice. She was asking if he was all right, but he couldn't respond. The outline of Crotty's face floated above him. Then, Sam and Crotty were gone.

Michael lies on concrete covered in dust and grime. The only light comes from a window that has been screened with a towel. The window is inches below the ceiling. A basement? Yes, but not one he's ever seen before.

How the fuck did I get here? *Muffled groans carry into his ears. His breath catches in his throat; he lies perfectly still. Someone else is here with him.*

In the hazy light, he sees the back of a metal chair with a head and shoulders above it. They belong to a woman, or at least he thinks it's a woman because the hair is long for a guy. The head is separated from the shoulders by a metal robot neck.

For a moment, he trembles quietly, waiting to see what the cyborg will do. She does not stand, nor does she turn to face him. Still, he keeps his distance, not knowing who she is, why she is here, or whether she is a friend or an enemy. He rolls onto his belly, rises to his feet, and creeps closer for a better look. Her neck isn't robotic at all. It's held in a vice. She cannot move, yet Michael is still scared. She looks creepy. He gathers his nerve and walks closer. The contraption around her neck has teeth on its inside, small triangles stabbing her skin.

"Hello? Are you okay?" His voice comes out so low that he can't even hear it. He clears his throat and tries again. "Miss? Who did this to you?"

The woman remains silent, save for her soft moans. He reaches for her bare shoulder, her white blouse having slid off it, exposing a white bra strap upon which Michael's eyes absently fixate. Inch by inch, his hand lowers unsteadily to that patch of naked flesh.

"Miss?" He knows he's speaking, though he still can't hear his voice. Can she?

She might be dead, *he thinks, even though he can hear her sobbing.* Maybe we're both dead.

"Please... just say something."

No response. Michael's shoulders droop. He backs away then circles the woman in a wide arc.

Her black skirt is hiked up to her hips, almost to the point of showing Michael something he definitely doesn't want to see for the first time on this stranger. Her panties are wrapped around her ankles and stained yellow with flecks of red. The sight makes him aware of a foul odor, like that of a dog kennel, and he wonders just how long the woman has been here. Shredded nylons run up the length of her legs, ending at mid-thigh where circular black spots on her skin look as though someone has put out a few cigarettes there.

Her blouse is slit down the middle from collar to belly button, exposing womanly curves filling out a lace bra. Bruises and bite marks are scattered across the tops of her breasts. Michael realizes he's staring, and as his face heats, he raises his eyes to her face.

The woman appears to be in her mid-forties. Makeup is smeared across her cheeks and chin. Her tears have caused part of the mess, but the rest is hand drawn. Black mascara streaks beneath her eyes. Candy-red lipstick coats her lips, clownlike, as if whoever had applied it couldn't stay within the lines. It clumps on her teeth. Her eyebrows are missing, the brown dot stubble in their place suggesting they were shaved off. Blush is applied so heavily to her cheeks that it almost hides the bruises. The worst of it is the word "filth" written across her forehead in what looks like permanent black marker.

Even though she has a gag in her mouth, Michael can tell that under normal circumstances, she has a kind face and striking features. Leather straps are fastened around her forearms and wrists, binding her to the chair. She is crying, emitting this gut-wrenching sound as sobs force their way past the ball gag. She keeps her eyes closed even after Michael tries to talk to her again.

Aw, man, this is so fucked up. What's going on? *Michael wants out of this basement. He doesn't belong here. He prays that whatever force put him in this cellar will soon put him back where it found him. Then, almost as an afterthought, he prays for the woman, too, even though he has to question whether she's real or a figment of his imagination.*

Voices sound from overhead. Michael spots a staircase with a door at the top. An escape? He sidesteps toward it, keeping his eyes on the woman as if she could go somewhere. Her eyes shoot open, freezing him in place then drawing him back to her like a tractor beam. He trips over his feet when they refuse to cooperate with his mind, and he stumbles back onto the unforgiving concrete. Bracing for the impact, he cringes, but he feels no pain when he hits the floor. In fact, he doesn't feel anything at all.

The woman stares at him, and the fear he sees in her eyes makes him equally afraid. On palms and heels, he scurries backward. Is she afraid of him or someone else? He wonders if the owners of the voices upstairs are friendly.

No, she isn't looking at me. *Something about her gaze is off. She isn't looking at him but through him. He waves his hand in front of her face. She doesn't react. He is certain now that he is invisible to her, that more than shock is at play.* What's happening? Where's Sam?

"Sam?" *Michael calls.*

But no sound passes his lips. Why can't anyone hear me? *He shivers, arriving at the theory that maybe only he is dead. Frightened and angry, he punches the floor, but he feels no impact. Part of him thinks his knuckles passed through the floor as though it were water. The concrete seems to ripple. But his rational mind assumes his eyes cannot be trusted. After all, he is sitting on that very floor.*

A door closes upstairs, then footsteps and voices come from outside the building. Michael is thankful that at least one of his senses seems to be working properly. He runs to the window, thinking he'll tear down the makeshift blind, but every time he reaches for the towel, his hand misses it. Everything remains slightly hazy, so Michael chalks up his bad aim to cloudy depth perception.

He peeks through the slit between the duct-taped towel and the framing around the inset window. The outside world looks vaguely familiar: grass and a cement walkway leading to a street, someone's front lawn. Sam's black Toyota Camry is parked at the end of the walkway. A tall, slender woman with a long, charcoal-colored wool coat and knee-high black boots walks into Michael's line of sight.

Sam! *Michael tries to yell, his lips forming the words, but his vocal chords stay unresponsive. Is she leaving? How can she leave without him?* I'm still here, Sam, trapped in the basement. Something's wrong. Something's terribly wrong. Damn it, Sam! Help me!

He pounds on the window and swipes at the towel covering it. No matter what he does, the window remains unchanged. Sam keeps walking away from him. She doesn't hear him. How could she? Michael can't even hear himself.

Am I a ghost? *His hands certainly seem intangible. He slowly pokes the towel with his finger. When it appears to be touching the towel, he continues his finger's motion toward the window. Even though he half expects it, Michael has to stifle a scream when he sees half his finger disappear behind the towel. His mind searches for an explanation, some way to make sense of his situation. His panic is quickly getting the better of him.* How did this happen? How did I die? Was the soda poisoned? Did I even drink it?

Hysterical, Michael watches Sam climb into her car. She's going to leave him trapped in this basement forever, his only company a stranger who doesn't know he exists when he's standing right in front of her.

Then, Michael sees someone else opening the passenger-side door of Sam's Camry. Though it makes no sense and chills him to his core, he cannot deny what he's seeing. It's him! He's getting into the car.

As Sam and the doppelganger who has somehow stolen his life drive away, Michael hears a creak from the basement door. A light overhead flickers on. Work boots, then pant legs, then the rest of a man descend the stairs. When John Crotty reaches the bottom step, Michael wonders again if the man poisoned or drugged his soda. The last thing he remembers before the basement is Crotty handing him a drink.

Crotty approaches the woman. His chest is puffed out like a gorilla warning a trespasser to back off. He struts by Michael without a glance.

The woman struggles to break free when she hears Crotty behind her. Crotty combs his hand through the woman's long, straight hair. She flinches, closing her eyes. Tears leak from their corners.

"You've gotten me into a world of trouble, darling," Crotty says. He lifts the chair from the floor while the woman squirms, displaying his strength

for no other reason than to terrorize her. Then, he puts the chair down, walks in front of her, and squats so that he and the woman are at eye level.

"You're nothing but a cheating whore. I didn't want this. I didn't want any of this. I've always been faithful. Wasn't my love good enough for you?" Crotty lets out an exaggerated sigh. "I guess not, since you've been tainting our bed with some other man's scent." With each word, Crotty's face grows a darker shade of red. The veins in his arms pulsate, coursing with hot blood. Michael can see Crotty physically restraining his rage. It threatens to explode. Michael has felt the same way before. Rage like that needs an outlet. Michael shudders at the thought. The woman would serve as Crotty's outlet.

Michael runs at Crotty with all his might, thinking to tackle him and not worrying about what would come afterward. But he hurtles through *Crotty without even feeling any contact at all.*

Why can't I help her? *Michael begins to realize what's happening, even if he can't understand his part in it. He can see what Crotty has planned.* Am I really going to be forced to watch this, unable to do anything about it? Why is this happening to me? *The last question makes Michael feel selfish, then ashamed. He looks at the woman in the chair, restrained and inconsolable and about to feel so much pain. She has it far worse than he does.*

Crotty walks over to a workbench propped against the far wall. His every step is slow and methodic. He spends several minutes going through his tools, searching for one in particular. The right tool for the job, Michael assumes. The thought makes him want to retch. Helpless as he is, Michael can only watch and pray. Maybe Crotty won't be able to go through with it. He doesn't look like a killer. Then again, neither did Jimmy.

"Fuck it." Crotty picks up a cordless drill. Then he grabs a bit that looks to be a foot long, one of those swiveling kinds shaped like ribbon candy.

Carrying the drill over to the woman, Crotty fixes the bit into the chuck. He gives it a few test spins, seemingly content with his choice. A wry grin worms its way across his face.

"Oh, my sweet, faithful wife..." Crotty makes a tsking sound. "What's a scorned lover to do?" He begins to pace in front of her, spewing curses. He says things Michael would never dare say to anyone, much less a woman. But Michael figures that the longer the guy paces and swears, the longer he keeps his hands off the woman. Time enough to let out his anger, rethink his

plans, Michael hopes. But his hope is faint because of the nagging thought that he wouldn't be seeing this if Crotty was going to let the woman go.

This has to be a vision. The first time it had happened, though, he had been able to interact with those in it. Now he is collateral damage, forced to watch, unable to stop it. But it has to be a vision. The alternative is far more frightening. He saw himself leave the house. The woman's death isn't an event he's supposed to be attending.

Crotty suddenly stops pacing and raises the drill. He clicks the trigger, letting the bit spin in the air in front of his wife's eyes. A low moan works its way out of her mouth. Tears bubble on her eyelashes as she presses her eyes closed and cringes away from the bit.

"Well, playtime's over, I guess. It is for you anyway." Crotty straddles her lap, leans forward, and plants a kiss on her clown lips. "I loved you."

The whir of the drill ceases. The woman stops sobbing and stares at her husband. The silence is so heavy that Michael thinks it impenetrable. Maybe if no one stirs, they could all stay frozen that way forever.

Crotty raises his head. A single tear trickles down his cheek. He wipes it away. The whirring of the drill begins again.

He roars as he wraps his left arm around the woman's head. With his right hand, he brings the drill in hard and fast, straight at the top of her head. He bores a dime-sized hole into her skull. The ball gag mutes her screams but not enough. They echo off the basement walls.

Bits of flesh and hair fly like mud off a merry-go-round. Crotty's wife's eyes roll back in her head. Crotty stands and jams one foot into her stomach, while the other is firmly planted beside the chair. He has more leverage and uses his own weight to push the drill through her skull, all the while clenching his teeth, his eyes full of hate.

Blood and bone spatter, and Michael screams soundlessly. He moves out of the way, even though none of it touches him. Hair twists around the drill and rips from her scalp. When the large drill bit is most of the way in, Crotty swirls it around inside as though whipping cream.

He finally pulls the drill out and steps back.

Then he starts a second hole. More and more hair and pieces of scalp tangle into the drill bit.

"Shit!" Crotty says when the drill stops working.

He tucks the drill into his armpit and starts picking the pieces off the bit. His wife's eyes are blank sheets as she convulses in the chair. The spiky triangles of the clamp tear her neck to shreds with every involuntary movement. White foam bubbles from her mouth. Her head droops, blood oozing in globs from the holes.

Michael averts his eyes. He hears Crotty drop the drill on the floor and turns to look at the man, the killer. Crotty gazes at his wife as though critiquing a sculpture. Michael doesn't see remorse, fear, or even happiness in the guy's face. The killer's eyes are just blank. But Michael has seen enough. He runs to the stairs and starts up them. When he opens the door...

Michael was lying on a couch. *Back in Crotty's living room?* The copper odor of blood lingered in his nostrils. He assumed he must have had another vision, but he had no way of knowing if he'd seen the past or the future.

Crotty's face appeared above him. "Hey, kid, are you okay?"

"You!" Michael drew his knees up to his chest then kicked at Crotty. "Get back!"

Frowning, Crotty stepped out of the path of Michael's feet. He threw up his hands. "What's wrong with this kid?"

Sam moved between them and placed a hand on Michael's knee. The expression on her face resembled what he imagined a mother's worry might look like. "Are you all right?" she asked. "Did you have another... incident?"

"Keep that sicko away from me, Sam." He scurried to the far end of the couch, as far as he could get from Crotty.

Sam moved down with him. Keeping his eyes on Crotty, Michael reached for her service pistol, holstered at her side.

She slapped his hand away. "What is it, Michael? What did you see?"

Michael glanced at her then quickly turned his gaze back on Crotty. "I saw us! My God! We were there—I mean *here*. That means..." His head started to spin. "I think I'm going to be sick."

Crotty sat in the chair across from the couch. "Will someone tell me what the hell is going on here?" Beads of sweat formed on his forehead, and he couldn't sit still, crossing and uncrossing his legs, switching his gaze between Sam and the door.

Michael swallowed and took in a breath. "It was horrible. It's like

I was brought here just in time to…" An idea suddenly came to him. "Wait a minute!" He took his eyes off the murderer long enough to glare at Sam. "Did you bring me here on purpose?"

"Michael, I—"

"'Cause I know that you—the one person I trust, the one person I can always count on— would never, ever bring me here and try to make that happen on purpose."

Sam averted her gaze. "Now's not the time to discuss it." She shook her head. "Just tell me what you saw."

Michael jabbed a finger at her. "You did, didn't you?" He scooted away but only a little, mindful of the drill-wielding psychopath nearby. "You fucking set me up! You knew I would see something. That's why you brought me here."

"Michael—"

Crotty leaned closer. "I don't know what you're going on about, but maybe it's time you two—"

"You are such a bitch!"

Sam straightened. "Michael!"

Michael slumped back into the couch, exhausted and defeated, betrayed by his only real friend. "I can't believe you would do that to me." He growled, pounded his fists into the couch, and glowered at her with animalistic rage. His stomach felt hollow. His heart ached in his chest. As the fight left him, he bit his lip, holding back tears.

She knew. I can't believe her. He pounded his fists into the couch. Oh, how he wanted someone to slap her, since he would never do it himself. *She wanted me to have another vision, even though she knew how much the first one bothered me. How, though? How did she know it would work?* Michael sneered at her. *I don't know. But she knew it would happen. She wouldn't have brought me here if she didn't.*

"Are you two quite finished?" Crotty asked. "As I was saying, I think you should—"

"Michael," Sam said softly, "we'll discuss why I brought you here later. From the way you reacted when you… um… woke up, I'm guessing we have more urgent matters to attend to." Her hand rested on the snap of her holster. "Please, for now, just tell me what you saw."

Michael wiped his nose with the back of his sleeve. Remembering the poor woman in the basement made him ashamed that he'd put his own problems first. "He's got a lady tied up in the basement."

"What?" Crotty slapped the armrests of his chair, rocking forward in his seat. "You have some nerve coming into my house—"

"Do you?" Sam asked. She stared at him with her piercing green eyes, sharp like jade daggers.

Crotty rose, his hand extended out before him. "Now hold on a second." His words came out fast, excited. "You're not making any sense. I've invited you into my home, treated you like guests, and—"

"It's a simple question, really." Sam unbuttoned her holster. "Do you or do you not have Amy Crotty tied up in your basement?"

Crotty's nose twitched. His body shook. "Do I have...? Get out! You hear me? I know my rights. You get out of my goddamn house right now, and take your little freak bastard with you."

"Michael," Sam said, still cool as ice, "do as the man says. Wait in the car."

Michael got up and tiptoed backward to the door, too terrified to take his eyes off Crotty. He fumbled behind his back, searching for the doorknob.

"That means you too, Officer." Crotty's fingers curled into hooks at his sides.

"We know you have her, Crotty. We found her car where you dumped it."

"You got no right being here, lady. I'm gonna ask one more time, nicely, for you to leave."

Michael found the doorknob. He turned it with a shaking hand.

"All I have to do is say I heard screaming." Sam chuckled. "Who's the jury going to believe, me or some no-good wife beater?"

Crotty raised his fist. "I'll show you wife beater, you... I mean, I got nothing else to say to you. Now get out of my house before I call your superiors."

"Call them. Meanwhile, I'm having a look in that basement."

Michael froze as the door creaked open behind him. Cold air blew in, raising the hairs on his neck. He wanted to leave, but he didn't want to leave Sam alone with that awful man.

Crotty dropped his fist and slapped his thighs. He quieted, his eyes studying Sam. "I don't... she's not..."

Sam took a step toward him. "Let's go have a look-see in that basement, shall we?"

Crotty huffed and turned around slowly, as if the weight of the world was his alone to bear. Michael, still frozen by the door, relaxed a little. He wondered if the man hadn't abducted his wife yet or, worse, had already disposed of her body.

Sam followed Crotty, keeping a few feet between them as he walked around the coffee table. As he reached the opposite end of the table, Crotty grabbed a vase of flowers and hurled it at Sam's head. She turned at the last second, and the vase hit her left shoulder, bounced off, and smashed against the floor. Crotty sprinted out of the room.

Sam drew her service pistol with the speed of a seasoned gunslinger and pointed it at Crotty's back. "Freeze, asshole."

Crotty didn't stop. He ran into the kitchen and yanked open a door Michael hadn't noticed earlier. He disappeared through the opening, slamming the door behind him. Sam ran over, yanked open the door, and followed him.

Michael heard her running down some stairs then metal clanging against concrete. It sounded as if Crotty had knocked over his entire workbench. He wondered if Crotty had gone for the drill.

"Sam?" Michael called softly. *She said to wait in the car.* He shivered. Despite his anger, he couldn't leave her down there with that monster. He crept toward the basement door.

He heard a lot of banging, like silverware thrown against a wall. "Get down on the ground, and put your hands behind your back!" Sam's voice echoed up the stairwell.

Michael smiled. *Sam can handle the guy a lot better than I could.* He turned the corner and looked into the basement. He couldn't see them from the top of the stairs, so he crept down a couple of steps and crouched.

Sam had her gun aimed at the bound woman because Crotty was hiding behind his wife. Michael was glad to see that she was still alive. For the moment, anyway. Crotty was holding an ice pick to the woman's ear.

"Come any closer, and this bitch bleeds!" Crotty's hand shook violently.

Amy's head tilted away from the weapon. Tears made mascara fans under her eyes. She looked just as she had in the beginning of Michael's vision.

Crotty glanced up at Michael, and a sort of calm washed over the man's face. He even smiled.

Oh God! He's gonna do it!

The killer brought his arm back and let out a primal yell as he swung it forward, aiming for his wife's ear.

A gunshot made Michael's ears ring. Crotty fell. The ice pick spiraled out of his hand and vanished somewhere beyond Michael's view with a few final clinks against the floor to mark its passing.

In an instant, Sam was on Crotty, rolling him onto his belly, driving her knee into his back, and ratcheting on the handcuffs. Michael ran the rest of the way down the stairs and began to unscrew the vice around Mrs. Crotty's neck. Her eyes pleaded for him to hurry. "I'm trying," he told her. She stared at him the entire time he undid the straps on her arms, which wasn't long, he knew, but felt like forever.

Once her arms were free, the woman jumped out of her chair, ripped off the ball gag, and pummeled Crotty's head with it repeatedly while Sam was trying to stand him up. He fell face-first onto the hard floor. A soft whimper whistled out of a flattened nose. Still, she kept hitting him, holding the straps and swinging the ball into his skull again and again.

"That's enough," Sam said.

The woman looked at Sam as if considering starting in on her, then threw the ball gag against the wall, took a deep breath, and ran upstairs.

Crotty coughed as Sam pulled him to his feet. His nose looked more messed up than a veteran boxer's. He spit blood onto the floor.

Michael didn't feel the least bit sorry for the guy. He took one last look around the basement, noting all the details he had seen in his vision and knowing how close Mrs. Crotty had been to death. Confused, unsure how he was supposed to feel about it, he headed back upstairs. He waited at the top for Sam, wanting to make sure she stayed all right.

After reading Crotty his rights, Sam marched him up the stairs and thrust him into a chair. Then, she called for backup and an ambulance. Mrs. Crotty stood near the front door and stared out the window.

As the four of them waited for Fall River's finest to arrive, no one said a word. Michael had difficulty seeing Crotty's eyes behind the swollen purple cheeks, but he could feel them glaring at him. Michael concentrated on his hands as he waited.

Soon, sirens were blaring outside the house. Sam had placed a ton of faith in his vision. She had placed a ton of faith in him. That meant something he couldn't ignore no matter how angry he was with her. She would have been in a boatload of trouble if he had been mistaken or had misinterpreted what he had seen. *Kinda hard to misinterpret a drill to the head.* He would never be able to erase from memory what his vision had shown him. Michael had not been mistaken, and the fate of Crotty's wife had been altered, a fact he did not take lightly.

The first officers to arrive escorted Crotty to their patrol car on Sam's orders. They then walked Mrs. Crotty over to an ambulance.

Sam disappeared down the cellar stairs with the next arriving officers. Plastic bags were filled, and yellow tape was plastered everywhere.

Around Michael, officers were conversing, taking evidence, or otherwise going about their police business without so much as giving him a nod. Why did no one notice or care about the fourteen-year-old boy sitting in the middle of their crime scene? The thought that he might still be invisible made him uncomfortable. The way he was being ignored, he might as well have been. He pinched himself to make sure he was awake and solid. The pain reminded him that he was real.

After a half hour passed, Sam emerged from the basement, wearing rubber gloves. Michael watched her pull them off and throw them on the kitchen counter. She glanced about the room until her eyes met his. Then, without a word, she escorted him outside. They got into Sam's car, where he sat in silence the entire way back to his foster parents' home. Apparently, going to dinner was no longer an option. Sam seemed anxious to be rid of him.

"I'm sorry," Sam said as she pulled up to Helen and Greg's house.

Michael snapped. The ten-minute ride had not been long enough to quell his anger. "How could you? He... he was going to drill a hole in her head! You knew I would see it. You made me watch it."

"I didn't know," Sam said. "I had a hunch. I've heard of this kind of psychic phenomenon before. Some guy up in Maine supposedly helped police solve a number of cases just by touching objects at a crime scene. But I never really believed it until you predicted what would happen to Glenn Rodrigues. So I planned this little experiment. I also thought you would want to know if your vision regarding the school shooting was a fluke or if you actually do have the ability to see the future."

"So it's my fault I had to witness a man drill through his wife's skull? I'm sure there are other ways we could have tested whether my brain is a crystal ball. You could have at least had the decency to give me a heads-up. I'm not your damn guinea pig, Sam."

"I know. You're right, and I'm sorry. What I did was wrong, inexcusable. But you did save a woman's life today. What neither you nor Crotty knew was that we dragged his wife's automobile out of the Taunton River yesterday. Of course, that kind of thing screams foul play. And when a wife goes missing, the first suspect is the husband. Ninety-nine times out of a hundred, he's the one with blood on his hands."

"The end justifies the means? Is that what you're telling me? That shit I saw is going to give me nightmares for a long time."

"I put being a cop before being your friend. You feel betrayed by that and understandably so. Again, I'm sorry. I really am. But I would do it all again if it was necessary to save Amy Crotty's life, and I think you would, too. As long as you would be okay, I mean. Saving one life isn't worth destroying another's."

Honesty. If nothing else, he could always expect that from Sam. Yet honesty didn't make her betrayal hurt any less. Remembering the many times she'd been there for him, Michael could feel himself already forgiving her, but it would be a little while before he went with her on another ride-along. "I'll get over it," he said. "Just please don't do it again."

Sam smiled warmly. "I won't. At least not without warning you first."

Michael shrugged and opened the car door.

As he climbed out, Sam said, "You did an amazing thing today. You won't get any credit for it. In fact, if my bosses find out I even brought you over to Crotty's, they'll have my head. How we caught him could jeopardize the prosecution, Fourth Amendment rights and all that other mumbo jumbo."

"You mean he might actually go free?" Michael was shocked. John Crotty was a murderer as far as he was concerned, whether the rest of the world saw it that way or not.

"Don't worry about that. We'll find a way of making something stick. We obviously won't get him for murder and maybe not even attempted murder, but kidnapping his wife and assaulting an officer will get him a heck of a lot more than a slap on the wrist. And even in the extremely unlikely case that he somehow walks, I'm sure Amy Crotty will still think our intervention was well worth it."

Sam paused, staring at him that way she did when she probed his mind. It made him feel as if he were being dissected. "Still," she said, "you've got some amazing skills, kid. If you wake up tomorrow feeling good about saving that woman's life, maybe you'll want to lend your services to the Fall River Police Department again. What do you think? The people of Fall River could use someone like you on their side."

"I wouldn't count on it." Michael was grateful Mrs. Crotty hadn't been killed, but he felt he would be better off if he never had any other visions. They were nothing more than nightmares while awake, and he experienced plenty of those when he slept. He would be thrilled if he never had one again.

Michael waved to Sam as she drove away. *Sorry, Fall River. You'll have to rely on good old-fashioned police work to solve your crimes. I'm not cut out for that sort of work.*

CHAPTER 10

TESSA STARED ABSENTLY INTO HER locker, hugging her biology book against her chest. She didn't feel like going to class, and she definitely didn't want to get called on again by dumb Mrs. Lautner, who always seemed to know when Tessa was daydreaming. The other kids would snicker when Tessa asked her to repeat the question, not that she ever knew the answer anyway. *That idiot Lonnie Danvers will laugh loudest, hee-hawing like the jackass he is.*

It made her blood boil, his obnoxious cackle. Not that she would ever do anything about it. Still, she could almost hear it now. *Wait... I do hear it now. Is he laughing at me?*

She hugged in so close to her locker that she had practically stuffed herself inside it. She tilted her head back just enough to see Lonnie hee-hawing his way toward her with Stacy Fields by his side. What that seemingly normal girl saw in that moron, Tessa couldn't guess.

Lonnie's laughter boomed into her ears as he and Stacy formed the beginnings of a line outside the nearby classroom, just four feet away from Tessa's locker. Only a bent and rusted aluminum door separated her from them.

He must be keeping Stacy company before classes start. Better her than me.

Without a sound, she gathered her things, planning to tiptoe all the way to biology just to not have to deal with him. As she grabbed the locker door to swing it closed, she heard Lonnie say, "I heard from Nick Rennert that Nancy Pettigrew was there when Glenn was shot. According to Nancy, Michael Turcotte had tried to stop Jimmy from shooting Glenn. The rumor is that Michael knew about the shooting before it happened."

Tessa's hand fell away from the door. She leaned into her locker again but concentrated on Lonnie's voice. She had heard the gossip and the stories, that Jimmy shot Glenn for dumping him and Michael in the toilet or something like that. But up until now, Michael had been only a footnote in the story.

She didn't think much of Michael and barely knew him. He was kind of cute, in a little-brother sort of way. *Humph.* She giggled softly, covering her mouth with her hand. *Awkward, like me. Only he wears the hand-me-down's hand-me-downs.*

Tessa didn't know Michael, but she knew that foster kid stigma and the hurt of losing a parent. Other than that and their solo lunchtime habits, she doubted they had anything in common. She didn't know Jimmy or most of the others involved in the crime or the gossip trail either, but the thought of another potential student killer on the loose touched something deep within her. Maybe there was another student at Carnegie who kept as much pain locked up as she did. Still, she'd been forced. She never wanted to hurt anyone. Tessa wondered if this Michael guy was a different sort of animal. Pretending to flip through a notebook, she hesitated in the hallway to hear the rest of the conversation.

"He probably knew about it because he was in on it," Stacy said.

"Don't be stupid," Lonnie responded. "If he intended to shoot Glenn, why would he tell Principal Alves beforehand?"

"Maybe he got cold feet. Maybe he tried to stop it because he realized he couldn't go through with it."

"That's possible, I guess, but that's not what I heard. I heard he told them what was going to happen right down to the last detail. He said when and where it would happen, how it would happen, and who would be there when it happened. And he told Principal Alves about it two days before it happened."

"Probably because he planned the whole thing. Think, Lonnie. Michael Turcotte is not psychic. Don't tell me you really believe that?"

"I don't know. He even knew what Jimmy and Glenn would be wearing that day. Are you going to tell me he called them up to ask? Only girls do that."

"What were they wearing? T-shirts and jeans? Every guy wears that every day. Your gender has no imagination, never mind fashion sense."

Tessa stifled a giggle. Then, she looked down at her pink long-sleeved T-shirt and her blue jeans. Still, Stacy made sense. Lonnie's belief sounded silly.

"Besides," Stacy continued, "if the school knew about it before it happened and did nothing to stop it, wouldn't there be a lawsuit?"

"Give it some time," Lonnie said. "I bet there will be, probably a whole bunch of them. Anyway, I'm not the only one who thinks that kid is psychic. Ask around. You'll see."

"Maybe I'll just ask him." Stacy gave a sly grin. "He's kind of cute, for a freshman."

"Go ahead, but keep me out of it. That freak's got some sort of power, and who knows where the hell he's getting it from? He could be dangerous. I wouldn't go anywhere near him if I were you."

"It's all stupid gossip blown out of proportion," Stacy scoffed. "Just because you can't explain something doesn't mean it isn't explainable by someone smarter than you. And trust me, there's a perfectly rational explanation for it. Michael Turcotte is *not* psychic."

"I know better than to argue with you," Lonnie said.

Then, Tessa heard them kissing. She didn't think there was supposed to be so much smacking. A moment later, Lonnie strutted by as if the world gave him all the things he wanted, none of the things it would ever give her. He walked past her without ever looking her way.

She spent most of the afternoon thinking about Michael Turcotte and his superhero powers. On the bus, with kids yelling and screaming and shooting spitballs past her head, she daydreamed about what it would be like to see the future and how she would alter it.

Her true future involved grocery shopping. Tessa hated being out in public with Father. She hated being anywhere with him, but in public, she had to hide in plain sight. She always felt as though people were watching her, examining her for signs of the secrets she so desperately wanted to reveal.

When Tessa and her father got to the checkout line, the couple at the register had just finished unloading their basket onto the conveyor belt. A gorgeous Hispanic woman put the divider bar down and started putting her groceries on the belt. The woman was so beautiful that Tessa knew life had to have been easy for her. Father stepped up behind the Hispanic woman, swinging their basket behind him.

The exit of the grocery store was less than fifty feet away. *I could run. Just run and never look back.* Tessa shuddered. *Even if I managed to get away, he would find me. After that, things would be much worse.* She surveyed the shelf of candy bars and ran a finger along the edge of a box of Butterfingers, her favorite. She sighed. She knew better than to ask Father for one.

Father was quiet, as usual, and his gaze was intently set upon the Hispanic woman unloading her basket. Tessa couldn't blame him. Even she wanted to stare at the beautiful woman. But then she realized that Father's eyes were following the woman's hands and the items she was purchasing. He watched as a carton of eggs, a jar of peanut butter, and a bunch of celery were all placed on the conveyor belt.

He cleared his throat. "That's fourteen items," he said loudly.

The woman turned, and Father glared at her. If looks could kill, the woman would have died fifteen times over.

"Excuse me?" the lady asked.

"That's fourteen items," Father repeated. He pointed at the sign above the register. "This lane is for twelve items or less."

"I'm sorry," the woman said, obviously taken aback by the reproach. "I picked up a few more groceries than I had originally intended when I came in here. I'll put two of them back if it bothers you. Perhaps you could forgive me this one time?"

Father didn't answer right away. The question seemed to spawn conflict within him. The cashier, a pimply-faced girl with braces hopefully intended to fix her giant overbite, stared at him with her nose crinkled and mouth gaping. For the girl's sake, Tessa was thankful Father didn't seem to notice. But his expression remained hostile. Tessa was afraid the customer's beauty was about to fade much faster than life had planned for her.

Oh God. Not another one. Not this soon. Tessa straightened the boxes of candy on the shelves, trying to appear busy, disinterested. *Please don't kill her.*

The express lane violator seemed uneasy, too. Father had a way about him that made him appear more threatening than his small frame justified. His steel-hard glare, stiff posture, and low, monotone voice—and the way he always seemed to stand an inch or so closer than he should—unsettled anyone unfortunate enough to converse with him. The woman's apologetic smile began to fade.

Then, the unlikely happened. Father grinned. "No need to put anything back," he said. "Mistakes happen."

The woman gave a courteous nod and went back to her groceries.

Mistakes happen? Tessa wondered if the man next to her was the same man she'd always known, at least as far back as she could remember. Father didn't smile. He didn't forgive. Did he think it was Christmas? Was he suddenly willing to overlook menial rule violations? "Rules were meant to be enforced," he always said. He had said it so much that Tessa could hear him saying it in her head exactly as if he'd said it aloud. Rules weren't meant to be broken.

Father's uncharacteristic leniency was cause for alarm. Surely, the woman's subtle charms hadn't won him over. Something else must have been going on in that head of his.

The woman paid for her items, flashed Father another, somewhat nervous smile, and left. Father's eyes stayed on her until she traveled out of their view. The lady was gone. Tessa hoped she would never have to see her again.

On the way home, Father seemed to be in an unusually good mood. Nearing a light, he waved in a car waiting to exit a convenience store parking lot. When its driver didn't offer him a courtesy wave or nod in return, Father's grip on the steering wheel tightened. His hands twisted around the grip, then he slapped the dashboard. He mashed down the horn and stepped on the gas until he rode the car's bumper. He slammed his hands against the steering wheel.

Minutes later, they passed Winchester Street, the street they lived on, without turning. A sickly feeling rose in Tessa's stomach. He planned on teaching that driver a lesson.

CHAPTER 11

GLORIA'S FEET WERE LIKE IRON plates, each step made heavy by the task before her and the boundaries she was overstepping. It was nearly two p.m. when she ascended the stairs to an immaculately maintained, battleship-gray-painted house on Winchester Street. She knew she had no true business there. Officially, Gloria was forbidden to be there.

"We can't invade their privacy or make accusations without more substantial evidence than your hunch," Janet at the Department of Children and Families had said. "I'm sorry, Gloria, but we just don't have the resources to follow up on every suspected case."

She forbade my intervention as gently as she could, but "no" means "no," however the Commonwealth says it. It doesn't change the fact that this child needs me. Tessa could be dead before I can get state approval to ask a few questions.

But DCF was the least of her worries if either the father or the student should call the school to complain. *If Roger finds out I'm here, he'll kill me.* She shook her head. *He'll definitely have to fire me. How could the school's principal justify keeping on a guidance counselor who shows such blatant disregard for protocol.* She sighed. Roger was a good man, and she loved him, but she knew he would do whatever he thought necessary to maintain the integrity of his school.

He won't even let people know about us. Gloria's lips pressed into a flat line. *So what if he's my boss? It's not like either of us is married.*

"Always so concerned with policies," she mumbled. "The stupid policies are what got that Rodrigues boy gunned down. I'll be damned if I sit back idly and watch another kid sent to the slaughter."

She clenched a manila folder tightly beneath her arm, thinking about how she might have helped Glenn if she had just been a little less concerned with playing by the rules. Sure, he had denied the abuse at home, acting tough and being disrespectful toward her. But the signs were there—aggression bred aggression—and would have been obvious to a first-year psych student. She had met with his parents, as she did with all parents of suspended students, after he had dunked that poor boy in the toilet. She had seen Mr. Rodrigues cast his eyes away when his wife slapped Glenn's face so hard it left an imprint. Then, the woman had twisted Glenn's ear until the teen dropped to one knee, tears forming in his eyes.

Gloria had started to say something, but Mrs. Rodrigues glared and smiled wickedly as if to say she could do whatever she wanted to her boy and there wasn't a damn thing Gloria could do about it. Without another word, Glenn's mother dug her press-on nails into her son's arm and led the boy away, Mr. Rodrigues following meekly at her heels.

I should have done more then. I should have taken him out of that home and out of school, at least for a while longer, away from those he had hurt and those who wished to hurt him. I failed Glenn, and I failed the boy who shot him. Two lives ruined, all because of my inaction.

She stared at the smooth wood of the Mastersons' front door, convinced she had a moral duty to help Tessa Masterson, even if her official duties prohibited it. *Yep, I'm bound to get fired over this.* She shrugged. No one knew she was there, not even her boss and partner. Given the delicacy of her work, Gloria preferred to keep things that way. Whatever negative consequences would come her way, she was willing to accept them. She couldn't live with herself if something happened to Tessa while she sat back and did nothing. She rang the bell.

Tessa opened the door and gaped at Gloria. She paled and asked, "What are you doing here?"

"Who's at the door, Tessa?" a man asked from somewhere inside the house.

Gloria assumed the voice belonged to Christopher Masterson, the girl's father. She tried to catch a glimpse of the man she'd come to see by peeking around Tessa. The teenager closed the door to a crack.

"It's no one, Father," Tessa replied. She bit her thumbnail as she turned toward the voice.

"No one doesn't ring the doorbell," he said with a hint of irritation. "I'll ask again. Who's at the door?"

"A friend from school. She was just leaving."

The look Tessa gave her made clear that she wished it were so. "Leave," Tessa whispered. "Quick. Please," she whined, appearing on the verge of tears.

A moment later, the door swung all the way open. A man stood behind Tessa. No more than five-ten, with thick-rimmed glasses set high upon a crooked nose and a widow's peak that made him look a little like the Count from Sesame Street, Christopher Masterson wasn't particularly intimidating. He looked thin, almost feeble, as if he wouldn't put up much of a fight against most men his age. *Only the weak prey on the weak.*

Still, something about the way he stood there, staring at her as if measuring her, made Gloria shiver. She tried to figure out what she saw in his eyes that was so creepy until she realized that it was what she didn't see. His eyes were flat and dead.

Gloria was determined to have the stronger will. And if push came to shove, she could shove pretty hard. *I can't let this guy intimidate me. I won't.*

He stepped in front of Tessa and extended his hand to Gloria. "Christopher Masterson."

She shook his dry hand and released it as quickly as possible without being rude. "Gloria Jackson. I'm pleased to meet you, Mr. Masterson."

"Please, call me Chris."

"Certainly, Chris. I'm your daughter's guidance counselor at Carnegie High School. May I come in to speak with you about Tessa?"

"Tessa didn't tell me I should be expecting you. Is she in some kind of trouble?"

"No, not at all," Gloria said, smiling reassuringly at Tessa.

Tessa slunk away like a beaten dog, disappearing into the house.

Gloria's students never did have much faith in her to do her job. Most children of abuse saw no escape from it.

Chris didn't seem to notice his daughter's fearful behavior as he gestured for Gloria to enter. "Come in, but please take your shoes off." The corner of his mouth curled wryly. "First rule of the house."

Gloria stepped into the foyer and slipped off her shoes, grateful that she hadn't worn ones with laces that would take time to get on and off. Then, she followed Chris deeper into the house, having already lost sight of the girl she had come to help.

CHAPTER 12

THE DOORBELL RANG, AND MICHAEL raced out of his room and down the stairs. With the allowance he made from doing chores around the house, he often ordered comic books over the Internet, which he burned through faster than he could earn the money to buy more.

He nearly hip-checked Helen out of his way, smiling as he shouted, "I got it!"

Helen frowned, but he didn't care. Comic books were his escape, his chance to live in a world where he didn't have to worry about his foster parents rejecting him, school bullies attacking him, or other kids making fun of him. In those comics, he wasn't alone but part of a team of superheroes fighting the bad guys of a simpler reality. In those comics, he was strong and admired, not the weak little freak everyone thought him to be. He ripped open the door and grabbed the package out of the startled mailman's hand.

The guy laughed. "Whatcha got this time?"

Michael rotated the box in his hands. It looked as though it could hold up to ten comics. "I'm not sure. Some I subscribe to, and others I just get when I feel like it or if it looks like something big is going to happen, like when they killed off Wolverine for a while."

"Oh, so you're a Marvel guy. I'm a DC man myself. Been reading Batman and Superman for years, and Aquaman, too."

"Aquaman's lame."

"He used to be, I admit. But now he's pretty badass. Ever since he lost his hand."

"I don't know… I do like DC, but I mostly stick to Batman. I kinda have a thing for Harley Quinn, if you know what I mean."

"You and me both, bro."

"Anyway, Batman's gotta be in here, and Avengers and X-Men, too." Michael leaned in closer. "I get Deadpool, too, but I don't want my foster parents to know that. The last ones I had went ballistic."

"Over Deadpool?" The mailman rubbed his chin. "That's like Dr. Seuss when compared to all that Japanese shit."

"You're telling me." Michael stared longingly at the package in his hands, wishing Willie would leave so he could tear it open. "Well, thanks, Mr.…"

"It's Willie. And next Saturday, I'm bringing you some Aquaman for you to borrow. Read it. You'll be thanking me later."

Michael's eyebrows raised. *Free comics?* He liked that idea. "Thanks, man. I mean… Willie."

"No problem, bro." Willie held out his fist.

Michael rolled his eyes at the ridiculousness of how some adults tried to be cool. But the guy had offered free comics, so Michael put out his hand and bumped the fist anyway.

Suddenly, Michael was sitting in a mail truck. In the driver's seat, Willie was humming a tune Michael didn't recognize. They were at the intersection of Spruce and Route 6, stopped at a red light. The light turned green, and they proceeded into the intersection.

A loud crash, like that of a refrigerator dropped off a hundred-story building and smashing onto pavement below, threw peace into chaos. Metal crinkled. Glass shattered. Willie flew from his seat toward Michael, the side of his head colliding with the roof and jarring his neck almost completely sideways as the truck rolled onto its side. The metal rim of a wheel stripped of its tire spun like a table saw over Willie's limp body and headed straight toward Michael, who brought his hands up to try to protect his face.

When nothing happened, he lowered his hands and realized he was standing in his doorway again. The box lay at his feet. Beads of sweat rolled off his forehead.

"You okay there, buddy?" Willie frowned. "You look like you've seen a ghost."

Michael took a deep breath. "For a minute there, I think I might have." Still shaking, he bent over and picked up his package. "I'm okay. Thanks again."

The mailman turned to leave, and Michael started to close the door, but he couldn't let it close. He pounded a fist against the wall then ran outside and down the steps.

Willie turned. "You sure you're okay?" he asked, looking at Michael as if he had sprouted a third eye.

"Yeah, just... wait a second at the light on Spruce after it turns green before crossing Route 6, at least for the next couple of weeks. People have been running that red light a lot lately."

Willie looked surprised then shook his head. "Um... okay."

"That is part of your route, isn't it?" Michael stomped his foot. "Listen to me! You know how some people believe in God just in case there is a hell? Well, believe me now when I say to wait there, just in case I'm right that another car will run that red light and kill your sorry ass if you don't fucking wait!"

"Okay, okay. Man, you're a strange little dude."

"Maybe. But remember what I said." Michael huffed. "You'll be thanking me later."

It happened when I touched him, he thought as he marched back into the house. *That's just effing great. I'm going to have to wear gloves for the rest of my life, just like Rogue. At least she gets to fly. Is that what I am? A mutant?* The idea of being a superhero like Wolverine and Rogue might have been cool except for one thing: in the X-Men comics, most humans generally hated the mutants. *Just like they generally hate me.*

After the incident with the mailman, Michael was convinced his visions had become a part of his life he would have to learn to deal with... fast. He didn't know how much contact was required to bring one on or why he saw only terrible things. He wondered why his visions couldn't show him someone getting a new puppy or maybe a young couple doing sixty-nine, because no matter how many times he looked at those two numbers, he couldn't figure out how they related to sex.

At dinner that night, he cringed when Helen's hand brushed his as she passed him the mashed potatoes. Nothing happened. The next day, in line at a burger joint, he could have sworn he never touched the employee who gave him some extra napkins. But some itsy-bitsy follicle of that strung-out, yellow-toothed creep must have made contact somehow. Michael fell to the floor, convulsing in a vision that seemed to last for hours. He had to watch as the junkie shot up, then had sex with his boyfriend's corpse.

When Michael "woke up," he was in a hospital bed. Helen and Greg were there and seemed genuinely concerned, and for that, Michael was appreciative. Maybe they no longer considered him the devil's apprentice.

He told the doctor he had been overwhelmed by what had happened at school and wasn't getting much sleep, and that seemed to satisfy her. She recommended he speak with a "professional," and Michael knew exactly what that meant.

Embarrassed, he said he just needed things to get back to normal. The lie seemed to placate the doctor and his foster parents. He didn't know how he could tell them the truth: that he was still having visions and that all he saw was death and more death. The visions seemed to be coming easier, more frequently. The short one he'd had with Willie was simple, like an ugly daydream, horrific but over before he knew it. The scene with the junkie corpse-fucker was like a marathon nightmare filled with graphic details he hoped *never* to witness again.

He was amazed by how often he came into physical contact with complete strangers while going about his everyday business. Under normal circumstances, he would never have noticed, but for whatever reason, Michael's circumstances were no longer normal. On Monday morning, he would be back to funneling through the doorways of his classrooms and through crowded hallways, standing in line at the cafeteria, and participating in all the touch-filled sports Mr. Humphries made them play in gym class. The motions of daily life came with a considerable risk of human contact. And even though a vision didn't happen every time someone touched him, Michael vowed to stay alone as much as possible. He would become a shut-in, leaving his bedroom only for necessities and education. He would share his curse with no one.

Except Sam. Only she would understand.

When he got home from the hospital, he called her and told her about both visions. He cried, too depressed to care how much of a baby he was being. He told her how he loathed the visions. He had never asked for them. If only he knew where they came from, then maybe he could make them stop. Sam tried to console him, but there really wasn't anything she could do.

Monday, Michael lagged behind after some classes and showed up late to others. He had always kept to himself, but he was still worried his teachers might notice and send him in for another meeting with Ms. Jackson. Just the thought made Michael furious. He wasn't about to tell some random guidance counselor about his visions. Ms. Jackson was probably no different than all the other adults, dismissing his visions as products of the wild imagination of a lonely kid needing attention.

As usual, his fellow students gave him a wide berth, only in his new reality, he welcomed their avoidance. They whispered as he passed them, and he could feel their stares. Some seemed in awe of him; others seemed to fear him. Those who lacked volume control said things like "warlock" or "harbinger of death." Those were the prettier terms. Michael wasn't quite sure what "harbinger" meant, but he wanted nothing to do with death. But mostly, he heard "freak." He didn't like that word, probably because it described him perfectly.

After Robbie had cornered him in the lunchroom—even if it was only to apologize—Michael had begun eating his lunch on a bench outside, never minding the late fall chill. Eating outside was against school rules, but no one stopped him. Actually, no one even seemed to know or care where he was, so he was startled to look up from his sandwich and see a girl standing over him.

The tall, thin girl seemed as lost inside herself as she was in her two-sizes-too-big hooded jacket. He paused mid-bite, his teeth clenched firmly into his sandwich. His saliva turned the bread in his mouth into mush as he waited for her to speak.

He sat. She stood. Neither said a word.

The silence made her presence infinitely more awkward. *Why is she waiting for me to acknowledge her? What the hell could she possibly want?* He didn't ask for her company, and he certainly didn't want it. It quickly became evident that if he was going to get rid of her, he would have to be more proactive.

Slowly, Michael chewed the ball of roast beef, lettuce, and bread, then swallowed hard. "Yes?"

"Your name is Michael, right?" Nearly every part of her fidgeted, and she kept her gaze pinned somewhere on his chest.

It made Michael jittery just watching her. "Yeah. So?"

"I heard…"

Michael leaned forward, waiting for that mouse-quiet voice to finish the sentence. He set his sandwich down then tilted his neck to crack out some of the tension rising within him. But his muscles balled up in knots. Her uninvited appearance had gone from minor nuisance to huge irritation in a matter of seconds.

Oh, this is just great. I bet I know where this is headed. Can you tell me my future? She probably wants to know if she'll end up with some stupid guy. It was either that, or she was there to mock him for the whole bathroom incident.

Either way, he wanted nothing more to do with her. "Can't you see I am trying to eat my lunch here? I want to be alone." He sneered. "Why else would someone come out here to eat in the freezing cold?"

For the first time, the girl looked at him. Tears shimmered in her hazel eyes. "I'm sorry for disturbing you." She turned to leave.

Michael felt lower than a grave. "Wait." Before that moment, he hadn't realized he was a sucker for a girl's tears. His conscience scolded him for being a heel. The least he could do was hear her out. She had obviously reached out to him for a reason. "What's your name?" he asked.

She half turned back to him and mumbled, "Tessa."

"Are you a freshman?"

"Sophomore."

One-word answers are better than no answers, I suppose. "Well, Tessa, what can I do for you?"

Tessa approached the bench with hesitant steps. She stopped before sitting and glanced at him. He nodded, and she gingerly sat on the edge, as if prepared to jump up and run at a moment's notice.

Looking at the ground, she said, "They say you can see things, things that haven't happened yet."

There it was. Michael had known someone would eventually confront him and taunt him about it. He had thought it would be someone like

Ryan Taylor or some other jerk. Never did he expect a timid wisp of a girl to be the first to broach the subject.

Michael shrugged. "Is that what they say?"

"Of course, I don't believe it, but—"

"Then why are you pestering me about it?"

"Because if you can, I need to know something. I need to know if there's anything in store for me. You know, if things will ever get better for me."

Suicidal? The thought made Michael's head spin. He wasn't equipped to handle that. *What does she expect from me? Shit, I can't cure depression. I've got enough problems of my own to deal with.* "Tessa, I would like to help you, but—"

"Then try. That's all I ask. I'll do whatever you want. Just please, try to see what kind of future I have waiting for me."

Michael thought about lying to her, telling her that he was a fraud or that what had happened with Glenn Rodrigues was a fluke. He wouldn't even have to lie if he told her that the rumors had blown things way out of proportion. Also, he didn't know why his visions happened or if he could actually make one occur. He did know that he didn't want to see any more of them.

But he could see she'd had to summon a lot of courage to come to him. He wondered what could be so important that she would seek him out and beg for his assistance. Grudgingly, he held out his hand. "Um… I don't know if this will work, but I have to touch you. Give me your hand."

She seemed as reluctant to put her hand in his as he was to take it. "Does it hurt?"

"I don't think you'll feel anything." He shook his head. "Look, I can't promise I'll see anything. In fact, I doubt I will. The only reason I'm agreeing to try is so I can prove to myself that what happened with Glenn was all just a strange coincidence." The last part was a lie. Nobody at school knew about John Crotty or his other visions, and no one needed to know.

Tessa closed her eyes but kept her hands clenched in her lap.

"Okay," Michael said. "Your guess is as good as mine how this fortune-telling bullshit works, but you still want me to try?"

"I think so."

"Then stop wasting my time, and give me your hand."

Something wild flashed across her face. Michael couldn't be sure, but for a moment, he felt a connection to her. It excited him, and briefly, he was thrilled to have her company.

Then, she reached out and placed her hand in his.

Michael felt fear creep into the back of his mind, the part still anchored in reality. As an alternate universe unfolded before him, Tessa and his surroundings withered and peeled like an old painting.

Michael is sitting in a room with a sofa, two chairs, and a large television, an old one with a triangular back. He doesn't recognize the place.

Knickknacks are positioned on shelves with perfect spacing between them. Every horizontal line—from the bottom of a portrait to the edge of a wall shelf or the borders of a coffee table—is perfectly parallel or perpendicular to the four walls of the room. End tables are equidistant from each arm of the wrinkle-free sofa, identical lamps standing dead center on each. Everything is set with steadfast accuracy. Everything has its place.

Everything, except for the blood.

Michael gasps. He jumps from his seat and circles behind it. A mammoth-sized tick squirms in the spreading blood. Michael blinks in an attempt to get his eyes to adjust in the dim light. The tick is actually a man in an unzipped ski jacket. His legs and groin are difficult to see as they match the color of the floor beneath them—black with shades of red where light from outside hits a liquid surface. The man is clutching his belly as if his guts might spill out.

It's just a vision. I have to remember that.

The man's eyes are hidden behind thick-rimmed mirrored glasses. He appears to be in his late forties or early fifties, with skin so pale he could pass for the dead. Sweat gathers like air bubbles, one each side of the man's widow's peak. Spit slides down his lip as he breathes rapidly through gritted teeth, and the veins in his neck bulge.

The man stares upward, looking somewhere to Michael's left. Michael turns to see a naked girl standing a few feet away from him.

Tessa.

Michael gapes at her. He can't help it. She's the first naked girl he's ever seen that wasn't on a late-night cable show, in a magazine, or on the Internet. Somehow, Tessa seems so much better than all those starlets and porn queens. She is real, both flawed and perfect. He bites his lip, frightened, excited, and ashamed, all at once.

But the shame isn't enough to make him look away. He starts at her eyes—and he prides himself on that—then works his way down to her chapped but full lips. There, he lingers, thinking himself spying and knowing it wrong, able to see her breasts but trying not to ogle them. Temptation strips him from the horror around him. For a moment, he and Tessa are alone in the universe.

His penis throbs against the zipper of his jeans as he takes in her breasts, wanting more than anything to touch them. They are small, the nipples like erasers on the ends of pencils.

He likes the way her shoulder bones form bulges beneath her skin that look like the caps over the air valves on the Huffy he had before it got stolen. He lowers his eyes to the smooth, flat plains that close the distance from her hips to her blond pubic hair.

What's that in her hand?

She's holding a butcher knife, and by the looks of it, the biggest one from the rack. And the blade is dripping blood.

Fuck. *Michael's hormones die in a fiery crash, but his heart skips faster. He raises his eyes to meet hers and sees an animalistic ferocity on her face. The wildness he'd seen in her earlier has returned with a vengeance. Its intensity is amplified, and she scares the shit out of him.*

He rubs his temples and tries to stay calm. "It's just a vision," *he mutters, pacing.* "It hasn't happened yet."

Pictures lining the wall show Tessa with two adults. Her parents, Michael assumes. They look happy. They look like the type of family Michael used to wish he had, until he just stopped caring.

The man on the floor, a bit older now, is definitely the same man in the photographs.

She's killing her own father!

A part of Michael knows he is rushing to judgment. But the man is defenseless, and he's dying. Michael glances at the woman in one of the pictures and wonders where she is. Has Tessa already murdered her?

"Tessa, honey," *the man whines. Dark, almost black blood seeps through his fingers. "Haven't I always taken care of you? Haven't I always been there to provide for you?"*

Tessa's heavy breathing makes her chest and shoulders heave like a cartoon ape's. Her muscles flex. The wildness she exhibits continues to mount, a fury burning as blue as the hottest part of a flame. Michael fears that, like fire, it might consume her. He wonders if it already has.

With a howl as bloodcurdling as it is primal, Tessa lunges at the man. The knife rips through his shirt and pierces his skin just below the rib cage. Again and again, the blade rises and falls, leaving two-inch slits wherever it strikes. Each groove bubbles out more blood.

A sound blares in the background. Sirens.

Back on the bench, Michael lurched violently over the rusty metal armrest. He leaned over and vomited.

"Are you okay?" Tessa asked, placing a hand on his back.

"Don't you touch me!" Michael jumped to his feet, knocking her hand away. "Don't ever touch me."

He pulled a napkin from his brown lunch bag and wiped his chin. Angry and embarrassed, he turned from the mess he'd made and slung his backpack over his shoulder.

"Wait." She reached for his arm but stopped short of making contact. "What did you see?"

"I saw what kind of person you really are." He started walking away.

Behind him, Tessa started crying. "I can't do it again," she said through sobs. "Please don't make me do it again."

Michael didn't stop or turn back. He was through trying to help.

CHAPTER 13

SAM PINCHED HER NOSTRILS AS she descended the slippery stairs. Her black boots weren't the right footwear for managing the wooden steps eaten away by years of rain, wind, and ocean spray. The city hadn't spared any resources for cleaning up the waterfront, and no one had swum at the beach for decades. Only junkies and teenagers looking for a secluded place to fuck or drink hung out in the shadows of the rocky shoals.

Junkies, teenagers, and the occasional disposer of a dead body. Sam shrank from the cold wind, reaching out for a handrail that wasn't there. Like a tightrope walker, she held her hands out by her sides as she made her way down to the sludge-covered coastline. The scattered seaweed reminded her of an old Charlton Heston movie about a disturbing food product.

The thought made her miss her former partner, Bruce, who would've gotten the reference immediately. He had been a surly detective who seemed to like no one but her. He had also been her mentor, but he had fallen in the line of duty. She'd never requested another partner, never wanted one, instead preferring to pull uniforms in to serve as backup or assist with footwork. She didn't know why the department had never forced another partner on her—a young apprentice, perhaps—but she guessed it had something to do with politics and budget cuts or some other bureaucratic bullshit.

The tide was coming in. The beach was mostly rocks and mud, and a salty garbage stench hung over her like a thick cloak. The rancid dark water frothed with brown bubbles, making it look a little like soda, but Sam would have drunk her own urine before swallowing Taunton River water.

Sam ducked under the tape that cordoned off the crime scene. A tent had been erected over a small patch of surf, its tail end jutting out a few feet into the water. She headed toward it, knowing the body she had been called in to see lay beneath it.

As she approached, a heavyset man in a bulky winter jacket, knit hat, and waders stepped into her path. "It's not a pretty one," Dr. Prentiss said.

Sam rolled her eyes. "You and I both know I've probably seen worse."

The medical examiner chuckled. "So you have." His bifocals fogged up as he stuck out his lower lip and released a breath. "Okay, then. Right this way, Detective. This one is... mostly intact."

Dr. Prentiss led her to the tent. "We haven't moved the body yet. No ID or personal effects were found on or near the remains, but we'll take a closer look once we get her on the table. We've bagged her hands but otherwise left her where we found her. We're going to have to pull her out soon, though. The water is rising."

"What can you tell me about the victim?"

"Female. African-American. Approximately five-foot-nine, mid to late forties. Hard to nail it down on account of all the missing skin."

"Possible homicide?"

"Most certainly homicide."

Dr. Prentiss unzipped the tent flap and stepped inside. Before following, Sam surveyed the area. Most of the uniformed officers were outside the tape, some questioning the Department of Transportation crew that had been working on the nearby bridge, others keeping reporters and busybodies away from the scene. She had instructed Sergeant Rollins and Officer Bova to scan the vicinity for possible weapons and evidence, with instructions to photograph and bag anything of interest. Officer Cromartie gave her a nod then scribbled on a notepad. He was tasked with recording the names of all those who entered the scene and the times each came and went. So far, no one had reported sighting anything of note, not even a footprint that didn't belong.

Sam braced herself and stepped inside the tent. Two feet beyond the entrance, Dr. Prentiss crouched near a corpse that lay half out of the water like a shipwreck survivor crawling onto shore. Except this victim wasn't crawling or moving at all, save for the rolling tide's sloshing her repeatedly against the rock to which it had her pinned. Whether the body had washed up between those rocks or been dumped there, Sam could only guess. On publicly owned land situated between a polluted river and a highway with a landfill beyond, the rocky shoreline was as good a place as any to dispose of a body. A corpse blended well with the rest of the decomposition. If not for the nearby construction workers, the body might never have been spotted. The landfill might have been the smarter choice, but perhaps the killer couldn't get past the fence and thought the river his next best option. If so, he was right. The river eroded evidence as easily as it did the shore.

Sam walked as close as she could without stepping into the water. Her heels sank into the wet sand. With every minute shifting of her weight, air bubbles gurgled up from the resting place of some underground mollusk.

"We're ready to move the body," Dr. Prentiss said.

Two members of his staff carried over a stretcher. One waded into the water and grabbed the body under its knees, while the other reached under the victim's arms, and together, gently but quickly, the two lifted the corpse from the water with a plop, as if the river didn't want to let the body go. Seaweed fell from dark, matted hair. A tattered blouse dripped with liquid ranging from clear to black. The doctor rolled the body over, revealing the face.

Sam gasped and covered her mouth. "How long has the victim been in the water?"

Dr. Prentiss grunted as he positioned the legs on the gurney. "Hard to say. I'll know more after further examination, but if I had to guess, not more than a day."

Sam had seen what a body looked like after it had soaked in the Taunton River for a long time: bloated, gray skin covered with a mucus-like film, an assortment of creatures making it their home. Neither the water nor its indigenous life had laid claim yet, not even the worms.

But the victim's head was missing one eye, half an ear, and portions of the upper lip. The nostrils were slit, and huge swaths of hair were gone, along with the scalp beneath them in some places. In its somewhat preserved state, the corpse's lacerations were horrific. Sam's years on the force had prepared her for nearly everything. She had seen ritualistic sacrifice, explosions, and bodies broken and contorted by accident or intent, a host of unclean ways to die. Just by looking at the body, Sam understood why Dr. Prentiss had been so confident that a murder had been committed. What the killer had done to this victim was abhorrent.

Filleted. That was the word that came to Sam's mind. The left thigh was missing strips of skin and, in some places, chunks of muscle. The right thigh was worse, the femur exposed like a spiral ham that had been carved down to the bone. Her left arm was much the same, skeletal, the meat stripped away like ribs gnawed clean. Pieces were missing from just about everywhere.

The polluted saltwater had infested the wounds, turning the meat into what looked like ground beef left out to gray and rot. The stench of the sea, already worse than death, hid any odor the body might have been releasing. Sam held in her lunch and went about her work with professionalism and as much detachment as she could muster. Her detective mind was already considering the usual suspects—husband or former lover, most likely—but she couldn't shake the feeling that the killing was something more than heat of passion, that a darker motive was at play. She had long ago learned to trust her hunches.

Only someone truly fucked up would do something like this. Fortunately, people this batshit crazy usually stick out like elephants at a raccoon dance party. The thought did not improve Sam's gloominess. Solving a murder without knowing the motive was rarely as easy as picking a face from the crowd. She would need to learn everything there was to know about the victim, and the sooner, the better.

"Can you give me anything, Dr. Prentiss? Time of death? Murder weapon? Anything that might help me identify her killer?"

"I can't say much without a full autopsy, I'm afraid. Although, the victim does appear to have been carved." He pointed at the exposed bone of the victim's left arm. "See those little divots? The way their walls are sort of shredded suggests a serrated blade, perhaps a saw, but I can't be certain. I do know one thing for sure: some of these wounds were made pre-mortem."

"She was tortured?"

He nodded. "It appears that way."

Sam shook her head. "Sometimes I wonder if the crazies and sickos outnumber us ten to one."

"Only in our lines of work, Detective." Dr. Prentiss laughed. "It could be worse. I'll take dealing with dead bodies any day over my thirteen-year-old's horrid taste in music. If I have to hear one more song about teenagers in love or falling out of love or re-finding love or learning how to love or whatever other lovesick crap those boy bands spew, you'll be visiting another crime scene real soon."

Sam faked a chuckle. She saw something familiar about the victim. Then, it came to her. "I know this woman! She is… she *was* a guidance counselor over at Carnegie High. Gloria. Gloria Jackson. Yeah, that was her name."

Sam had met Gloria Jackson several times in the course of past investigations. She'd even had a few arguments with the counselor concerning the proper punishment for criminals that were both products of abuse and alumni of Carnegie High School.

She wanted to save them all, Sam remembered. She wondered if Gloria would still have wanted to save them all if she could have seen what somebody had done to her. *Some people aren't worth saving.*

"Well," Dr. Prentiss said, "it looks like you have a starting point for your investigation, Detective. I should have a full report for you within a couple of days. Schedule a time with Charlotte, and I'll meet you at the morgue to go over it." He gestured for the two staff members to lift the gurney. "Let's go."

Sam followed Dr. Prentiss out of the tent with one question on her mind. *Who would want to kill a high school guidance counselor?* She sighed. *Gloria, what did you get mixed up in?* She cleared her throat and, with it, her attachments. At that moment, Gloria Jackson ceased to be a person and became a puzzle to be solved. Sam's detachment gave her focus. It was time to work.

CHAPTER 14

MICHAEL SLOUCHED IN HIS SEAT, his eyes turned away from Sam, watching rain droplets slide down the car window. He had only a half day of school that Wednesday before Thanksgiving, and he agreed to spend it with her at the morgue. In the window, he caught sight of his own reflection: tousled brown hair that he had combed with his fingers, eyes red at the corners and encircled with purple smudges. The shirt he had picked up off the floor where it had lain for more than a week was wrinkled and crooked at the collar. He pictured Tessa's face—not wearing the feral expression from his vision but that of the timid girl who had come to him for help. He sneered. *The face of a liar.*

He jolted upright. His bitterness woke him up a bit, but not much. He would have to tell Sam all about Tessa and his vision, but that could wait until after he poked a dead body.

"This whole thing seems stupid," Michael said.

Sam smiled softly. "You never know."

"She's dead. Whatever happened to her is in the past. And as far as I can tell, I only can see what might happen in the future. I sure ain't an expert on this, but... all I'm saying is, I think you're wasting your time."

"You can learn a lot from a corpse... if you know how to read it. I guess I'm hoping maybe you can read it even better than the rest of us. Besides, I was heading down here anyway for the medical examiner's report." She rubbed a spot under her lip. "But if you don't want to do this…"

"No, no. I'm fine. A little creeped out, maybe, but other than that, just fine." He shrugged. "I mean, how bad can it be?"

"You'll be happy to know that John Crotty pleaded guilty to kidnapping charges," Sam said as she pulled up to a red light at an intersection. Charlton Memorial Hospital loomed tall on their right. She turned to Michael. Her mouth looked as though it was threatening to smile, one side of it having the slightest curl. "He won't be going away forever, but it will be a long time before he has a chance to put his hands on another woman."

"Good," Michael murmured.

"Good? You don't sound too pleased. Is something wrong?"

"No, that's good news about that psycho." He fiddled with the strings of his hoodie. "I have something else I need to talk to you about, though."

"Michael, you know you can tell me anything. What is it?"

"It's this girl at school. I had another vision." He paused. *Might as well just say it.* "She's going to kill her father."

"Are you sure?"

Michael shot Sam a look. After all they had been through with Glenn and Crotty, he couldn't believe she could still doubt him. The insult hit deep.

"Okay," Sam said. "Easy. I'm sorry. But you have to understand that accusing someone of murder without proof—the kind of proof that holds up in court—is one thing. Accusing someone of murder before it even happens is infinitely more problematic. The law is not equipped to handle psychic visions. We have to go about this carefully. That's why I need to know you are one hundred percent certain of what you saw. There's no room here for misinterpretation."

"Believe me, I'm sure. I saw her stab him like thirty times. He didn't have a weapon or nothing."

"Okay. What's the girl's name?"

"I can't remember her last name, but her first name is Tessa. She's a sophomore."

"When is the murder supposed to happen?"

"I don't know."

Sam pulled into the hospital parking lot. "So her father could be dying as we speak?"

"I... I don't know."

"Can you recall any details that may help us determine when it might occur?"

He tried to picture the scene. "Nope."

"No television programs playing, newspapers in the room, calendars, clocks?"

"No. Nothing that I can remember. I was more focused on the girl plunging a ginormous knife into her father."

"No need to be sarcastic. Was it day or night?"

"Night, I think. The lights weren't on, and it was pretty dark inside the house, but some light came in through a window. I thought it was moonlight, or maybe a porch light or streetlight, too."

"Was it Tessa's house? How can you be sure the man was her father?" The questions came without hesitation. The way Sam stared, all stone-faced and stern, made Michael's hands clammy.

He wiped his palms on his pants, trying to collect his thoughts, wondering if she were treating him the same way she treated her suspects. "Th-There were pictures all over the walls of Tessa with the man and a woman. I'm pretty sure they were her parents. Who else would they be?"

"Was her mother there, too? Anyone else?"

"No one that I saw, but I didn't see the whole house."

"Anything else you can remember?"

"There were sirens. I think they were getting louder toward the end."

"Well, at least we've pinned down the probable location." Sam sighed. All at once, the sternness seemed to leave her. "I'll be honest with you. I'm not really sure how to handle this situation."

"That makes two of us."

"Try not to worry. I'll figure something out. Maybe I can put a police detail in the area. At least if they hear it going down, they might be able to save him or give him a fighting chance by getting an ambulance there quicker."

"That doesn't sound very promising."

"No, it doesn't. I'll keep thinking about it. But do me a favor. Don't go meddling in her affairs. Let me handle it."

"I won't." But he wasn't remotely satisfied with Sam's idea of crime prevention. He remembered Glenn's death with crystal clarity. He wondered if another person would have to die when he could have done more to prevent the death. His conscience wouldn't let him just forget it and move on. Why did he have to foresee murder? Each time he did, that voice inside pestered him until he did something about it. He was batting .500 when it came to saving lives, not a terrible average. Couldn't he retire with that stat and leave the life-saving duties to those who weren't failing algebra?

Michael wanted nothing to do with Tessa or her father. *Her face had been so...* Michael couldn't think of the right word to describe it. *Haunted?* Tessa had looked so lost, as though she was the one in need of saving. For a moment, he had wanted to be her knight, her savior. Then, his vision showed him what Tessa was really all about, slapping any notion of chivalry right out of him.

"Maybe... she's the victim... somehow?" He wanted to believe it, but he couldn't, not after what he had seen. He sighed. "I don't know."

"You care about her, don't you?" She reached toward his hand.

Michael pulled his hand away and scolded her with his eyes. "No, I don't. I don't even know her."

Sam grimaced and pulled into a parking space. "We'll do what we can, for both of them. Maybe we can get her some help."

He slapped his thigh. "Yeah! Help. That's what she needs. We can find her a psychiatrist or maybe get her some pills. One of the kids in the Sutter Home used to take antidepressors or whatever they're called, and he was never violent."

"You never know. She really could be the victim in all of this."

"Yeah. Maybe." Michael kept his doubts to himself. *Victims don't stab defenseless people thirty times when they're already bleeding on the floor. Besides, Tessa seemed to enjoy it.*

Sam got out and led the way to the door. Michael had never seen that part of the hospital. It looked more like a loading dock than an entrance to a hospital. He didn't like hospitals. He thought they always smelled funny, as if they were constantly being sprayed with air freshener to mask the stink of death. The thought of corpses all lined up like sardines in a tin can in the morgue chilled him to the bone. *It's just a dead body*, he told himself over and over again. *There's nothing to be afraid of.*

"We don't have to do this," Sam said for what seemed like the ninetieth time. "If you're not up for it—"

"I'm fine." Michael took a deep breath, puffed out his chest, and held the door open for Sam.

"Welcome back," a portly woman said from behind a too-tall reception desk. "Here to see Gloria Jackson? Dr. Prentiss said you would be coming and that I should just show you right in."

"Hi, Charlotte," Sam said. "Yes, we're here to see Ms. Jackson." She grinned. Michael had known her long enough to know when her smile was phony.

Charlotte's eyes fell on Michael. He felt small beneath her stare. Her gaze lingered long and hard, as though she was sizing him up. But if she questioned his presence, she kept it to herself. She rose and stepped out from behind the monstrosity of an oak desk to lead them down a hallway.

With the exception of the reception desk, which at least had a few personal touches, the morgue was somber and uninviting. Michael wondered if there was a policy against staff members having pictures of their families or posting awful art pieces their children made like most workspaces on TV seemed to have. The morgue was so dreary, Michael thought its atmosphere had to be intentional, and he didn't know why anyone would want to work there. *Even cemeteries have nice green grass and lots of flowers.* He gave a mental shrug. *I guess it's not like the dead care.*

Near the end of the hall, Charlotte led them into an area much bigger than the average-sized door suggested it would be. The room gave Michael the chills, and not just because of the freezing temperature. He felt as though he were standing in a walk-in refrigerator. Hugging himself tightly, Michael wished he had worn a jacket over his sweatshirt.

Large drawers lined one wall like a gigantic system of file cabinets. Michael had seen enough movies to know that he and Sam had reached their intended destination. *The dead bodies are stored in those drawers.*

He wondered how many of them were occupied. *Will I end up in that wall someday?*

Sam reached for Michael's shoulder. Even if she were only trying to comfort him, he wasn't having it. He stepped away from her.

"What are you doing?" he asked, almost yelling. "You can't touch me. You know that, and that's the second time you've tried. You can never touch me."

"I'm sorry," Sam said, eyes downcast. Meekly, she turned away. The always strong, always confident Sam looked as though someone had just bitten the head off her favorite kitten.

Michael instantly regretted snapping at her. "Just... don't touch me is all. I don't want to have another vision."

"If it bothers you that much, maybe we shouldn't be here. I don't want to upset you, Michael."

"No. I'm okay. Let's get this over with."

Charlotte had to have found their conversation strange, but again, she didn't say a word. Her expression was as stoic as a professional poker player's. She walked over and opened one of the drawers. Michael noted that it was marked "Number 16."

Sam looked at her watch. "Will Dr. Prentiss be here soon?"

"Yes," Charlotte replied. "Any minute now." She mock dusted off her hands and let out a long breath. "Well, I'll leave you to it." She turned and left the room.

Michael followed Sam to the open drawer. There, on a cold metal slab, lay what he assumed was the body of a guidance counselor he hadn't really liked but had certainly never wanted to see dead. Most of her was hidden under a white sheet. The contours of her face and body shaped the sheet covering her. As still as she was, she looked as though she were encased in plaster or maybe a cocoon. He found the idea of death being some sort of one-way bus ride to something different, something better, pleasing. He had never really believed all that religious mumbo jumbo, but he wished it for Ms. Jackson. She didn't deserve to be tucked away in that wall drawer. She didn't deserve to have that be her final destination. Yet there she was, one foot jutting out of its covering at the end of the slab. A large tag was fastened around the big toe.

"You sure you can handle this?" Sam asked again. Her voice oozed concern. It made Michael feel like a child. "Her body, uh, it's not in the best condition. Some of her wounds are really disturbing. You shouldn't have to see them if I'm careful. I need to look her over, but I can do that with Dr. Prentiss after you're out of the room."

"I can handle it," Michael said, trying to keep annoyance out of his voice. He knew she was just trying to help. "Besides, I don't need to see her body to touch it."

"All right." Sam yanked open the drawer the rest of the way.

Ms. Jackson's foot came closer. Michael stared at it. The skin was gray and wrinkled, as if it had been underwater for too long. He stepped toward it, thinking he would just touch it quickly and be done with it.

But as he got closer, Michael thought of toe jam and oozing blisters and Ebola and zombies and all sorts of other foul things that had nothing to do with that foot, but he linked them just the same. "I don't want to touch her foot."

"Her hand then?" Sam asked.

"Okay."

Sam slid the sheet gently across Ms. Jackson's body, exposing her right arm. The arm was naked up to the shoulder. Michael figured the rest of the body was naked, too. He was seeing naked girls in all the wrong circumstances lately and briefly wondered if it might turn him gay.

"That's enough," Michael said.

Sam dropped the sheet and stepped out of the way. Michael moved in beside the body, his thighs inches from the bottom of the drawer.

This is so damn stupid. Why put me through all this for nothing? His hand trembled as he reached for the exposed forearm. A mischievous idea popped into his head. He turned away from Sam and grinned. *I'll show her.* The instant his finger touched the dead flesh, Michael started to shake. He stared blankly at the wall of drawers.

"Michael?" Sam called. "Michael? Are you okay? Michael?"

After a few moments, Michael relaxed. He gasped, releasing the breath he was holding.

"What is it, Michael?" Sam asked, a sense of urgency underlining the question. "Did you see something?"

Michael slowly turned to face her. "Yes. I caught a glimpse of Heaven, and it was beautiful, so beautiful that I didn't want to leave."

"Seriously?"

Michael burst into laughter. He laughed until he could hardly breathe. He couldn't believe Sam actually fell for it. When he was finally able to talk again, he said, "Of course not. It's like I told you, this is a waste of time. She's dead. I didn't see a thing."

She scowled. "You're a jerk." But her grumpiness soon wavered, and she laughed along with Michael.

"Sam?" someone called from the doorway.

Michael was so startled that he nearly fell on top of Ms. Jackson's body. That was the end of his laughter.

"I'm sorry I'm late," the man said, strolling over to where they stood. He wore a white lab coat and carried a black leather bag. He extended his free hand to Sam.

She shook it. "Hello, Dr. Prentiss." At once, she was the adult again, and adults didn't laugh around dead bodies.

"I've brought Sixteen's file with me. Shall we begin?" Then he seemed to notice Michael. "And who might you be?"

Sam acted naturally. Her demeanor suggested that a fourteen-year-old boy had every right to be there. "Michael, meet Dr. Louis Prentiss, resident medical examiner extraordinaire. He's helped me solve more cases than I would ever like to admit."

"I do my best," Dr. Prentiss said, extending his hand toward Michael.

"Michael, here, is an intern of sorts," Sam added.

Her last comment distracted Michael, and without thinking, he put out his hand to shake. Dr. Prentiss grasped Michael's hand.

Michael stands next to Dr. Prentiss, who looks sad. The doctor stares down at the white sheet covering Ms. Jackson, who is no longer in a drawer but on a table.

More odd details confuse Michael. A tray set up beside the table is covered with what looks like an electric pizza cutter and a bunch of other shiny, sharp utensils. Dr. Prentiss shakes his head and pulls back the sheet. Instinctively, Michael turns away.

The body seems to call out to him. He needs to turn, needs to look, though the more the need increases, the more he doesn't want to do it. It feels wrong.

From the corner of his eye, he sees Dr. Prentiss pick up a scalpel.

Michael starts to panic. He wants to run, to be anywhere but in that room. Still, he cannot stop his head from turning, his eyes from seeing.

It is not Gloria Jackson on that table.

Screaming and gasping, Michael returned to the present. For some reason, all he could see was a bright circle of white light that practically blinded him. He squinted, clawed at the air, and tried to get to his feet.

"You're okay," someone said in a soothing voice. "You're okay. We're here."

Sam? Michael's heart pumped fiercely. He tried to make out the shadowy figure standing behind the light. That need returned—the need to see who was there, who stood behind that god-awful light. He swatted the light away, and something that looked like a pen flew across the room and hit the far wall.

Michael began to collect his bearings. His eyesight slowly improved. His body felt cold and clammy. For some reason, his knee hurt. Had he fallen on it? The shadowy figure became Dr. Prentiss.

Michael's heart started to race again. He leaped to his feet. "Sam? Where's Sam?"

"I'm right here," she said from behind him.

He twisted around to see her. "Oh, thank God you're okay."

"Me?" She chuckled. "You should be more worried about yourself. This floor isn't exactly soft. You're lucky you didn't bang your head. The doctor thinks you must have fainted. I told him that it has been happening to you sometimes lately and that your doctor says you just need more rest. Not to mention, this place is probably a lot for someone your age to absorb. I shouldn't have brought you here. I'm sorry."

Michael understood what Sam was saying between the lines. *Don't mention the visions.* But he couldn't keep quiet. "I saw something... something awful." He pointed at Dr. Prentiss. "It was his future."

The medical examiner scratched his head. Michael didn't care what he thought. He only cared that Sam listen.

"I saw *him*, Sam," he said, jabbing his finger at the doctor. "He was in a room kind of like this one but with operating tables. He had a scalpel in his hand."

"It's okay, Michael," Sam said. "He's the medical examiner. That's what he does. He conducts autopsies."

"No," Michael said sharply. He started to cry. "You don't understand. Yes, he was performing an autopsy. But *you* were on the table."

CHAPTER 15

"**W**HEN?" SAM CROAKED. BUT BEFORE Michael could answer, she cleared her throat and said, "Never mind that for now." Any crack that might have been present in her shell, she completely sealed up.

Michael looked as if he might vomit. He fidgeted uncontrollably. His cheeks were blotched from crying. He'd had more than his fair share of scares for a kid his age—hell, he'd had more than enough for anyone.

Sure, Sam was afraid to die. The risk of injury or death was already high enough in her chosen employment without a psychic kid predicting it. What Michael saw in his visions became reality. She believed that. So she knew that without appropriate interference, she would be lying on an examining table, her cold, rigid body the canvas for Dr. Prentiss's crude art.

But looking into Michael's tear-filled eyes, she knew her life had had some worth. Her work had always been good enough, and it had to be then. *Focus on the case.* She took in a breath, stood up straight, slid her loose hair behind her ears, and pushed the thought of her own death as far back in her mind as she could.

As if she had flipped a switch, Sam was back in cop mode. She looked Michael in the eyes. "Are you going to be okay?"

He sniffled but gave her a nod.

"Give me five minutes with Dr. Prentiss, then we'll talk."

"But, Sam, I—"

"Wait out in the hall. I promise, just five minutes."

He hung his head and plodded toward the door. When he reached the door, he glanced back, and she gave him a nod. She didn't like sending him off alone after he had just experienced a terrible vision, but she had a job to do. That had to be her primary focus.

"What was that all about?" Dr. Prentiss asked as soon as the door closed behind Michael.

"It's… nothing. Michael's had a difficult time lately. He doesn't have many people looking out for him these days. He… worries about me. Anyway, what do you got for me?"

"Quite a bit, actually. But you're not going to like it. This is some nasty business." Dr. Prentiss shook his satchel. "Just let me get my notes."

He reached into his bag and pulled out a clipboard with a pen tucked behind its clasp. He flipped through the pages, stopping occasionally while muttering and nodding.

When he was through reviewing the pages, he tucked the clipboard beneath his arm, walked over to the remains of Gloria Jackson, and drew back the sheet. "I estimate her time of death somewhere between four p.m. Saturday and two a.m. Sunday morning. She doesn't appear to have been in the water for more than twenty-four hours. Cause of death seems rather obvious. This lady was butchered. Official cause: blood loss."

"You couldn't just tell me this was the work of a shark or maybe a really off-course school of piranha and make my job a whole lot easier, could you? I saw what some coyotes did to the remains of a child once. That was some gruesome stuff."

"You don't seem the type to be satisfied with anything less than the truth, Detective."

"My cross and my curse. But make no mistake. An animal did this, even if it's the bipedal kind that lives in the suburbs. So tell me, Doctor, what exactly did our perp do to this woman?"

"Well, aside from some scratches on her right arm, the victim has few defensive wounds." Dr. Prentiss lifted the corpse's head. "She sustained blunt force trauma to the back of her skull, creating a fissure. The weapon used was something cylindrical like a pipe or a bat." He pulled the pen from his clipboard and used it to point at some inch-thick purple strips of smooth skin circling each ankle. "Rope burns here and on her right wrist. The skin of her left wrist—and of most of her left arm—is missing, as you can see. That appears to be where the killer made his first cuts. My assumption at the beach was correct. Many of these wounds were pre-mortem. He sawed through her skin as if he were slicing roast beef."

"Torture. You're certain?"

"Absolutely. I've analyzed the wounds thoroughly. The notches in the bone indicate the use of a serrated blade."

"A saw?"

"No. We dug metal fragments from the bone that turned out to be polarized steel, the same composition as an average kitchen knife. Whoever did this took his time. I'm no psychiatrist, but..."

"Go on."

"The method of torture was precise, done by someone in control of his emotions and his faculties. It took a steady hand and an even steadier heart." He leaned over and tapped his pen against the skeletal arm. "Here, you can see the progression of the attack. The striations on the left arm are two inches apart. The killer removed segments in intervals. The skin was carved, little by little and slice by slice, almost up to the shoulder. The slashes on the rest of the body appear more random. The victim probably had been alive for a good part of it, but it appears that the killer continued cutting pieces from her even after her death, particularly those from her legs."

Sam flinched. She didn't want to know what had happened to the missing pieces. "Where's the logic in that? Better yet, where's the logic in torturing this woman? What could she possibly have known that was worth torturing her to find out?"

"I'm afraid the answers to those questions lie well outside my area of expertise, Detective."

Sam rubbed her chin. The answer to her last question was simple enough to figure out: nothing. If information had been the killer's goal, he would have gotten everything he needed long before he had desecrated the victim's body to the extent in which Sam now found it. By the second cut, the guidance counselor would have been telling more tales than Scheherazade.

A chill ran down her spine. *No one could have done this for personal enjoyment. Surely, no one could be that sick.* But experience had taught her better, no matter how many times she tried to deny it.

"Anyway," Dr. Prentiss continued, "from the measurements of the lacerations, I was able to determine the size and type of the blade to a reasonable degree of medical certainty. It's all in my report." He tapped on his clipboard. "I'll have a copy sent over to you as soon as I finalize it."

"Thank you, Dr. Prentiss." Sam smiled and shook his hand. "I'll call you to discuss it further once I've reviewed your full report. I've kept that boy waiting long enough."

"Did you need him to identify the victim? Because that was already—"

"No, nothing like that. He's a… student ride-along."

Dr. Prentiss smirked. "If you say so. Anyway, I don't think he has the stomach for this line of work." He laughed.

Sam shook her head. "Well, I'd best be getting back to him. Thanks again."

"Any time, Detective. Any time."

Sam headed out of the morgue and nearly panicked when she didn't see Michael in the hallway. She hustled out of the building and found him kicking around a rock in the parking lot. His hood was up, one of the strings pulled tight and hanging out of his mouth. She could tell he had been crying by the puffiness of his eyes.

When he saw her, he ran over, wrapped his arms around her, and buried his face in her jacket. "I tried, Sam. The whole time you were in there, I tried to think when it might happen. As much as it scared me, I replayed that vision over and over again in my mind. It was just me and you and Dr. Prentiss—"

"It's okay, Michael." She hugged him back, careful to avoid touching his bare hands. She didn't want him to experience the pain of having another vision about her, even though she desperately wanted to know what he'd seen.

"I couldn't see any calendars or clocks or newspapers or nothing."

"Sh… it's okay."

Michael pulled out of her embrace. "It's not okay! You're going to die, and you don't even give a shit! I saw you lying there, dead. You're going to die and leave me just like everyone else does."

A knot formed in her throat, but she kept up her face. "I'm not going anywhere. I'll be more careful. But Michael, you don't know when or how I die. There's nothing more I can do than to be on my guard."

"You were stabbed, I think." Michael stomped his foot. "And your hair seemed longer. Ugh, I don't know. I barely saw you before the vision ended." He froze. "Wait a minute. That's it!"

He lunged and grabbed her hand. He held it for a moment, then his face fell. "Why does it only fucking work when I don't want it to?"

Sam grabbed him by the arms. "Listen. I'm going to be okay. We'll figure something out. I promise."

Michael went quiet then. She knew she had failed to convince him. Not knowing what else to do, she took him home. He hid his face behind his hood the entire ride. When she pulled into the driveway, he barely waited until the car stopped before jumping out and slamming the door.

Sam let him go. He needed some time to process what he'd seen, and she had a case to solve. Her case gave her the chance to do what she was trained to do: solve murders, not predict and prevent them. Delving into the work would help her get her head on straight.

Since she still had an hour before sunset, she headed straight to Ms. Jackson's apartment, ready to start from ground zero. On the way, she called for backup to help her toss it. An hour of searching revealed nothing out of the ordinary, aside from a second toothbrush and some male undergarments in the dryer. Any records pertaining to the kids or families of schoolchildren she had tried to help must have been kept at her office. Other than a few newspaper articles on the table, the apartment revealed little about the victim's work and no insight at all into why anyone would want to kill her, much less torture her for information.

Questioning Jackson's friends and neighbors proved just as fruitless. All described her as gentle spirited, amicable, and sweet. Like trained parrots hesitant to speak ill of the dead, most used those exact words. The guidance counselor had no lover, male or female, that any of them could recall, though her next-door neighbor reported often seeing a strange car in her driveway late at night. Jackson had no criminal record and, it seemed, no enemies—except for the obvious one who had carved her into steaks. No one Sam questioned gave her any information about Jackson's death or even her whereabouts the day she went missing, not a single lead worth following up, aside from the possibility of a secret lover. From what Sam could gather, Gloria Jackson was everything right with society.

So why would anyone want to kill her? That was the billion-dollar question.

In their few dealings in the past, Sam remembered the guidance counselor's fierce dedication to her work, a trait to which Sam could relate. The school seemed the next logical place to investigate. And with the holiday break beginning, no one would be around to protest her snooping.

Sam made a quick phone call to Principal Roger Alves, who agreed to meet her at the high school early Thanksgiving morning. She didn't know his plans for the holiday—she had planned to spend it with a TV dinner and some Three Stooges reruns—so she greeted him in front of the school with a smile and thanked him for his time.

Despite the cold and it being a day off, Alves seemed eager to help. "Gloria was a respected member of our faculty," he said after shaking Sam's hand. The skin over his knuckles was dry and cracking. He was a meek professor type, an older gentleman with salt-and-pepper hair parted on one side, gaunt features, and a butt chin. "She was loved by all who knew her." Alves's voice softened, and he looked away, but not before Sam caught the face of a man dealing with great sorrow.

Our mystery man? Sam kept her deduction silent. Alves was hiding something, but it wasn't guilt.

He sniffled as he fumbled with his keys, hands trembling. At last, he pushed the right key into the keyhole and unlocked the door. He raised his head and straightened his tweed jacket. His sorrow had regressed but could not retreat beyond the wrinkles at the corners of his eyes. After holding the door open for Sam, he followed her inside and locked it behind them.

Alves opened a gray panel in the faux-brick wall and flicked what looked like a half dozen breakers. The hallway illuminated with a sickly yellow light and hum that sounded like a cranked-up amplifier. "Please, follow me." He waved an arm. "Her office is just down the hallway here."

Sam crossed the lapels of her coat. For some reason, she found it colder in that empty school than it had been outside. The shiny waxed floors contrasted with speckled, stained, and in some places, broken white ceiling tiles. An air of somberness made her feel as if she had entered a crypt instead of an institution of learning. Every echoed footstep brought more gravity, as if the walls were closing in on her despite the spaciousness of the hallway.

Alves stopped and turned to her with defeated eyes and drooped shoulders. "I know you probably can't tell me much, but do you have any idea who might have done this?"

"It's too early to tell, but we have some leads," she lied.

The principal set his jaw. It reminded Sam of all the times she clenched her teeth tightly while she fumed inside, knowing that feeling anger and hate was always preferable to letting loss and longing take hold. She wondered if she was perhaps only projecting her own emotions onto him.

He shook his head and continued walking. "I wouldn't say this in front of the students, but I hope you find the son of a bitch and fill him with holes."

Sam hoped so, too. "We'll do everything we can to see that justice is served."

Alves sighed. "Well, we're here." He stepped around her and riffled through his key ring once more.

Sam looked at the gold placard on the door: Guidance. *Guide me, Gloria. Guide me to your killer.*

Alves opened the door and turned on the light. "Now, professionally speaking, I can't let you see the student records, any psychological evaluations—even the opinions of Gloria herself—or any other private information that may be held in their files." He pointed at a large filing cabinet against the far wall. It had eight drawers arranged in two columns. "So that cabinet is off limits. Please feel free to go through anything else. Glo—Ms. Jackson was a very meticulous woman, so I'm sure everything will be organized and easy to find."

Sam moved over to the desk. On it, she saw older pictures of Ms. Jackson with a chocolate lab that aged in each photo until it was replaced by a gorgeous baby girl with curly black locks and dimples the size of craters. A niece, Sam presumed. Other than a letter opener, a few stacks of Post-it notes, some blank legal pads, a stapler, and a jar full of pens and pencils, the desk was sparsely covered. She was not surprised; the juicy stuff was rarely kept in plain view.

She had a tried-and-true process for conducting an investigative search. When someone was murdered, the first documents she would seek were schedules: calendars, diaries, appointment books, or anything else that could pinpoint the victim's location or companions at a time closest to the murder. Most people kept a considerable amount of information stored in their cellphones, so they would be Sam's go-to sources. But cellphones were left on the victims only by stupid—and easy to catch—criminals. More often than not, the victim's cellphone was never found.

Next she tackled the desk drawers. In the top drawer were Gloria's personal bills and some office supplies, nothing of note save for a set of keys. In the top left drawer, she found what looked like a diary. It was bound in pleather with a latch and lock. She pulled it out.

"I believe that's her day planner," Alves said. "I'm not sure why she locked it, but I assume it was to keep her sometimes blatant disregard for my instructions hidden from me. Gloria could be so... stubborn. She really cared about these kids. About everyone, really. It was one of the many things I... we all loved about her."

"Had she disobeyed any of your instructions recently?"

Alves's eyes glistened with tears. "Not that I'm aware of. You would know better than me, I'm guessing, if you can get that open." He gestured at the planner in her hand.

Sam grabbed the key ring. All four keys on it were far too large to fit the lock.

Alves was sniffling more frequently. A noise emitted from his throat that sounded as though he was trying to hold back a cough. "Excuse me," he said as he headed out of the office. He stopped at the doorway. "I'll be back in a few minutes. In the meantime"—his eyes shifted over to the file cabinet—"I hope you find what you're looking for."

Sam nodded, and the principal exited the room. She had read him loud and clear—the keys, or at least one of them, were to the filing cabinet. But that knowledge did her no good if she didn't know what to look for.

She glanced back at the planner. Its lock looked so cheap she could probably pick it with a paper clip. "Fuck it." She pulled on the flap until the fabric tore away from the metal clasp.

Ms. Jackson was a bit archaic in her calendaring system. The details of her work and personal life were spread across the pages in calligraphy-like handwriting. Nearly every weekday was marked by at least one set of initials. Some days had multiple pairings of letters, each corresponding to a specific time of day.

Dr. Prentiss had estimated the time of death at no earlier than four p.m. on Saturday, October 23. Sam slid her finger down the calendar. She saw only one marking on October 23. "T.M. – 2:00 p.m." The letters had to be initials. *But whose? Who was she meeting on her day off just two hours before she was killed?*

Sam grabbed Ms. Jackson's keys and ran over to the filing cabinet, shoved the first key into the keyhole, and turned it. *Success.* She pulled open the drawer. The inside of the filing cabinet was filled with manila folders, many of which were teeming with papers. Despite their volume, each folder was arranged neatly and alphabetically—last name first. Over the top of the files lay a single sheet of printing paper. In large, bold letters, it read, "CLOSED FILES."

Sam smiled. Gloria's organizational skills were making her job easy. She closed the drawer, removed the key, and hurried to the adjacent drawer. When she opened it, her smile grew larger. She couldn't have more accurately predicted what she would find. Across the top of the files contained inside, Sam found a similar sheet of printing paper. That one read, "OPEN FILES."

Sam thumbed through the folders. The last names on them went up only to *F*. She found *M* two drawers below. Quickly, Sam scanned the files until she found her first match: Thomas Marconi. The name meant nothing to her, nor did she expect it would. Sam pulled the student's file and continued to the next one.

"Tessa Masterson," Sam read. The name caused several bells to ring inside her head, but it took her a moment to realize why. "Tessa!" She felt as though the evidence she needed for her case had just been gift-wrapped and handed to her. Tessa was the name of the girl Michael claimed would soon kill her father. The coincidence was too amazing to ignore. The name wasn't that common. There couldn't be many Tessas at Carnegie. Maybe the girl had killed Gloria Jackson as a precursor to stabbing Daddy.

Sam pulled out Tessa's file. Leaving nothing to chance, she fingered through the remaining *M* names and found two more sets of matching initials. She grabbed both, tucked all four files beneath her arm, and carried them over to the desk. She opened each one and photographed every page with her cellphone. She would have a techie blow up the pictures once she got back to the precinct.

As she finished taking her last photographs, a man's whistle came from down the hall. She hastily jammed the files back into the cabinet as close to alphabetically as she could and slid the drawer shut. After locking it, she tossed the keys back into the top desk drawer.

Principal Alves walked in a moment later. Sam made a show of looking through emails on her phone, trying to appear as though she had ended her search and been waiting for his return.

"Did you find what you were looking for?" he asked.

"Let's hope so." She shook his hand again. "Thank you, Principal Alves. I'll see myself out."

For the first time since Michael had prophesied her death, Sam felt something just shy of joy. Finally, she had a promising lead. Tessa Masterson was somehow involved with the guidance counselor's death. Sam was certain of it.

Speeding away from the school, Sam couldn't wait to tell Michael what she had learned and how he'd helped her. Maybe the news would cheer him up. She was well aware that she was not supposed to share details of an ongoing investigation with a civilian, but Michael was more than that. And he was shaping up to be quite the little detective.

Besides, what's anyone going to do about it? I'll be dead soon enough, and it's kind of hard to punish a corpse. But at least I'll have solved one more case before I go. With that thought, the certainty of her impending death—and her helplessness to prevent it—finally set in. All Michael knew was that she would be stabbed. She couldn't help but notice the similarity her death would share with that of her most recent murder victim.

As much as she wanted to see Michael, Sam feared that any delay could lead to her death and a murderer going free. She needed to corroborate the evidence she had discovered, to ensure that even if she didn't solve the case before her own demise, she would leave enough breadcrumbs for someone to follow through with what she had started.

She shrugged. *Half the drug dealers, muggers, and rapists in Fall River carried knives.* Her death could be at the hands of any number of potential deviants. She doubted she would have any chance of seeing it coming. *Maybe it's better that way.*

Sam had lived more lives than a dozen cats. Just as she had a precarious knack for getting into life-threatening situations, she had an equal knack for getting out of them. Her years on the force had pitted her against killers and madmen, and not the quirky-funny kind. Her arrests earned her many enemies. Her aptitude and strength earned her many more within her own male-dominated profession. Each experience helped define what she had become: cynical and untrusting, cautious but wise. Those qualities made her a better detective but had dismantled her personal relationships. Sometimes, she wondered if she had such a hard exterior to prevent others from cracking it and seeing how empty she was inside.

Without knowing when or where her end would come—or even who would cause it—Sam felt powerless. That was the part she hated most. In the next few days, she was sure she would jump at dog barks and car horns and constantly be looking over her shoulder. She wondered what it would feel like when the blade entered her. *Will there be a lot of pain? Will I die quickly?*

In the meantime, she had a case to solve and the determination to solve it, no matter the cost.

CHAPTER 16

TESSA CELEBRATED HER THANKSGIVING IN her room, thankful for every moment Father stayed out of it. Unlike most families who were gorging themselves on turkey legs, cornbread, and sweet potato pie, as she had done back when Mother was still alive, Tessa hadn't eaten a thing. The thought of food turned her stomach. It brought with it the smell of blood, the taste of her own vomit, and the sounds of torment—the begging, the whimpering, the suffering—of a dying woman.

A woman who had died because of her.

Distractions were hard to come by at home. Surprisingly, school on Monday and Tuesday, then the half day on Wednesday, had been a blessing. It had allowed her to be out of the house and away from Father, and the work kept her mind at least partially occupied. But while all the other kids were cheering as they hopped onto their buses to go home, Tessa was thinking of ways to get after-school detention. She had even flipped off a teacher, but the woman let her off with a warning, and Tessa hadn't found the courage to do it again.

In the end, she had missed the bus on purpose and walked home the long way. She crept upstairs, put on her headphones, and tried to sleep. But she could reach only that in-between stage where objects seen through barely open eyes blurred and formed Rorschach-like shadows. In those shadows, she saw Ms. Jackson and the cookie guy and even some others Father hadn't killed but might have just as easily, like the pretty woman in line at the supermarket. In those shadows, she also saw her mother.

Screaming.

She jolted awake just as Father entered the room. She bet other girls' parents knocked, but she would never dare to ask Father for some privacy.

"Are you going to sleep all day?" he asked. "Don't think that just because it's Thanksgiving you have a day off from your chores."

"Thanksgiving?" *How long was I asleep?*

Father either didn't notice or didn't care about her confusion. "Were you asked about her?"

Tessa knew exactly who "her" was. He'd asked the same question every day this week. "No. I didn't see one cop at school either." She gulped. "Maybe they haven't, you know, found her yet."

"Are you wearing headphones?" He raised his hand. "Take those damn things off when I'm talking to you."

She was slow to act, her hands already trembling as they removed the speakers from her ears. She turned to place them on her nightstand.

Whap!

The slap was hard enough to bring a metallic taste into her mouth. She shrank back against the headboard, squeezing the life out of a pillow.

"And if they do come around asking?" he snapped. "What do you say?"

"Sh-Sh-She never came here. I know nothing."

He smiled. "That's right. Good. You're just a dumb kid who knows nothing."

He leaned closer. Tessa hid behind the pillow, averting her eyes. She could feel his breath on her ear.

"You and I have been together a long time, Tessa." All the anger had left his voice, yet the low, calm whisper was somehow worse. "It would be a shame if you didn't show me the proper respect. Your mother—God rest her soul—she didn't show me the proper respect. I can't help but think that maybe if she had been a more respectful person, a more dutiful wife... well, maybe things might have turned out different."

Father sat down on the bed beside her. "You're not your mother, are you, Tessa?"

He ran his fingers through her hair, and she started, her whole body shivering as she shied as far away from his hand as she could. She ducked her head. The pillow folded in the middle as she pulled it against her.

Father leaped to his feet and tore the pillow from her hands. "Answer me!"

Tessa scurried back to the farthest corner of the bed.

He leaned over and gripped her jaw. "Well?"

Terror had taken her voice away. She wagged her head back and forth.

After she stopped, he wiggled her head for her. "No." He laughed. "You are not your mother. You will respect me. You will obey, like a daughter is supposed to."

A knock came to the front door.

"Who in the world...?" Father glared at Tessa, then his expression went blank. She knew that blank face, the one he wore for strangers. "You'll stay in here if you know what's good for you. And you'd better pray this has nothing to do with that guidance counselor. She had no right meddling in the affairs of a family. No goddamn right."

His mask started to slip. He let out a breath and said flatly, "No one does." He stormed out of the room, leaving her bedroom door open.

Tessa remained on her bed. For some reason, she thought of that boy, the one who claimed to see stuff. *What did you see, Michael?* She smirked through her tears. He had probably seen the day Father went beyond bruises, burns, and breaks—the day Father would finally kill her.

A day her pain and suffering would be over.

A day that couldn't come soon enough.

CHAPTER 17

BACK AT THE PRECINCT, SAM reviewed Tessa's file. If Ms. Jackson had made any significant observations pertaining to the girl, she hadn't placed them in the folder. *A woman as organized as Gloria Jackson would likely have stored her notes in the file. Unless her life was cut short before she could.*

In fact, Tessa's file lacked anything of significance. Whatever the guidance counselor's thoughts were, she took them to her premature grave. But the file did have one useful piece of information: an address. Though that would have been easy enough for Sam to look up, its inclusion within the file saved her the bother.

Tessa lived at 78 Winchester Street in what Fall River folk called the Highlands. The Highlands were the Ritz-Carlton section of the city. But being the wealthiest part of Fall River was like being the cleanest chicken in the coop, still full of shit. The houses in that area were mostly single-story ranches. Modest homes at fair prices, the kind where a single father might try to give his daughter a quality upbringing, even if that daughter wanted him dead.

But why the guidance counselor? Sam evaluated every possible answer to that question. Revenge was always a possible motive, by far the most common. Since a high school guidance counselor had taken an interest in Tessa, Sam suspected that either abuse was the impetus behind the girl's murderous intent, or Tessa was simply a disturbed teenage misfit.

The abuser seemed obvious. With no other relatives in Massachusetts and living alone with her father, Tessa had only one likely abuser: the lowest kind. Daddy issues like those had no cure.

Sam needed to summon up her commitment to the law and remember that Christopher Masterson was the victim, at least in Michael's vision. *Murder is murder, no matter what the reason for it.* In truth, she believed some men deserved to die. Sam would try to gauge if Masterson was one of them.

But Masterson's death was a crime not yet committed, so it would have to take a backseat to Gloria Jackson's. Besides, she figured her presence at the Masterson residence might already be altering the course of future events. Then again, the counselor's death would have led Sam to Masterson's house with or without Michael's vision. The only difference was that she had a more definite suspicion to go on. Only one question remained: would that knowledge make things better or worse?

Sam had never met Tessa, but she knew there weren't many teenage girls who could move a one-hundred-eighty-five-pound body by herself. Still, she believed Michael's vision and that the girl would murder her father at some point. *But Tessa hadn't necessarily murdered Gloria Jackson*, Sam reminded herself. Even if the girl was responsible and the Masterson house had truly been Ms. Jackson's final stop, Tessa would have needed help cleaning up her mess. Her father eclipsed all other potential candidates. Regardless, Sam made sure her gun was loaded.

With only her gut feeling, a teenage boy's psychic vision, and a notation in a day planner, Sam lacked the evidence she needed for probable cause and a search warrant. Other cops might have held off on questioning Masterson or his daughter until they had more to go on, but Sam's initial instincts were usually right.

So after letting several coworkers know where she was going, Sam drove to the Masterson home. *There's no law against talking to people. Maybe he'll even invite me in.*

As she got out of the car, Sam scanned the front of the house and the yard. She could tell a lot about a person by the way he maintained his property. Masterson's house screamed "perfectionist." It was something to be admired, not because of its grandeur, but because of the attention to detail its owner obviously showed it. She looked to the left of the steps then to the right. Sam bet if she drew a line down the middle of the house, the two halves would be strikingly similar.

No. They're identical. The house was more bisymmetrical than a human face and sort of looked like one, too. Windows on each side of the front door served as its eyes, gazing upon the outside world while their shutter-lids kept the outside from looking in. The door was its long, flat nose, the stairs its clenched teeth. *Not a face. A skull.*

What at first glance was almost poetic symmetry became somehow perverse and unnerving upon further inspection. Sam couldn't find a single flaw, not so much as a run in the cold gray paint. The steps and walkway looked as though they had been vacuumed and power-washed then scrubbed free of blemishes with toothbrush precision. Neither a single leaf nor a smudge of dirt invaded the pathway up to the structure. Like a still life, the house seemed trapped in time, unaffected by wind and weather.

The landscaping exhibited the same kind of anal-retentive maintenance. Hedges of identical height and shape, trimmed flat across their tops, jutted from dual rock gardens bordered by ornate brick. Even each of the hundreds of white rocks seemed equivalent to its neighbor in size, shape, and gradation. Every blade of grass, still thriving despite the onset of winter, stood erect and cut to precisely the same fairway height.

Everything was perfect, too perfect to be real. Yet somehow it was. If it weren't for one glaring difference, Sam would have thought mirrors or special effects were deceiving her. On the left was a statue of Jesus, set within a break in the row of bushes. On the right, in a similar break, the Virgin Mary stood in what resembled a bathtub cut in half, a popular lawn ornament among the local Portuguese. Masterson wasn't a typical Portuguese name, so the decor seemed odd.

She didn't like that house, but she couldn't think of a specific reason why. She frowned. If the home was the crime scene, she doubted she would find anything of use. The person living there didn't seem the type to leave evidence behind. Sam could almost smell the bleach already.

Feeling mischievous, she stomped her size-seven boot into the grass and twisted her foot. Her heel dug out a small divot, while her sole flattened a small area of grass. Her willful vandalism provoked a chuckle. She walked up the front steps and knocked on the door.

As she waited for someone to answer, she did an about face and studied the neighborhood. It was eerily quiet, the type of street where she imagined everyone kept to themselves.

"May I help you?"

Startled, Sam turned to see a man no taller than her standing in the doorway. With tightly cropped hair, mostly gray, and black-rimmed glasses, he wouldn't have stood out in a crowd. Sam hadn't even heard the door open, yet there he was. Had he caught her juvenile act? Part of her hoped so. "Mr. Masterson?" she asked, putting on her professional face.

"Yes?"

"I'm Detective Samantha Reilly of the Fall River Police Department. I'm sorry to bother you on Thanksgiving, but if I may just have a moment of your time..."

"What about?"

"Your daughter." Sam spoke the truth, even if what she said was only a part of the whole.

Masterson glanced over his shoulder. Sam leaned to the side, hoping to get a look at Tessa, maybe even have a chat with her. With younger kids, it was sometimes that easy, but Sam wasn't holding her breath. Teenagers were inherently wary of authority.

Masterson's mouth formed a flat line across his face. He opened the door and waved for Sam to enter. To her amazement, the interior was more orderly than the exterior. The living room was like an optical illusion, with every object arranged at right angles to the wall and each other. Nothing appeared out of place. Sam found its museum-like rigidity austere and uninviting, a reflection of its owner. She felt as though alarms would blare if she touched anything. She wondered how anyone could live there. The house did not look lived in at all.

"Please," Masterson said, "make yourself at home."

He pointed toward a sofa that, together with two chairs and a television set, formed a rectangle. Sam chose the chair at the far end. It gave her the best view of the room, its exit into the kitchen and dining room, and the staircase leading to the second floor. Masterson sat across from her, his back to the staircase.

"These chairs are comfy," Sam said. Her words were meant to draw his attention to her bouncing, which displaced the cushion just enough to annoy an obsessive personality. She then slid the chair about an inch to the left, purposely drawing it out of sync with the rest of the decor. She watched Masterson closely to see if the mistreatment of his chair bothered him.

He stared back with a placid expression. If her actions bothered him, he revealed no sign of it. "So, Ms. Reilly, what sort of trouble has my darling daughter gotten herself into this time?" His tone held a hint of disappointment, as if a police visit wasn't the least bit strange. But Sam had checked both of their records and found no past dealings with law enforcement for either.

Sam put on a surprised expression. "I wasn't under the impression that Tessa had been in trouble before."

"Does a cow shit in a pasture? Tessa is like a magnet for trouble; she attracts it everywhere we go. It's never been anything major, but we've moved a few times with the false hope that a fresh start and some new scenery would do her some good. I love my daughter, but sometimes I wonder if all I do for her is worth the effort. It would be a shame to think of her as a lost cause."

As Masterson spoke, a shadow emerged on the staircase behind him. Someone was at the top of the stairs, listening to their conversation. *Tessa*, Sam assumed. *Good.*

"Where's Tessa now?" she asked.

"I rarely know with her. Do you have children, Detective?"

"No."

"Well, I can assure you, keeping tabs on a teenage girl is no easy task. The tighter I close my grip, the more she slips through my fingers. She's probably out with friends, smoking or causing more trouble."

"Is anyone else here? I would like to talk to you in private."

"No, it's just me."

He's lying. Tessa was upstairs and had likely been instructed to stay there. *He doesn't want me to talk to her.* Sam set her jaw. *Let's find out why.*

Masterson shifted in his seat. "The suspense is killing me. What has Tessa done this time?"

"Nothing. Not yet, anyway. Mr. Masterson, I don't know how else to ask you this, so I'll just come out with it. Can you think of any reason why Tessa might want to kill you?"

In her years of interrogating suspects, Sam had learned that sometimes the best way to evoke a genuine response from her target was to sandbag him with a seemingly out-of-the-blue question that struck close to the heart. Reactions, particularly those from criminals harboring guilt or the fear of getting caught, were usually impulsive and defensive.

Yet Masterson didn't even raise an eyebrow. Sam had implied that his daughter had given some indication that she planned to kill him or at least had wanted to, but Masterson took the news as if it were idle chitchat. Sure, he didn't get defensive, and he didn't cry foul. There was no fear in his eyes, no blubbering of the guilty. But his was not the response of an innocent. His was the response of one without compassion. *Without a soul.*

"None." Masterson's voice was low and steady. His hands remained folded in his lap; he was calmer than a windless sea.

Sam sent the next question out like a bullet to throw him off guard. "Do you know Gloria Jackson?"

"No," Masterson replied without missing a beat. "Should I?"

"Ms. Jackson is a guidance counselor at Carnegie High School. Her calendar noted a meeting with Tessa last Saturday at two p.m. Was Tessa home Saturday?" She didn't speak of Gloria Jackson in the past tense, not wanting to offer any implication that Jackson might be dead, hoping instead that he would slip up and let that fat cat out of its bag.

Masterson smiled wryly. "Like I said, teenage girls are impossible to keep track of, but let me think." He shifted his gaze to the ceiling and put on a thoughtful expression.

This guy thinks he's good, Sam thought, confident he was putting on a show for her. *But I'm better.*

"Saturday. Hmm... I saw Tessa in the morning. We ate breakfast together. I made pancakes. After that, I can't be certain."

"And I suppose Ms. Jackson never visited?"

"Not unless she came by when I was out back raking leaves."

"So you were home then? All day?"

"Yes, all morning and afternoon."

"And in the evening?" She wanted to lock him into a story, one he couldn't squirm out of later.

"I may have run some errands."

"Where?"

He shrugged. "The grocery store. McDonald's to pick up dinner. What's this all about, Detective? What does this Gloria Jackson have to do with my daughter?"

"Ms. Jackson was murdered. Witnesses say that they last saw her here." That was a lie. She had no witnesses, yet. But it wasn't the first time she had lied to get at the truth.

"Well, your witnesses need to get their eyes checked." Masterson widened his eyes. The shock on his face looked real enough, but Sam wasn't buying it. "Wait. Are you saying that I'm a suspect? I've never even met the lady." He paused as if he'd had a sudden epiphany. "Oh. Do you think Tessa's done something?"

"At this time, I'm not accusing anybody of anything, Mr. Masterson. I'm simply conducting a murder investigation, interviewing anyone who may have knowledge of Ms. Jackson's whereabouts in the hours leading up to her death. Your cooperation has been appreciated."

He jumped to his feet. "This conversation is over. I was happy to speak with you, but your questioning has become grossly inappropriate. Tessa is a troubled girl, yes. But murder? No, she's not capable of it, and before you ask, neither am I."

"Well, you see, the curious thing is that so many people knew Ms. Jackson was coming here, yet nobody saw her leave. Tessa couldn't possibly have dumped a woman of Jackson's size all by her lonesome. She's not strong enough."

"I know what you're driving at. You're gravely mistaken. I would like you to leave now." He pointed at the door.

"If your only part in this was aiding in the disposal of the body so you could protect your daughter, I can understand that. I may be able to convince the prosecution to go easy on you if—"

"I've heard enough of your silly accusations!" He marched over to the door and opened it. "Unless you're going to charge me with something, it's time for you to leave. I will not answer any more of your ridiculous questions without a lawyer. Neither will Tessa."

"Have it your way." The conversation had run its course, but it hadn't been fruitless. Masterson had invoked his right to an attorney even though he hadn't been charged with a crime. Sam had learned plenty, not so much from what was said but from what wasn't. "If you think of anything else you would like to tell me—"

"I wouldn't wait by the phone for that call. Go," Masterson said, jabbing a finger at the open door.

Sam grinned smugly. "Thank you for your time." She buttoned her overcoat and headed out into the cold. "I'm sure I'll be seeing you," she said as she passed him. As she walked down the steps, she heard the door close behind her.

After getting into her car, she glanced back at the house to check the windows. She thought she saw a curtain drop in one upstairs, but she couldn't be sure. She almost waved, in case Tessa was looking, but she kept her hand on the wheel, in case Masterson was, too.

As she drove away, Sam knew she had her man. Christopher Masterson was guilty of murder, as well as kidnapping and torture. But as Sam had found out early in her career, her cases were never about what she knew but what she could prove. Just then, she didn't have a whole lot of proof. The evidence she needed was probably in that house somewhere. Maybe it had been right under her nose. But she would need a search warrant to get it.

Unless… maybe the key to solving this case is Tessa. Whatever is going on between those two, one of them is in danger. I better build my case fast before I have a second homicide to solve. Masterson's not going to let me anywhere near his daughter, but maybe there's another way.

Sam closed her eyes and took a deep breath. She was reluctant to go down that road again, but the urgency left her with little choice. Preventing murders was something altogether new to her, but for sure, she had to try. If Masterson was the type of man she thought he was, it was only a matter of time before he did to someone else what he had done to Gloria Jackson, if he hadn't already.

People like him, once they start, they can't stop. Sam cursed. She had to play her new trump card sooner and more often than she had intended.

Damn it. Michael is going to be so pissed.

CHAPTER 18

MICHAEL HAD WALKED AWAY SEVERAL times already, but each time, he returned to that same spot against the concrete pillar. *What the hell am I doing?* He couldn't understand what had possessed him to go through with his plan. Again, he thought to leave. Again, he reminded himself that if he did, he wouldn't get another chance to enlist the help he needed.

The final bell separated most students from the hallowed halls of Carnegie High. Only athletes, musicians, and troublemakers stayed after it, and Michael didn't fit into any of those categories. Carnegie was the last place he wanted to be.

The football team was nearing the end of its season. With its successful romp against their Turkey Day rival, the New Bedford Whalers, and with seven players already named All Stars and another three just waiting for the official announcement, the Carnegie High Hurricanes were going to compete at the state competition. They were gearing up for a fistfight against a vicious team over in Rockland. After they were given the Friday after Thanksgiving off, the student athletes were back to running drills and slamming into big blue punching bags that Monday.

Under the guise of being a freshman interested in joining the team next year, Michael went to the practice and watched from the bleachers. The sport seemed barbaric. Any grace it might have had at the college level was undermined by its pimply teenage practitioners ramming into each other like stubborn goats and trying to muscle each other without heed to leverage. Phrases like "bootleg" and "I formation" made little sense to Michael. When he saw one kid snot rocket on another after tackling him with what looked like a crippling hit, he turned away, disgusted.

Some of the athletes noticed Michael in the stands. They began yelling insults at him, calling him every slur he knew for "homosexual," then twice as many more he'd never heard. Their meathead minds conjured barely intelligible threats, and they promised all sorts of graphically painful penetrations as they grappled and groped each other, constantly slapping each other's asses for the most minor of accomplishments. Michael wondered if half of them were in the closet, acting overtly homophobic to cover up the fact they were getting boners from touching each other. The rumors of what went on in the locker room just might be true.

Coach Pelletier looked on with seeming approval. He kept his players on a leash, but it was a long one. He kept them safe from each other when the 'roid rages hit, but anyone not on the team was fair game. His silence pretty much encouraged their hostility toward Michael.

Michael ignored the taunts. None of them mattered. He hadn't gone there to see idiots fight over a ball. He wanted to see only one player, Robbie Wilkins.

Unlike his teammates, Robbie went about practice with cool-headed methodology. If he saw Michael, he never let on. Given his teammates' constant hazing of Michael, Robbie's ignorance of Michael's presence had to be willful. The team's starting center, he towered over most on the field, yet he seemed the meekest.

Coach Pelletier dismissed the players, and they headed for the showers. Michael got up and walked over to wait outside the locker room. When the door opened, he braced himself for more hazing.

One by one, the athletes filed past him. Oddly, their mouths remained closed as they passed. A few gave him strange looks; most ignored him altogether. Robbie was one of the last to come out. With a gym bag slung over his shoulder, he walked by Michael without even glancing his way.

He's going out of his way to pretend I don't exist. Michael again doubted his reasons for being there. *Maybe I should just let this volcano stay dormant.* But Michael's fear wasn't as potent as it once might have been. He'd seen what true evil looked like, and Robbie wasn't it.

"Robbie?" he called.

Robbie froze. For a moment, he seemed to be debating how to respond or whether to respond at all. Slowly, he turned to face Michael.

Is he afraid of me? That would be weird. Maybe he thinks I'm going to shoot him.

Robbie's obvious discomfort made Michael feel much more at ease. He felt surprisingly in control of the situation, as if Robbie might actually listen to him and maybe do what he requested. To think that so soon after bullying Michael in the school restroom, Robbie was now scared of him almost made him laugh.

"What's up?" Robbie asked, obviously trying to sound casual but tough. The slight squeak in his voice betrayed him.

"Hey. I just wanted to talk a second, if you got one."

Robbie's shoulders dropped. He exhaled a long breath. "Michael, I feel terrible about what I did to you. If I could take it all back, I would. But I can't." He glanced around the empty area, then asked, "Are you going to shoot me now?"

"What?" Michael laughed. "No, I'm not going to shoot you. Look. You said that if I ever needed anything, well... I need your help with something."

"Okay." Robbie seemed a little relieved but not much. "What do you need help with?"

Michael took a deep breath. "This is going to sound crazy," he said, thinking too many of his conversations were starting the same way lately. "I'm sure you've heard all about my, um... dreams?"

"Are you kidding me? Who hasn't?" Robbie stepped closer. "That must be so awesome. What's it like?"

"It's not nearly as fun as you might think." Michael rolled his eyes. He supposed he should be thankful Robbie at least believed him. The conversation would be a lot harder if Robbie scoffed and thought the rumors were nuts.

"Anyway, I had one about this girl, Tessa. She's in your class."

"Tessa Masterson? Yeah, I have dreams about her, too, but I doubt they're the same as yours. She's hot, dude."

Michael shrugged. "I guess. I really didn't notice."

"Are you gay or something? I mean, it's okay if you—"

"Can we get back on track here? Tessa's in a bit of trouble. I need to warn her. She needs my help, but I can't do it alone. I'm... scared."

Michael hoped Robbie would see helping as a way to make amends for all the crap he'd pulled with Glenn, not to mention the literal crap he'd put Michael through. He didn't seem like a terrible guy, just impressionable. Maybe playing the good guy might actually suit him. Michael didn't care as long as he helped.

Robbie stood straight, confident, and ready for business. "When?"

"The sooner the better."

"I got practice all week, then I gotta go straight home to babysit my baby sister. How about Saturday afternoon sometime? I have practice in the morning."

"If that's the earliest you can do it..."

"It is."

"Then that will have to be soon enough." *I hope it will be soon enough.*

"What do you need me to do?"

"Nothing dangerous. Can you come with me to Tessa's house this weekend so I can tell her what I saw?"

"What did you see?"

"Nothing specific," Michael hedged. He certainly wasn't going to tell Robbie that he'd seen Tessa kill her own father. And Robbie also didn't need to know what Sam had told him about Ms. Jackson's murder and Tessa's possible connection to it.

"Find out what you can as discreetly as possible," Sam had told him. "But do *not* go anywhere near that house."

Michael had promised to do both, but the instructions were at odds with each other. *What better way to learn more about Tessa and her father than to go to their house?*

He knew the excuse was weak. But ever since he'd met Tessa, he couldn't get her out of his mind. His heart went out to that fragile, quiet girl. And he was filled with terror at the thought of what she might become. He didn't want that for her, though he couldn't understand why he cared so much. Michael felt responsible for Tessa, whether she was a victim or a murderer. Even if his practical side could dismiss it, his conscience couldn't.

His plan was easy enough: go in and get her out. But Robbie might screw it up if he knew any more than necessary. Worse, if he knew about the murder, Robbie might decide not to help at all. Michael didn't like keeping the truth from someone who willingly offered his assistance, even a mongoloid like Robbie, but he wasn't brave enough to do it alone. He needed Robbie there with him, no matter how he had to paint the truth to get him there.

"I just know she's in trouble," Michael said. "We've got to help her."

"All right. I'll go with you. But after that, we're even. And you'll forgive me for what happened in the restroom. Sound fair?"

Michael felt the tiniest bit sorry for Robbie. He knew he was about to lie to the guy again. He doubted he would ever forgive Robbie for dunking him in that toilet, his most humiliating life experience to date.

"Yeah, we're even. And I'll, um… try to forgive you. I can at least promise to never try to kill you."

"Deal," Robbie said, smiling goofily and holding out his hand.

As they solidified their bargain, Michael's hand looked like a gumball inside a catcher's mitt. Robbie had committed himself without even knowing what he was supposed to do, not that it was a long way off from what he used to do for Glenn Rodrigues. *Cheap muscle.*

"Meet me at the top of the Seven Hills at three o'clock on Saturday. President Avenue is only a few blocks from where she lives. We can ride our bikes from there." Michael hated having to wait until Saturday, but he had seriously doubted that going alone was a good idea, and Sam wouldn't allow him anywhere near the place. If he wanted to help, and he did, he would have to wait. In the meantime, he would have to rely on Sam's squad's emergency response time.

"I don't have a bike."

"Then we'll walk it. You've got feet, right?"

Robbie nodded. "Three o'clock. President Avenue. Got it."

"Good. Don't forget."

"I won't." Robbie turned and walked away.

I hope not. Michael sighed as he watched Robbie leave. *I hope he's more honest than I've been.*

CHAPTER 19

TESSA WAS IN HER BEDROOM with the door closed when the doorbell rang. She'd been pretending to do homework while listening to Taylor Swift as loud as she dared. Swift and other upbeat pop singers were her favorites, though at the same time, their songs choked her up. She wondered what made them so happy they wanted to sing and dance about it. She swallowed. *I never feel like dancing. Not that anyone would want to dance with me.* She would have given her soul to be like all the fabulous people—the singers, the actresses, the models. They were living real-life fairy tales. She thought she might like to see Hollywood someday but doubted she would ever get much farther than her front door.

With one speaker buried in her right ear and the other lolling over her shoulder so she could hear Father coming, she hummed the tune so softly that it sounded like a bee was buzzing around in her head. Father didn't approve of modern music, or any music really.

She couldn't concentrate on homework until he was asleep. While Father was awake, Tessa wasn't safe. While he was awake, she made no noise, spoke only when spoken to, and stayed out of his sight as much as she could. Her only relief from anxiety came when he slept. With her own dreams plagued by nightmarish memories, Tessa didn't find any relief in sleep.

Father expected her to answer the door, another one of his inexplicable rules, something about being a proper lady. It made her feel more like a butler. But with the way he whipped her for the slightest infraction, maybe "slave" was the better term for her position in their household.

Father wouldn't care if she'd truly been concentrating on homework. Tessa would upset him if she allowed the doorbell to ring a second time. She sprang from her bed and hustled down the stairs, keeping her footsteps as light as possible. No stomping down the stairs. Violating *that* rule had once earned her the punishment of having her hand pressed against the stove burner. She wouldn't make that mistake again.

Tessa was reaching for the knob when the doorbell rang a second time. Terror washed over her. Father sat in his chair in the living room, not more than ten feet away. He was staring at the *Fall River Herald* as though trying to decipher a hidden code within one of the articles. He must have heard the doorbell, yet he didn't stir, even though Tessa never had visitors.

Tessa opened the door. *Michael and Robbie.* Her heart thumped harder, and she tried to keep the fear from showing. She had to get rid of them. She stepped outside and carefully closed the door behind her.

"What are you doing here?" she whispered.

"Since we were in the neighborhood, we thought we would come by and see if you wanted to come out and hang with us, maybe go down to the park." Michael spoke way too loudly, obviously trying to be heard by Father, but she had no idea why.

"Yeah," Robbie said, playing along but not well. "We were gonna toss around the football at the park."

"Neither of you are holding a football," she said, still whispering. "Please leave and don't come back." She stepped back and pushed open the door.

Before she could get inside, Michael said, "We came to warn you. We've got to get you out of here before somebody ends up dead. The police know about Ms. Jackson."

Tessa gasped but then caught herself. She was immediately skeptical. If the police knew about Ms. Jackson, they would be at the door instead of two boys she hardly knew. Maybe Michael had another vision? She still didn't know what he'd seen in the first one. Tessa remembered how he'd stormed off, leaving her desperate and lonely. She had already gone to him once for help and had been shot down, left to fend for herself until Father finally killed her.

"Oh yeah?" she said. She glanced back and forth between the boys and Father, who was still sitting in his chair. She was surprised he hadn't come over to see who was at the door, but she knew she didn't have much longer. Blood pumped into her head so fast, she thought she might faint. She slid out onto the front steps and closed the door again. "What happened to Ms. Jackson?"

"He killed her." Michael said it so confidently, so matter-of-factly, Tessa was certain they had been found out.

She looked out at the street, fully expecting to see a police car, maybe even a SWAT team. But the street was the same old quiet place it always was. She glanced back at Michael. Perhaps he was wearing a wire, trying to trick her into confessing. Father had done the killing, but she had been right there beside him, whether she'd wanted to be or not.

"We can talk about that later," Michael said, tugging on her sleeve. "Right now, we've got to get you away from him."

"Wait a minute." Robbie held up his hand. "Did you just say what I think you said? No one said anything about anyone killing anybody!"

"Could you keep your voice down, genius?" Michael glared up at Robbie. "I told you she was in trouble. What did you think I was talking about?"

She suddenly realized how strange it was to see the two of them together, much less on her front porch. She was pretty sure Robbie had been at least partly responsible for dipping Michael into a toilet.

Robbie shrugged. "I don't know. I thought maybe some ex-boyfriend was harassing her, and you needed my help to make him back off or something like that. I didn't know her father was a serial killer."

Michael sighed. "No one said he was a serial killer. Can we focus on why we came here?"

The two boys were arguing as if Tessa were invisible. Their voices grew louder. They would soon disturb Father, if they hadn't already. Even if they didn't, Father would come looking for her soon.

"Shut up!" Tessa blurted. They did. "You guys need to get out of here." Her voice conveyed urgency, but the message was too late.

"Nonsense," said Father from behind her. Like an assassin, he had a way of slinking around without a sound.

Tessa wondered how long he'd been there. She hadn't even heard the door open. She shivered. The hairs on her neck stood on end.

"Well," Father said, "aren't you going to introduce me to your friends?"

Robbie and Michael stood gaping. Tessa stammered but was unable to form anything that resembled a coherent response.

Father nudged her aside and approached the boys. He looked as though he were sizing them up. "Please forgive my daughter. She has a lot to learn about manners." His lips formed a sickly, wry smile.

Tessa's stomach fluttered, full of butterflies looking for an escape. The boys stared at Father as if mesmerized by him.

"Christopher Masterson," Father said, extending his hand.

"M-Michael. Michael Tur-colgate." Tessa almost snickered. *On the spot, the best Michael could come up with was toothpaste?* "Michael Turcolgate," he said again, as if repeating it would make it sound more convincing.

"Elijah Wood," Robbie said, shaking Father's hand and smiling.

Tessa wondered if he was really that proud of his pseudonym. She shook her head, part in fear and part in disgust. *This will not end well. The only chance they have is if they refuse to enter the house.* Her eyes blurred. *And me, I have no chance.*

"Well, Michael and Elijah," Father said, his own smile big and phony, "come in. It's far too cold to be outside. You boys look like you're chilled right through. I'll make you some hot chocolate."

Behind Father, Tessa shook her head side to side as fast as she could. Still, Michael and Robbie entered the house but remained only inches from the door. Father disappeared into the kitchen. Tessa was doomed by their uninvited appearance, but she thought she could still save them. In stepping away, Father had given them a chance to flee. They would not likely get another.

"Are you two stupid?" Tessa hissed. "Why aren't you running?"

"You asked for my help," Michael said. "I'm giving it to you now. We came here for you, and we're not leaving here without you."

Tessa almost smiled. She was touched by Michael's innocence and courage, but all they really amounted to was stupidity, the kind that would get him hurt, or worse. He and his double-stuffed friend had stumbled into a situation they couldn't possibly understand. A lion's den might have been the better of the two choices.

"I don't know," Robbie said. "Maybe we should listen to her."

"Don't be such a wuss," Michael scoffed. "You're easily three times that guy's size."

"You should listen to him, Michael," Tessa said. "You're not safe here. And anyway, I don't want you here. Go. Leave now."

The kettle whistled in the kitchen. Soon, hot chocolate would be on its way. But unlike most social visits, drinks at Father's house were never followed by friendly conversation.

Michael reached for her hand. "You have to trust me."

She didn't pull away, but he must have lost his nerve because he did.

He straightened. "You're not safe here, either. We all need to go."

"You think I don't know that?" Tessa had to fight back tears. "Do you have any idea how much worse you've made things for me?"

"Then come with us. You can stay with me until everything's okay. I'm sure my foster parents won't mind."

"How do you think things will ever be okay? Will the police come and take Father away? Will they find me a new life and a new home? I wish things were that simple. He'll never let me leave. He'll hunt me, and when he finds me, he'll make me wish I never left. A few days free of him, even a few months, are not worth what Father will do once he gets his hands on me again."

Tessa felt hopeless. The sincerity she saw in Michael's eyes only made her hurt more. He truly wanted to help her. She wanted him to have the strength to take her away from Father. But if Michael thought she could just walk away, or even run, without always having to worry and look over her shoulder, then he didn't really know anything. He certainly didn't know the monster that hid behind Father's face.

"Go," she said, sobbing. "I don't want what's going to happen to me to happen to you two."

"Here's hot chocolate," Father said, emerging from the kitchen. He sounded like a dad in a '70s sitcom.

He handed a piping hot mug to Robbie and another to Michael.

Tessa didn't get one, nor did he have a mug for himself. "Careful," he said. "It's hot."

He moved between the boys and the door then ushered them over to the couch. "Sit down. Relax. Friends of Tessa are always welcome." He bared his teeth in a grin.

Michael sat at the end of the couch closest to the door, which wasn't very close at all, and stared suspiciously at his mug. Robbie sat beside him, almost on his lap. Tessa perched on the edge of the chair closest to the boys. Father remained standing. He was the only person in the room who appeared comfortable.

Apparently not sharing Michael's intuition, Robbie raised his mug. Tessa noticed Michael nudging Robbie's arm, but the big lug didn't pay any attention.

Robbie poured half his hot chocolate down his throat. "Ouch!" He dribbled some of the liquid back into the mug. "That *is* hot!" He took another enormous gulp.

"Then why do you keep drinking it?" Michael asked. "Why don't you wait until it cools?"

"Because it's so good." Robbie licked his lips. "Damn, I already got that crud hanging from the roof of my mouth."

Michael shook his head. "Do you mean burned skin?" He rolled his eyes, glanced over at Tessa, then reached out to put his mug on the coffee table.

Tessa quickly intervened. "Wait! Uh, you can't put that there." She grabbed a coaster and placed it on the table in front of him. "Here. Please use this."

"Thank you." Michael plopped his mug on the coaster.

"Relax, Tessa," Father said. "They're our guests." His smile never wavered. He slapped his thighs. "So, boys, what brings you to see my daughter?"

"Um, we were at the park," Michael said, "the one on President Avenue, at the top of the hill. We thought we would come by and see if she wanted to... um... hang out. Oh, and to tell her happy Thanksgiving."

Father frowned. "Tessa and I don't celebrate Thanksgiving. Neither of us have anything to be thankful for."

"Oh, I'm sorry. I—"

"Nah, I'm just busting your balls, Michael." Father chuckled.

The boys let out some forced laughter. Tessa didn't know whether hearing the word "balls" from an adult had made them uncomfortable or if they were finally realizing that Father was a little off. Both of them began to fidget. She wondered how much more they would need before they decided to run... and leave her behind.

Father turned to Robbie with a grin. "What about you, fat boy? Is that the excuse you want to use, too?"

Robbie seemed confused by the question. "Uh... I-I..." He looked at Tessa. "Uh, excuse for what?"

Father chuckled. "Come on." His laughter stopped, and his expression turned sour. "Enough games. Let's hear it. Which one of you is fucking my daughter?"

Tessa moaned as her face heated. Even she hadn't expected *that*. Things had just gone from bad to worse. She couldn't tell whether Father really believed it or if he was just messing with the guys' heads.

Maybe it's a good thing. If that was all Father suspected, if he hadn't figured out the real reason for Michael and Robbie's visit, the boys might yet survive the encounter. They might, but she wouldn't. Premarital sex was a cardinal sin in Father's household. Not that he would ever let her get married, anyway.

Robbie and Michael looked at each other with wide eyes, speechless. Tessa could only guess at what was going through their minds. And if she couldn't tell whether Father was joking or not, she was pretty sure they couldn't.

"I asked you a question." Father scowled and took a step closer to the couch. "Which one of you boys is fucking my precious little daughter? Or is Tessa such a whore that she's doing both of you?"

Michael shrank back into the cushions, his face reddening. "Neither of us are having sex with Tessa."

"What about the Michelin Man over here? I want to hear what he has to say."

"I've never had sex with your daughter, sir," Robbie said, his lips quivering. "I swear it. Tell him, Tessa."

Tessa looked away. It didn't matter what she said. Speaking would only make things worse. Father would never believe her, even if she could somehow show him her unbroken hymen. He'd already drawn his conclusion. Right or wrong, Father would stick by it.

Michael stood, tugging Robbie by the arm. "We should probably get going."

Robbie got to his feet and allowed Michael to pull him toward the door. They did a kind of side-shuffle around Father, never taking their eyes off him.

So much for help. Tessa remained in her seat. *He's no hero. There are no heroes.*

As the boys got to the door, Michael blurted, "Tessa, you should come with us."

Big mistake.

"That whore isn't going anywhere with the likes of you," Father said, clenching his fists.

Tessa couldn't will her legs to stand. She could not oppose Father. Robbie reached for the doorknob.

"Where do you think you're going?" Father charged over and grabbed Michael by the back of his collar, his knuckles brushing the back of Michael's neck.

Michael fell to the floor.

CHAPTER 20

MICHAEL TRIES TO SUCK IN *some air. Cold sears his lungs. His legs are in motion.*

Am I running? *Michael chokes up.* Am I being chased?

His feet pound the sidewalk, one after the other, over and over again. He can hear himself wheezing. He wants to stop, but something compels him forward. Even in the freezing night air, he's sweating. He has no idea how long he's been running, but his legs are starting to cramp. His sprint turns into a limping gallop.

A vision of my own future? *It has to be. He feels it, interacts with it. That happened only once before, when he saw Jimmy Rafferty shooting Glenn Rodrigues. He can* stop running, *but then he might not make it to wherever it is he's supposed to be running toward.*

In a vision of his own future, Michael knows he has more control. He can alter whatever it is he's meant to see. Maybe he can use the vision as a sort of virtual reality training area. In life, people don't get do-overs, but with everything Michael sees now, he'll get a second chance to do it better, what his foster dad calls a mulligan. Or I could foul things up even worse.

But first, Michael has to figure out what needs fixing. He lets his legs carry him where they will. As he rounds a corner, he spots Sam a couple of blocks away. She's standing beside her black Toyota Camry. Her car is double-parked at the edge of a small parking lot. A short distance behind her, a big blue tarp with "ICE" printed on it is affixed to the wall of a building. Large overhead lights blur his view, and his eyes are slow to adjust. Oblong shadows of Sam and her car extend toward Michael like black holes longing to suck him into darkness. He tries to sprint, but he can't make his legs move any faster.

Sam opens the passenger door and reaches into her car. She appears to be talking to someone.

"Sam!" Michael is now crossing a grassy field. He leaps over a drainage ditch, wincing as he lands on the other side. Waving and calling her name, he keeps going. He has to reach Sam. He has something he needs to tell her, and it is urgent. But what he plans on saying remains a mystery.

Sam looks up at him. He's almost there, now so close that a glimmer of hope sparks in the despair eating away at his insides. Sam leans over the open car door and smiles at him as though she hasn't a care in the world.

Michael, on the other hand, is overrun with fear. His stomach churns, and he's afraid he might have to stop to vomit. Someone moves from the shadow of the building and walks up behind Sam. Michael clenches his fists. His thighs burn, but he lengthens his stride. He has to reach her. The urge is stronger than ever, though he doesn't yet understand why.

As the person moves swiftly toward Sam, a man's face becomes clearer. There is no mistaking that face. He saw it no more than a few minutes ago. And now Christopher Masterson is right behind Sam.

Less than ten yards away, Michael skids to a stop. Sam lurches forward as Masterson crashes into her, slamming her against the car window. Her smile is replaced by surprise mixed with pain. Her head flies back then falls forward. After bouncing off the door a second time, Sam collapses to the pavement.

Masterson stands over her, and a sly grin spreads across his face. For the first time, Michael sees the man is holding a large knife. The blade is coated with red. Masterson raises his hand and stabs at the sky. Blood drips down his arm, but he doesn't seem to notice.

Masterson lowers the blade to his side and tries to close the car door, but a lifeless arm gets in the way. Masterson raises his foot and kicks the door shut. The resulting grotesque snapping sound causes Michael to gasp.

Masterson looks up, smiles, and points the knife at Michael.

Michael turns and runs back the way he came. His weary legs don't make the jump over the drainage ditch, and he falls against the opposite bank. He can hear Masterson running after him. He scrambles to get back on his feet. Just as he manages to stand and stumble forward again, he feels a hand on the nape of his neck.

Michael screams.

Michael was still screaming when he realized he was no longer in the vision. Masterson had a viselike grip on Michael's jacket collar, and he was twisting it tightly around Michael's shoulders as he pulled him up off the floor. Michael was both surprised and frightened that such a small, nerdy-looking man could lift him so easily.

Michael raised his arms and wriggled out of his jacket. Masterson held the empty coat and stared at him with obvious irritation.

Panting, Michael shrank into the corner beside the door. *Get a grip. If I live long enough to see Sam die, then I won't be dying here. Of course, the future is one fickle son of a bitch.*

Robbie looked shocked, his mouth hanging open in a which-way-did-he-go-George expression. Tessa appeared completely terrified. The cushion she sat on trembled along with her as she sat curled up tightly, knees against her chest. For better or worse—Michael had quickly decided for the better—Masterson seemed less angry than he had before a teenage boy collapsed onto his rug like some unmedicated narcoleptic. At any rate, Michael was pleasantly surprised Masterson hadn't decided to kill him yet. He couldn't know Michael had seen his true face, the killer hiding behind a mask of normalcy.

I know what you are, Michael thought, glaring at Masterson. *I see you.*

Masterson stared back, eyes full of hate and loathing. They seemed to answer, *I see you, too.*

Michael was still trying to catch his breath. "May I please have some water?" He thought he might be having an asthma attack, even though he didn't have asthma.

"In the kitchen," Masterson said, tossing Michael's jacket at him. "There are some cups by the sink. Have your drink. Then, I want you and your pudgy friend out of here. If I ever see either of you around here or my daughter again, I'll kill you. Understood?"

Pulling his jacket on, Michael nodded. "I'll be right back," he told Robbie, who appeared rooted to the floor. Michael hurried across the living room and into the kitchen, which along with the dining room was only partly visible from where they had been standing. He went straight to the sink, turned on the faucet, and splashed some cold water onto his face. Once he got his breath back, he cupped some into his hands and drank.

Something to his left caught Michael's eye. A wooden block full of kitchen cutlery stood on the counter next to him. It was loaded with black handles. *The knife!* Michael moved toward the block.

"What are you doing in there?" Masterson called from the living room.

Michael ignored him as he reached for the largest handle. *This has got to be the one.* He pulled the large serrated knife from its slot.

Michael heard a sound behind him and spun around, instinctively holding up the knife. Masterson was storming toward him. The man stopped little more than a foot away as his eyes dropped to the knife pointed toward his stomach. All Michael had to do was stab, and Sam, Tessa, all of them would be safe.

Masterson seemed larger than he was, hovering over Michael like a wolf over dinner. He showed no fear. He didn't even question why Michael was holding one of his butcher knives.

The feel of the knife's triple-riveted handle, strong and sturdy in his hand, gave Michael courage. "Move aside," he said, flicking the knife at air.

Masterson sneered. "No."

Michael gaped at him. "What do you mean, no? Can't you see what I'm holding?" His courage was fading. Soon, he would lose it altogether.

"Little boys shouldn't play with such dangerous things." Masterson smiled and inched closer. "Little boys might end up hurt."

Not knowing what else to do, feeling trapped between an immovable object and an irresistible force, Michael charged, knife out. Masterson quarter-turned out of the way as Michael ran past, making a beeline for the door. As he skidded to a stop in the living room, he noticed the blade was wet. Judging by the amount of blood, he must have sliced the man pretty good. *Just how sharp is this freaking thing?*

He felt a twinge of guilt, but it passed quickly. There was no time to waste. "Robbie, get the door!"

Tessa sat blank-faced in her chair.

Michael grabbed her wrist and yanked her from her seat. "We're leaving."

Ordinarily, Robbie was slow, but he apparently took Michael's command as a matter of life and death. He hadn't seen what Michael had seen. As Michael pulled Tessa out of the house, he heard some clanging coming from the kitchen.

"Now you've done it," Tessa muttered. "You should have finished him off. He'll kill you for sure now. He'll kill us all."

Tessa's words registered, but their impact was lost. He heard her sobbing as she ran beside him and Robbie. He was thankful she was coming along willingly, or at least, she wasn't trying to free her arm from his grip. He never looked back to see if anyone was following.

When they finally stopped to catch their breaths, Michael realized they were near Plymouth Avenue, one of Fall River's busiest streets. Tessa bent over, panting. Robbie wasn't nearly as winded. He had pretty good stamina for a big guy. Michael figured it was all that football training.

Michael let go of her wrist. He could already see a bruise forming where he had held her. Robbie stared at him, apparently expecting him to know what to do next. Michael's fight or flight instincts had gotten them that far, with flight weighing much heavier upon the balance. For the moment, he was all out of ideas.

Then, it hit him, a solution so simple. *Call Sam.*

"There's a supermarket about a quarter of a mile that way," he said, pointing. "We should hang out there. I know a cop. I'll call her once we get there. She'll know what to do."

"Dude," Robbie said, "you cut that guy."

Michael shrugged. "Shit happens."

They headed toward the store. Minutes later, flashing lights whizzed by them. Sirens blared, but the police paid Michael and his companions no notice.

As soon as they stepped into the grocery store's parking lot, Michael's cellphone rang. He pulled it out of his pocket, saw Sam's name on the screen, and answered, "Hello?"

"Michael," Sam said, "what's going on? Christopher Masterson just called 9-1-1. He said you stabbed him and kidnapped his daughter."

Michael felt tears burning his eyes. He tried to answer her, but his throat closed up as a lump formed in it.

"Are you okay?" she asked.

"Yes. We all are," he managed.

"Where are you?"

"At the Stop & Shop on Rodman Street."

"Stay there. I'm coming to get you."

Michael waited in silence with Robbie and Tessa. He looked down at the knife he still held and realized something. What he had done might have improved Sam's odds of living. He had the knife Masterson would have used to kill her.

And nothing and no one could make him give it back. *Not to that piece of shit.*

CHAPTER 21

CHRISTOPHER LISTENED TO NURSE REYNOLDS chomp her gum. Her smacking sounded like handfuls of mud being slung against a wall. She wore loose-fitting blue scrubs that hung on one shoulder, baring her collarbone. He wanted to bite her there like a rabid animal and rip out her throat, anything to stop that smacking. The pressure mounted in his head. Holding back his rage caused the world to blur. He needed to release it.

Nurse Reynolds, didn't your father teach you not to chew gum like a slut? These are dark days when one can't even find common decency within the medical profession. He sighed. *Maybe her parents deserve blame.* The concession didn't make him want to kill Nurse Reynolds any less.

Apparently oblivious to his contempt, Nurse Reynolds went about her business in the sterile hospital room. Minor medical devices and some furnishings cluttered the room in no discernible arrangement—a chair, a television, and the bed in which he was lying. The television showed an aged Anderson Cooper fumbling through a piece on some political coup in Egypt. *Savages,* he thought as tanks rolled through Cairo and across the tiny screen.

"The doctor says you're free to go as soon as you feel up to it," Nurse Reynolds said between smacks. "Guess you're not gonna die today after all."

"Really?" Christopher shook the IV line pumping saline into the back of his hand for emphasis. "Do I take this with me?"

"Oops." She giggled. "I guess I forgot to remove that. Don't be such a sourpuss. I'll take it out, and you'll be on your way in a jiffy."

"Fantastic."

Nurse Reynolds didn't seem to be in any hurry to remove the line. She turned and started restocking a drawer with tissues, gloves, and biohazard bags, all the while prattling on about her personal life, and Christopher completely ignored her. His focus was on the gum. Her open-mouthed chewing never stopped. He couldn't block it out no matter how hard he tried. His headache worsened. He wanted to stop that smacking. No, he *had* to stop it.

"That's a disgusting habit," he snapped, wishing he could remove that gum from her mouth and half her tongue with it. Someone had to teach her manners. Someone had to teach her self-respect. *Why doesn't anyone in this goddamn world have any goddamn respect?*

"What?" She'd been rambling absently to whomever she thought was listening but finally shut up long enough to consider what he'd said. "Oh, my cigarettes?" She pushed the pack deeper into her shirt pocket. Christopher hadn't even noticed it. "I'm trying to quit," she said, blushing.

"That, too," he replied. Though he had been referring to the gum, the cigarettes were equally appalling. He wondered why someone who saw daily what cigarettes did to people would want to smoke them. *She'll never quit. Whores like her always need something in their mouths.* He sneered. *Like that fucking gum.*

"Huh?"

Christopher shook his head. He really didn't need to call more attention to himself. "Never mind."

She shrugged and went back to work. She didn't stop chomping, but at least her chattering had ceased. She moved a bit quicker, too. After pulling the needle out of his arm with as much delicacy as a wolf enjoying fresh rabbit, then slapping a bandage over the spot, she shuffled out of the room.

Minutes later, he heard a knock on the door. Before he could answer, a woman in a charcoal wool overcoat and knee-high black boots stepped into the room.

Christopher grinned. "Detective Reilly." He welcomed intelligent company, even if she was an adversary. "Have you come to apologize?"

"Not likely. I'm going to nail your ass to the wall."

"Such ugly words from such a pretty face. Aren't officers of the law supposed to serve as role models for our country's youth? It's no wonder most of them are wayward."

"Save your preaching for someone who gives a damn, Masterson. Maybe your cellmate will listen to you if he's not too busy fucking you up the ass. Of course, that's only possible if your mouth isn't stuffed at the same time."

"Why the hostility, Detective?" Christopher remained calm. He wasn't dumb enough to be provoked into saying something that could be used against him. Whatever she thought she had on him was nothing his lawyer, already on call, couldn't unravel. "Could it be because your little spy violated my rights as an American citizen? I have to admit, I'm a bit surprised to see you here. Is it because you wanted to make sure my recovery was going smoothly? After all, we wouldn't want your pet to go to prison on murder charges. Is your relationship with the boy causing some tension back at the office? Why is it my fault that you clearly don't know how to do your job?"

Reilly raised an eyebrow, but she didn't respond. "What are you talking about? I have you dead to rights. We're going to run some tests on that knife taken from your place. I'm sure we'll find Jackson's DNA all over it."

Christopher smiled. *Baited like a worm on a hook.* "Whose DNA? I haven't the faintest idea what you might be referring to, Detective. The only person's DNA you'll find on that knife is mine, unless you count that insolent brat's grubby handprints. But if you want to waste your time with that, feel free."

Reilly huffed. "It is going to be *so* satisfying when the jury gives you that big G-word. Every cop in Fall River knows what you did to Gloria Jackson. There's no escaping where you're going. You're a marked man."

"Are we going to do this dance, Detective? You've got nothing on me, despite all your tough talk. I, for one, am done talking. Neither I nor Tessa will be answering further questions without our attorney present."

"Tessa's beyond your control. Right now, she's a ward of the Commonwealth and represented by it. I can and will ask her anything I want."

She was right. Christopher found it humbling, for a moment, then as irritating as an itch in a hard-to-reach place. He had warned Tessa of the dangers of talking and the fate that would befall her if she did. Many times. Getting her to talk wouldn't be easy. But the female detective could be crafty. She'd already manipulated one kid to steal a murder weapon from his house. *Could she turn Tessa against me, too?*

For the time being, Christopher couldn't do a thing about it. He needed to get out of that damn hospital bed. His migraine was blinding.

He rubbed his temples, stopping once he noticed the detective's stare. In a moment, his problems would become moot. He would simply walk out the door, pick up Tessa, and gently remind her of her vow of silence.

Well, maybe not too gently.

"Anyway, I'm not here about the guidance counselor," Reilly said.

"Do tell, Ms. Reilly. What brings you to my modest hospital room?" *Did they finally find Mr. Girl Scout Cookies? That could be a problem. If she's here on behalf of that fat oaf, perhaps it's time to move again.*

"Michael Turcotte."

Christopher rolled his eyes. "Him? That little cretin can relax. I'm not pressing charges."

"Who's to say he's not pressing charges against you? By both his and Robert Wilkins's accounts, you assaulted Michael as he was trying to leave your home. You even knocked him unconscious."

Christopher couldn't suppress his laughter. *The boy fainted, just like Tessa did the first time I had her watch, and I never even touched him. Children are so feebleminded.*

"Did I say something funny?" Reilly asked.

He waved a dismissive hand. "By all means, go that route. But tell me, did you find any bruises on Michael? Did he spend the last few days in the hospital? Is there any disputing that he came to my house and stabbed me, an unarmed man, with my own kitchen knife? Stop pressing this stupidity. It won't end well for you or the boy."

"Is that a threat?"

"An observation. You should try making them from time to time. The cards, as they say, are stacked against you. I was trying to be merciful and move past all of this, give the child a second chance. Live and let live, so to speak."

"Why would you want to do that?"

"The boy is clearly troubled and could use some good old-fashioned corporal punishment. But instead, he would be introduced to the criminal justice system. By the time he got out of it, he would be a worse criminal than he was when he entered, deprived of any chance of a good, honest life."

"How altruistic of you."

"Say what you will unless, of course, you've already said it. Then you would just be wasting my time." Christopher avoided her stare, trying to keep his thoughts hidden. His decision not to press charges had nothing to do with the failings of the American penal system or that kid's future.

The real reason he didn't press charges was much simpler: Christopher wanted his knife back. The mere thought of his knife block sitting at home with just the one slot empty made his blood boil. He wondered how long it would take him to retrieve it from a police evidence locker. There would probably be a stream of paperwork to wade through, but the police would give it back eventually. In the meantime, he would have to make do with the empty slot, an inconvenience as irritating as Nurse Reynolds chomping.

"Are you even listening to me?" the detective asked, frowning.

Apparently, she had continued talking while his mind had drifted back to his knife. He hadn't heard a word of it.

"If you want a statement from me, speak to my attorney. Now, if you'll be so kind." He hopped from the bed, not caring that he wore nothing but a faded blue hospital gown, his bare ass hanging out the back. "Or do you plan on keeping me here against my will? I wouldn't enjoy reporting you to your department for false imprisonment. Honestly, I wouldn't." He grinned broadly for her benefit.

She looked almost amused by his assuredness. Christopher didn't like that. Cops were usually easy to read, even predictable. Her reaction to his goading worried him. He wondered if she was going to arrest him or shoot him. She walked closer and stood directly between him and his pile of clothing.

He stood his ground. "As I understand it, I'm free to go. If you would kindly step aside."

"Yes, yes, the doctor has cleared you for release. It's been an absolute pleasure talking with you, Mr. Masterson. Just one more thing..." Detective Reilly extended her hand.

With rising suspicion, Christopher reached for the proffered hand. But before he made contact, she grabbed his wrist, spun him around, and slammed him over the railing of the hospital bed. She wrenched his arm up toward his shoulder blades. He felt cold metal scratching at his wrist, then biting into it.

"Christopher Masterson, you are under arrest for the assault and battery of a minor."

"You can't be serious."

"You have the right to remain silent," she said as she yanked his left arm behind him.

Ice crawled up his spine, but he kept his cool. "For a moment, I thought you were smarter than this."

"Anything you say can and will be used against you in a court of law."

"You're making a big mistake."

"You have the right to an attorney. If you cannot afford one..."

Christopher started to blank her out. They had his murder weapon, but he didn't think they had any grounds to test it for the teacher's DNA. And Reilly wasn't arresting him for murder, which meant she still had nothing. The detective's strategy seemed wildly miscalculated, incompetent even, unless...

She's biding time. His jaw clenched so hard he thought he might chew through his teeth. *The bitch is going to try and turn Tessa.*

When Reilly turned him around, he saw that she was smiling. His upper lip began to twitch.

How dare they take what is mine? As soon as I'm out—and it will be soon, you stupid bitch—I will retrieve what you and yours have taken from me.

Both things.

CHAPTER 22

SAM STRAIGHTENED THE WRINKLES FROM her suit pants, then walked with her head high, trying to appear cool and confident. When Police Chief Frank Cotillard called her into his office, Sam knew she wasn't going to leave happy. The chief wasn't one for compliments. He never gave his subordinates a pat on the back for a job well done. He was far more likely to dole out walking papers.

She had been a cop at the Third Precinct longer than Cotillard had been police chief, nearly her entire career. She had climbed her way up from writing tickets and directing traffic to a position of dignity and respect. Her talents put her in line for command roles, but she would purposely sabotage her own advancement whenever talk turned that way. Sam just loved being a detective, and she was damn good at it. There was no greater satisfaction than putting bad guys where they belonged.

In all the years she'd been working under Cotillard, Sam had been called into his office only twice. Both times, she'd left it thinking she was going to lose her job. When it came down to saving a life or following proper police procedure, for Sam, the choice was easy. She would disregard the rule book every time. Twice, that disregard had landed her in front of Cotillard's desk. But she still never regretted her decisions.

They say the third time's the charm, she thought as she stepped into the chief's large corner office. Tension hung heavy in the air, and Sam detected a faint smell of mint, a lesser version of the chief's liberal application of aftershave each morning. An imposing figure, the chief loomed behind his desk as he always did right before he was about to dole out a tongue-lashing, using his girth and tree-trunk arms to intimidate. He was not the best and brightest among them, and Sam assumed he had strong-armed his way to the top. His bullying didn't work on her, nor did his temper tantrums.

What did make her nervous was the threat of losing her job, though she would never show it. So as impatient as she was, she kept her mouth shut and waited for him to tell her why he'd called her in there.

His wiry gray mustache hung like an awning over a sour grimace. Nostrils flaring, he peered down the end of his nose at her. "Please, have a seat," he said after a long, uncomfortable silence.

Sam squinted at him, searching for tells, then pulled back a padded blue chair with metal legs. She sat.

The chief remained standing, his gaze somewhere behind her. "Here he comes."

The door opened, and a young man, probably in his late twenties, barreled into the room, clutching a briefcase in one hand and some loose paper in the others. He put down all of it in a disorderly stack on the floor beside the chair adjacent to Sam's. His cheap navy suit and yellow tie were wrinkled, but the rest of him was kept up nicely, from his perfectly feathered hair and clean-shaven face to his polished dress shoes. He straightened and buttoned his jacket.

Lawyer. Sam stood to greet him. *This can't be good.*

"You fucked up, Reilly," Chief Cotillard said.

Well, hello to you, too. There's something to be said for small talk. Before her temper could get the better of her, she bit the inside of her cheek and put on an innocent face. That wasn't too difficult since she hadn't the faintest idea what Cotillard was talking about.

Cotillard gestured at the younger man. "This is Assistant District Attorney Leslie Quintara."

Sam shook the attorney's hand. Then, all three of them took their seats.

"Leslie, tell Detective Reilly what we're up against here," Cotillard said.

Leslie tugged his collar as if it were too tight. For an attorney, he was extraordinarily slow to speak. Usually, Sam couldn't shut them up, even those on her side. He couldn't have been a prosecutor for long. Most of his kind were cocky and unjustifiably self-assured, or they at least acted that way. Maybe they had to be to go up against the types they faced on a daily basis. Most cops were the same way.

Sam thought she knew all the prosecutors in Bristol County, yet she'd never seen Leslie. The DA looked as green as grass and did little to inspire confidence. Most newbies spent their time handling misdemeanors. Sam hoped Leslie wasn't the prosecuting force behind any of her felony arrests, especially not Christopher Masterson's case.

Leslie cleared his throat. "It's the Masterson case."

Oh bloody hell. Sam swallowed hard. Things were quickly going from bad to worse, and she hadn't even found out why she'd been called into the office.

"We've hit a snag, a rather serious one, actually." Leslie gave her a sheepish, awkward smile. "Masterson's attorney is moving to exclude the evidence and for the immediate dismissal of all charges."

Masterson's attorney's move didn't come as a surprise. Every suited monkey posing as a defense attorney with nothing but the slightest hope of getting his undeniably guilty client off on some imagined procedural violation filed motions like that on a daily basis. Ninety-nine percent of them failed, unless the goal was to waste everyone's time and the taxpayers' money. The remaining one percent succeeded because of horrendously bad police work. And since Sam wasn't in the habit of illegally wiretapping phones or searching vehicles without warrants or consent, charges against her collars generally stuck.

Under normal circumstances, she would have laughed at the news and sarcastically wished Masterson good luck. But she was sitting in Chief Cotillard's office, so things weren't normal. His and Leslie's unsmiling faces implied that the motion was no laughing matter.

No, Masterson's arrest was anything but normal. She knew she had nothing, yet she had arrested him anyway, all just to give her some time alone with Tessa so she could build a case for Jackson's murder. Masterson's attorney, however, wasn't playing fair.

She knew the motions were coming. She just thought she would have a little more time.

The chief shoved a finger in her face. "What were you thinking, arresting Masterson for attacking that kid? He was the one who got stabbed, for Christ's sake! If, and I do mean *if*, that knife was used in a homicide, its evidentiary value has just been flushed down the fucking toilet."

Michael had given her the knife, and she had taken it into evidence, using all the correct procedures. "If we could just get it tested, you'll see—"

"Forget it, Reilly. The guy's attorney has already requested its return three times, like it has some kind of emotional value or something. And I'm of the mind to return it to him. It ain't evidence, that's for sure. Isn't that right, Leslie?"

"I'm afraid so," the attorney said as he pushed his glasses up the bridge of his nose. Sam was beginning to hate that whiny voice. "The judge has already made his ruling on that regard."

"I just need a little more time." Sam had arrested Masterson barely two days ago. She hadn't even had a chance to work him for a confession or to get in to talk to Tessa. The social workers were stonewalling her, claiming Tessa was in shock. And maybe she was. The kid had seen her dad get stabbed. But Sam was determined to interview that kid while she could still get to her away from her dad. "It's the knife that killed Gloria Jackson. I'm sure of it. It was found in his kitchen. I know, the chain of custody is a little shaky, but it's been properly documented since the knife entered our possession and can be traced all the way back to his home. No judge in Bristol County would exclude it on those grounds. If we can just get it tested, we will have what we need to charge him with murder. We've got Masterson dead to rights."

She vaguely remembered telling Masterson the same thing. He had played it off as though it was a minor inconvenience. *That slimy son of a bitch*. She felt helpless, forced to watch as her chances to nail a killer crumbled around her. "I just need a little more—"

"Time?" Chief Cotillard finished. "We know. You've said that. You're out of time, Reilly. This prosecution is going nowhere. And that's not even the worst part."

"What do you mean? I can find corroborating evidence. Let me talk to him... or the girl. I'll get one of them to talk. Then we'll have the evidence we need to get the knife tested and put that bastard away forever. I don't understand why you're not willing to back me up on this."

Leslie coughed. "The knife is exactly the problem. Masterson's attorney is asserting chain of custody and a host of additional evidentiary issues, true, but those are the least of our worries. He's citing all sorts of Fourth Amendment violations with respect to your... the department's seizure of the weapon. Most contain the normal jargon, easy to handle. As you are probably aware, we are taking the position that Michael Turcotte and Robert Wilkins were invited guests of Tessa Masterson and seized the weapon after Masterson assaulted Turcotte."

"Right," Sam replied. "Masterson's daughter let them in. Michael grabbed the knife to escape from an attack by Masterson. Doesn't the knife have some probative value of Michael's perceived need to defend himself? Admittedly, his getting the murder weapon was an amazing stroke of luck. We should be thanking him for it."

Sam left out the part about Michael being sure he was grabbing a murder weapon because he'd seen it used in a vision. In doing so, he'd probably saved Sam's life, too. She no longer had to look over her shoulder every time she stepped outside. Michael was like an avenging angel. She didn't believe in all that religious stuff, but she sure felt blessed to have him around.

Even so, she had told Michael not to go to the Masterson house. He'd gone anyway, and she felt guilty for it. Had some part of her known he would? Had she manipulated Michael as though he were a playing piece in a game where losing could have meant death? The thought made her stomach turn. Suddenly, she didn't like herself very much.

Leslie said, "Masterson's lawyer claims that Michael acted as an agent of this department and, specifically, *your* agent. If true, Michael isn't afforded the same leniency as the average civilian. Rather, his conduct must adhere to the same standards as those of every officer in the Commonwealth of Massachusetts. Masterson's attorney alleges that as an agent of the Fall River Police Department, the boy entered his client's home without his client's consent and searched it without a warrant, after Masterson informed the boy that he wasn't invited and told Michael to leave."

Sam's face heated. "That's a load of horse—"

The lawyer held up his hand. "If the argument is to be credited, just as you, Detective, cannot waltz into Masterson's house without his permission or a warrant, neither can Michael Turcotte. Whatever evidence he seized as a result of such conduct is inadmissible."

"That's crazy." She couldn't believe what she was hearing. "The knife was in plain view for the entire world to see. Isn't there some principle like that that can help us here?"

Leslie scratched his chin. "A good thought, except only the handle of the knife was in plain view. Its handle is identical to several others in the set. The blade was not visible. Even if it had been, there are serious questions as to how Michael knew what to look for... unless someone told him what to look for. That would bring us back to the 'undisclosed agent' argument."

"Are you suggesting I revealed details of my investigation to a teenage boy?" Sam acted as outraged as she could. Grimacing, she glared at the young lawyer. She hadn't told Michael much, but she'd definitely told him more than she should have. The implication being tossed around by Leslie, however, put her career in jeopardy. She had to come clean, even if it meant falling on her sword. "All I told Michael was to see if he could learn anything about Tessa Masterson. I stressed that under no circumstances was he to go anywhere near that house."

"So you admit that you used a fourteen-year-old boy to help you investigate a fucking homicide?" Chief Cotillard slammed a fist into his desk. His office windows rattled in their frames. "Damn it, Sam! What the hell were you thinking?"

"Michael has served only in the capacity of a witness, a confidential informant at best. Since when has using an informant not been an essential part of detective work?"

"I don't care if the boy is Sherlock fucking Holmes. You should *not* have been involving a kid in a murder investigation. Christ, Sam. It's not like I'm telling you anything you don't already know." The chief's face turned so red, Sam thought he might have a heart attack. Her own face felt balmy, too.

"In any event," Leslie said, "whether or not you told Michael to go there, I'm sure you can at least see how it looks. This kid, whom you've known his entire life, called you with the evidence we needed to put Masterson away. Add to that Michael's baffling participation in the Crotty case, and defense counsel is painting him out to be a police profiler or consultant of sorts. It's even been suggested that you use Michael for... supernatural reasons."

"Michael had nothing to do—"

"Save it, Sam," Chief Cotillard interrupted. "Four officers were sent to Crotty's house when you arrested him. At least one of them talked. He told us all about the kid who was there. You sure have a strange way of entertaining that boy."

"He saved that woman's life!"

"And there's more," Cotillard continued, ignoring Sam's outburst. "Dr. Prentiss filled us in about your visit to the morgue. He said you called the boy your intern." Cotillard shook his head. "Christ, Sam."

Leslie sighed. "Right or wrong, the judge apparently wants to consider the defense's argument. She took the matter under advisement, but at this point, we have to assume the knife is out. Our whole murder case is built around it. Without it and some grounds to test it for DNA, Masterson will walk, unless you've obtained more evidence since his arrest."

"We haven't gotten enough for a search warrant," Sam said despondently. "I was banking on being able to talk with the girl before Masterson was released. She's gotta know something. We haven't found Jackson's car yet, either. I'm assuming he used that to move her. We should be trawling the river for it."

"There were no tracks anywhere near the location Jackson's body was found," the chief said. "Where would you have us look?"

"What about witnesses?" Leslie asked. "Did anyone see Ms. Jackson enter Masterson's house? Did anyone catch anyone leaving that evening? Did anyone call in suspicious activity near the dumpsite?"

Sam nodded. "A neighbor saw a car parked in front of Masterson's home at the approximate time of death."

"Did he or she get a license plate number? Make or model? Color?"

"She said the car was a black sedan. That's all she knew. Jackson drove a dark blue Chevrolet Cobalt." The questioning was becoming frustrating. If she had more to give him, she would have already told him. "We know she was going there to see Tessa," she added. "That has to count for something."

"The notation in her day planner, you mean? Yes, it can be used to show where she might have been heading, but it doesn't show if she ever got there. We need more."

"Tessa must have seen something. All I'm asking is that you hold him long enough to give me time to talk with her."

"Well, you'd better be quick. Once the case is dismissed, we can't hold him any longer. Besides, when she was told of her father's arrest, Tessa Masterson took full responsibility for the murder of Gloria Jackson. She confessed under oath and stated that she acted alone. Beyond that, she refuses to give any details."

"That's horseshit. Either her father did it, or they both did."

Leslie nodded. "I agree with you. She's obviously covering for him. More importantly, our psychiatrist agrees with you. But the problem is not what we know, but what we can prove. We're keeping her in juvenile hall, going at her day and night, but Tessa won't budge. She's spooked, and if you saw the scars on her, you would understand why. She won't even finger her father for the abuse. You've got to give me something I can work with here, Detective. I'm only here on a short recess. I have to get back to the courthouse, and unless I have more to offer the judge, Masterson is moments away from walking."

"Believe me, I wish I could." Sam felt like an ant beneath a magnifying glass on a sunny day. Masterson would walk, and it was on her. *All because I had to take shortcuts. I just wanted to see him imprisoned before he could hurt someone else.* She slouched, vaguely recalling a famous quote concerning good intentions. She straightened. "I'll find the evidence we need."

"No," Cotillard said, standing. "You'll stay away from him. You're off the case from this point forward. You're lucky I'm not suspending you. But there will be an internal investigation into the matter. You can bet your ass on that. If the recommended punishment comes back as termination, so be it. I would hate to do it, but you've really forced my hand here."

Sam didn't argue. She knew she had screwed up. She thought she understood how Michael felt when he said he always got in trouble for trying to do the right thing.

The chief ran a hand across his bald head. "In the meantime, keep a low profile, and stay the hell away from Masterson. And if I hear you're giving that kid any more ride-alongs, you'll be suspended immediately without pay. You got it?"

Sam nodded.

He pointed at the door. "Now, get out of here."

Sam left the room, then the precinct, only stopping by her desk to grab her overcoat and keys. She felt humiliated and dejected. She seemed to be losing her hold on the only thing in the world that made sense to her, being a cop.

She plodded over to her car, opened the door, and slid behind the wheel. She started the engine then sat there, unable to bring herself to pull away from the precinct. For the first time since her partner and mentor had passed away, Sam broke down and cried.

CHAPTER 23

I F THEY WERE TRYING TO speak so that Tessa wouldn't hear them, they were doing a poor job of it. She heard nearly every hushed word. She sat in an uncomfortable wooden chair with a placemat-flat pastel cushion, pretending not to be listening while she stared at a spot on the canary-yellow wall, wondering where her future lay.

Not with him, she prayed. *I can't go back to him.* She knew what returning to Father meant: punishment. And it would be brutal, potentially deadly.

When she was younger, Tessa didn't know better. She thought she had to do what Father said without question. That was what good girls were supposed to do. Father always said so. As the years passed, Father tried to keep her sheltered. She would have even been homeschooled had her mother not fought so hard against it, one of the few times Mom had dared to speak against Father's commands. And how Mother had paid, beaten so badly she couldn't get out of bed except to make him dinner and do other household chores. Maybe Mother was the lucky one. She got away from him, even if she had to die to do it.

When Tessa had found her mother in that tub, she knew Father was responsible, and not only in the he-drove-her-to-do-it kind of way. No, Tessa believed he had slit her mother's wrists and made it look like suicide. Of course, she didn't see him do it, and she would never dare ask him about it. But the way Father avoided questions about her death, skirting around the very mention of her, always made Tessa feel as though he was hiding something.

After her mother's death, Tessa began seeing the wrong in Father. Still, she did as he commanded, more from training than from fear. After all, he was her father. Good girls listened to their fathers. Good girls did as they were told.

The violence became worse with each passing year. Not only did Father direct it at her, but also he began lashing out at those he felt had slighted him. He lost his job as an insurance agent for tossing his boss through the office's plate glass window. Claiming post-traumatic stress disorder from his tour of duty in Iraq, Father avoided prison.

Father had to go to court-ordered psychiatric appointments, but he somehow managed to fool the doctor because he was eventually put on disability for PTSD. That meant that he spent much more time at home, all alone with Tessa. She could only imagine the ugly things war did to people. But Father's "condition" had nothing to do with his service. Recently, Tessa had decided that he had enlisted only for the chance to hurt people where he wouldn't get in trouble for it.

Her life had become a walk across a tightrope. The slightest slip, and Tessa was lost. Still, she did as she was told, even when she knew it to be wrong. As Father got worse, her fear of him was enough to keep her in line. She knew what he was capable of; she'd seen it firsthand. He forced her to help him clean up his "messes."

Then he began making Tessa watch. To her shame, she never protested. She felt as though Father had molded her into a monster just like him. With each kill she witnessed, she felt a little less human.

But she couldn't tell anyone. He would kill her if she did. He'd promised it many times. And she knew he would find her, no matter where she went or how well she was hidden.

She hadn't said a word to the cops other than to confess to Father's crimes. She'd told them that she had murdered Gloria Jackson, turning a horror to her advantage. Going to jail was far better than living with him. And maybe since she'd gotten him off the hook, Father wouldn't come after her.

Am I... free? Tessa found the idea peculiar. She was alive. She was unharmed. She was away from Father.

"Gloria called me about her, but at that time, she only had a hunch," said the young woman wearing an embroidered vest over a pressed black skirt. Her name was Janet. Tessa had met her only once, the day after she got to the center. Even at a whisper, Janet's voice carried through the reception area. "We couldn't do anything about it then."

"It could have been her instead of Ms. Jackson," Detective Reilly said. She seemed strong and sure, her voice uncompromising.

Tessa kind of liked the detective. The woman had appeared like an avenging angel after Michael called her from the grocery store that horrible night. And Michael obviously trusted Reilly completely.

But Michael had hurt Father. Tessa had seen the blood. *He's not going to let that go.* Tessa's knee bounced uncontrollably. Father would be coming for them—Michael, Robbie, the detective, and Tessa. None of them were safe. She squirmed in her seat. *He's coming for me.* She felt the warmth of urine between her legs. *I'm doomed no matter what I do.*

Tessa glanced at the detective. She didn't look like much. Average height and slim, Detective Reilly probably wouldn't have won a lot of ass-kicking contests. Some of the girls in Tessa's class were bigger. She had seen Father tear more intimidating adversaries to shreds. Without her gun, the detective seemed no different than all the soccer moms Tessa saw collecting their kids after school while she hung back, afraid to go home. What made her so different from Mother, who had sworn to keep Tessa safe? A lot of good that promise had done her. Tessa was sure Detective Reilly would soon make the same promise, but she wouldn't be able to keep it any better than Mother had.

"We do what we can, Detective," Janet said. "Same as you."

Detective Reilly looked as if she wanted to take a swing at the woman. "Well, Janet, we can't exactly put her back there. He's a killer. Have you not listened to a word I've told you? It's outrageous that you would even consider it."

"Where else would you have her go? Her father's already called for her. You said yourself there are no charges pending against him. Tessa shows no signs of recent physical abuse. The scars on her back are old, and she's not saying how she got them. She says the bruises on her wrist came from the Turcotte boy. The size and shape of the markings are consistent with her story. Her personality exhibits half a dozen signs of abuse, from flinching and timidity to introversion, but even combined, these symptoms can be indicative of a host of psychological or behavioral disorders. To top it all off, she's confessed to murder."

"She's confessed to a crime she couldn't possibly have committed. Her father is the prime suspect, and she's the key witness. Yet you want to send her home with him?"

"As I understand it, no charges have been brought against Tessa, either," Janet said. She shrugged. "We can't keep her here under the present scenario. I'm sorry, Detective."

"Let me talk to her," Detective Reilly said. It sounded more like a command than a request.

"I planned on it. She said she would only talk to you."

"Me?" The detective seemed surprised. Tessa wondered if she had made a mistake in thinking she could trust her. But she figured that Michael liking the woman had to count for something, and Tessa really didn't have much in the way of choices. She didn't expect much anyway. She hoped when Father got to her, he would make it quick, not like he did with Ms. Jackson.

Janet replied, "Yes, only you. But one of our people will need to be there with you. You know, for the sake of the child. It's policy. I've got time if you would like to talk to her now."

Tessa saw no need for a chaperone. She wasn't afraid of the detective. Nothing the law could do to her would even come close to rivaling what Father likely had planned.

Detective Reilly glared at Janet then apparently realized there was no point in arguing. "Whatever." Without waiting, she spun and strode across the room, over to where Tessa was sitting. "Hello, Tessa. I'm Detective Samantha Reilly. If you recall, I was the officer who picked you up at the supermarket the other day. You were a little out of it, and—"

Tessa nodded and whispered, "I remember."

"Good." Detective Reilly sat in the chair beside her. "I'm a good friend of Michael's, but you know that already. Anyway, Janet tells me that you wanted to speak to me. Is that so?"

Tessa nodded again. She could feel the dampness in the crotch of her pants and hoped it didn't show. But if Reilly noticed, she was kind enough not to say so.

The social worker coughed as she approached. "We have a room set up. It's just through there," she said, pointing toward a doorway.

Reilly stood, and Tessa followed. She took short steps to keep her legs together as much as possible, not wanting the women to notice her accident. They walked down a short corridor and veered into a small box of a room that looked like something right out of the movies, one of those rooms where cops would take turns yelling at a suspect while a commanding officer watched from behind a two-way mirror. It even had the blinding overhead light above the table in the center. Tessa stopped in the doorway.

Detective Reilly waved her inside. "C'mon in and sit down. We're just going to talk."

Pulling her shirt down over her crotch, Tessa strode past the adults and took a seat at the table. Reilly sat across from her.

Janet fiddled with a video camera in the corner. "We like to record our sessions. We find the practice keeps questioning more appropriate and helps our team evaluate... um, things."

The video camera made Tessa extremely uncomfortable. *What if Father sees the recording?* She turned her body to the side so she could face away from the lens.

Reilly must have noticed Tessa's discomfort. "Janet, can you hold off for a minute?"

"But—"

"Just give us a minute," Reilly said more firmly.

Janet looked ready to protest, but Reilly stood and pulled her outside. They shut the door, so Tessa couldn't hear, but Reilly came back alone. Tessa wondered how she'd convinced the woman to break the rules.

Looks like Detective Reilly will be playing the good cop. Tessa wasn't stupid. If she told the detective anything, it would only be because she wanted to tell her *everything*. She just wasn't sure she had it in her to cross Father.

Reilly sat down again, reached across the table, and placed her hands over Tessa's. She gave them a squeeze. "It's just you and me here. The camera's off. No one's listening. Nothing you tell me gets repeated unless you want me to repeat it."

"How do I know I can trust you?"

"You asked for me, didn't you? Part of you must think you can. Why don't you trust that part of you?"

"Fine. How do I know you can stop him?"

"Believe me, I've put away bigger and scarier men than your father."

"He's scarier than you know."

"How so?"

Tessa slid her hand out from beneath Detective Reilly's and slouched against the back of her chair. She studied her sneakers beneath the table. *I can't tell her anything. I just can't.* She bit into her lower lip, wanting the detective's help, *needing* it, but feeling more alone than ever. Once Tessa opened her mouth, once she spilled Father's darkest secrets, she couldn't shove them back in, no matter how much she might want to. Once she told, two things would happen: the police would be going after Father, and Father would be coming for her. His speak-no-evil policy was the only rule for which he had a definite penalty. That penalty was death. But first, he would make her hurt.

All that would stand between her and her father's tyranny would be this unimpressive woman sitting in front of her. Would a badge and gun be enough to stop Father? It had never been enough in the past. The detective would need more than that to face him. She would need courage, more than Tessa had, and the will to pull the trigger.

"Tessa, I can't help you if you don't let me."

"It's too late to help me. He's going to punish me for what Michael did to him. He's going to blame me for everything. They shouldn't have come over. I never invited them. They just showed up."

"So you're afraid of your father. That much is obvious." Reilly leaned forward. "What is not so obvious are your reasons for being afraid. What has he done to you?"

Tessa thought back to the burns, the scrubbings with the wire brush, the scalding baths, her white blouse wet and sheer, exposing her budding breasts and clinging to her lobster-red skin as she wailed and begged. Heat flooded into her cheeks, and she imagined her skin reddening, this time from humiliation. She wouldn't talk about those things, not those things, not ever. Father's hands knew no boundaries.

She thought back to the whippings and shuddered. Father's techniques had improved since those early days. He had learned cleaner ways to punish her, ways that didn't leave marks. But no matter what he did to her body, nothing came close to the pain she'd felt when Father took her mother away from her.

Mother.

Tessa couldn't swallow. He had beaten her mother, broken her, taken away her pride, her joy, her self-worth, even her love for Tessa. A store mannequin, hollow and soulless, was all that remained of Tessa's mother in her final days. When she had only her life left to give, Father took that, too. Years passed, but Tessa's pain remained.

Just then, she felt it resurging, as though she were a bicycle tire being pumped full of air and then pumped some more, until the stitches that tied her together bulged and ripped.

"I hate him!" Tessa slapped a hand over her mouth. She'd never dared to say that aloud. The release came with a mixture of terror and relief. Had Father heard her say it, he would have retaliated hard. But he didn't hear her. The world had not ended when she said those words. No repercussions came her way. "I hate him," she said again, almost smiling. "I hate him, and I want him dead."

"I can understand how you feel, Tessa." Detective Reilly pushed her hair behind her ears. "Unfortunately, it's not my job to kill him even if he deserves it. Would you settle for a nice long prison sentence?"

Something about the way the detective spoke seemed genuine. Tessa wondered if she might actually be able to trust the woman. But words were words, and actions were actions. Tessa was ready to talk and see where it would get her, but telling anyone about what Father had done to her and to others would pour salt on many wounds, old and new.

As if she could read Tessa's mind, Detective Reilly moved to a less personal topic. "Why don't you tell me about Gloria Jackson? We don't have to talk about everything all at once. We can start there."

Tessa nodded and took in a deep breath. "Ms. Jackson wanted to help me, to get me away from him, just like you say you do. I warned her. I told her to stay away from him, but she wouldn't listen."

"Do you know how she died?"

Tessa again found it difficult to swallow. Her barriers were crumbling as she recalled that Saturday. Tears came before she could stop them. "At first, he made me watch. He always makes me watch. It's like it makes it more fun for him." Her nose started to run, and she swiped at it with the back of her hand. "Father started cutting into her. She begged for help, for me to help her, but I just... I just sat there. Then... then..." Tessa started to sob.

"Then what, Tessa?"

Tessa buried her head in her arms on the table. Her body shook uncontrollably. "Then he made me do it." She started to heave and thought for sure she would vomit, but after a burp she was able to get her stomach under control. She looked up at Detective Reilly, and the room began to spin. A second later, Tessa was on all fours, vomiting all over the floor.

When her stomach was purged, Tessa felt the detective stroking her back. She remembered how her mother used to do that.

"We need to get him, Tessa. We need to put him away so that he never hurts anyone again, never hurts *you* again. You understand that, don't you?"

"Yes." Tessa got up and dropped back into her chair. Spots speckled her shirt, and the smell almost made her puke some more. Even then, she was frightened that Father would not approve of her appearance.

"Can you tell me something, *anything*, that we might be able to use to prove his guilt?"

"You have his knife. He keeps them all very sharp and—"

Reilly frowned. "Besides the knife. What about her clothes, jewelry, a purse... you know, did any of that get left behind? What did your father do with it? What about the... pieces of her that he removed?"

Tessa could taste the bile returning to her mouth. "I don't... he wrapped everything in plastic and threw it into her trunk—"

"Where's the car now?"

"He... *we* pushed it off the pier at the waterfront in Somerset. He sat Ms. Jackson behind the wheel, thinking it was funny. I guess he should have seat-belted her in. Where her lips were cut off, it kind of looked like she was smiling." Tears stung in her eyes. "She didn't have to die. She hadn't even broken any of his rules."

"I know, Tessa," Reilly said. She came around the table and crouched beside Tessa, taking her hand once more. "I know."

"So what happens now?"

"You'll have to stay here for a while," Detective Reilly said. "You'll be safe here. You've done the right thing, Tessa. Try to be strong, okay?"

Strong? Tessa had never felt strong. She used to have Mother to protect her, to take the punishment for her. Now, she had only a stranger with a badge and a gun. Tessa hoped the detective would use them both when she found Father. *If* she found Father... "Promise me you'll get him. He killed Mother, too, I think. And... there were others."

"Others?" Detective Reilly looked surprised, but then she shook her head. "There will be time to discuss that later, once we arrest your father. I'll be back, and we can discuss every detail you feel comfortable sharing. You have a long, tough road ahead of you, Tessa, but I promise things will slowly get easier from here on out, now that he's out of your life."

Detective Reilly stood. With a warm smile then an awkward closeness that almost passed for a hug, she left.

I'll believe it when I see it. A sudden chill came over Tessa. Again, she was alone. Father knew where she was. Detective Reilly didn't understand what he was like. Tessa wasn't safe there or anywhere Father might look for her. She needed to go.

She slid through the doorway, grateful that the detective hadn't thought to shut it, and followed Janet and Reilly back toward the lobby, ducking into doorways whenever she thought they might turn around. Living with Father had taught her how to move as quietly as a mouse.

Detective Reilly chatted with Janet in the lobby for a couple of minutes. Tessa wasn't close enough to hear the conversation, but she caught the gist of it from their body language. The detective spun and hustled out the front door. When Janet came back toward the hallway, presumably to collect her charge, Tessa slipped into an empty office and waited for her to pass.

A minute later, Tessa was standing on the street.

CHAPTER 24

WITHIN TWO HOURS, DIVERS HAD located the vehicle, right where Tessa had said it would be. It would take several more hours to tow it out, hours Sam wasn't about to waste waiting around and doing nothing. Masterson had already been released. He had claimed his things, and at that moment, he could be sitting at the gate for a flight to only God knew where. Sam certainly didn't know where, but she had her corroborating evidence. If only she had been a bit quicker, Masterson would still be in their custody. Still, he would not be squirming away this time.

She called Sergeant Jake Rollins and told him she needed two warrants: the first for the arrest of Christopher Masterson and the second, broadly worded, for an all-encompassing search of 78 Winchester Street. With any luck, Masterson was the sentimental type who wouldn't part with his knife, despite its incriminating nature. On the surface, he seemed too careful to do something so stupid, but he had obviously kept the knife after using it to slice and dice Gloria Jackson.

These sickos always need their trophies.

Sam hoped she would be able to serve both warrants at the same time. Masterson had to know she would be coming sooner or later, though. If he was smart, he would already be sipping umbrella drinks at a beach bar in Morocco or Brunei or some other watering hole where extradition to the US wouldn't be likely.

"What new evidence should I bring to the judge's attention?" Rollins asked.

"The daughter witnessed everything. She even confessed to helping Masterson carve Jackson." Sam winced, only briefly revealing her disgust before stoning her heart. Tessa was a victim, too. Sam recognized that, but she would have to treat the girl as an accessory. Her job demanded she enforce the law, but she would seek as much leniency for Tessa as that law permitted when the time came to do so. With an abusive, controlling father, Tessa might even prevail under the "he made me do it" defense. At the least, it should mitigate her sentence. "The victim's car is being exhumed as we speak. Tessa told us where to find it. With her story backed up by physical evidence, the warrants should be no-brainers. Let me know if you hit a snag."

"Will do," the sergeant responded and hung up the phone.

Sam rushed out to her car to go to Masterson's house. As she turned onto Winchester Street, she slowed to a crawl and dimmed her headlights. She parked at the end of the block to wait for the warrants and backup.

Four officers, the minimum she'd requested, arrived not even ten minutes later. Sergeant Rollins exited one of the cars and held up some folded documents so she could see them.

Good work, Rollins. Sam popped open her door and went over to him. "I see you got the warrants." Her tone almost sounded flirtatious, but her excitement had nothing to do with Rollins, despite how easy he was on the eyes. "Let's go arrest his sorry ass."

They returned to their respective vehicles and drove up to the house. A blue Crossfire was parked in the driveway. Sam and the drivers of the other two cars parked strategically—hers directly behind Masterson's car and the other two at the end of the driveway. She got out of her car and watched the men climb out of theirs.

The three patrolmen and Rollins looked like giant apes, muscles straining the buttons on their shirts. As they followed her onto Masterson's property and up to the front door, Sam felt like a celebrity with her team of bodyguards. It felt good, but the greater high would come when Masterson was stuffed into the backseat of one of those patrol cars.

Rollins sent one officer around the back of the house. *Cromartie*, Sam thought, recalling the officer's name. She prided herself on knowing her team. The other two officers were Ansari and Bostick. All were good cops and ready should Masterson put up a fight, which part of her wanted him to do.

Bostick leaned against the front storm door, propping it open. Sam peeked through a window but saw no signs of life inside.

"Christopher Masterson," she said while knocking sharply on the door. "This is the police. Open up."

Sam pressed her ear against the door. She heard a muffled bang, like the sound her shin made every time she hit it against the coffee table while stumbling around in the dark. Then nothing. She counted to fifteen in her head, much faster than seconds would tick off a clock. *Who actually says "Mississippi" between the numbers?* When she finished, she leaned against the railing, out of Sergeant Rollins's way.

One shoulder butt, and he had the door nearly off its hinges. The portion of the frame where the latch had resisted was a splintered mess. Sam laughed quietly. No one had even checked whether the door had been unlocked.

"You stay here," she whispered to Bostick. She shot her eyebrows upward and gestured toward the stairs, signaling Ansari to climb them. She and Rollins would clear the first floor.

Everyone drew their guns. Sam scanned the living room then led the sergeant through it and into the dining room. Rollins moved toward the kitchen while Sam started down the hallway.

After a few steps, she came to a closed door. She brought her gun in close to her body, stood to one side, and quickly turned the doorknob. Throwing open the door, she remained behind the protective shield of the wall. When no one popped out, she stepped into the doorway—a bedroom. Rollins strode past her to check the next room down the hall.

Now for the fun part. She glanced at the queen-size bed covered by a drab blue comforter. On the other side was a closet, door firmly closed. There weren't any other hiding places she could see in the room, but those two were popular and often deadly choices. She would have to make sure no one was using them before she could deem the room clear.

She knew no safe way to check under a bed for a suspect. Some cops flipped or kicked off the mattress, but that could be difficult and was ultimately pointless if the box springs were covered. Plus, the maneuver meant she would have to be close to the bed without knowing what lurked beneath it, inviting all sorts of injuries to her lower extremities. The thought made Sam's skin crawl. She preferred to yank off the bedspread if it hung to the floor, clumping it between the bed and her feet to block a potentially dangerous suspect's line of sight. Then she would step back, pretending to divert her attention from the bed, only to drop into a squat and peek beneath it. The whole process made her feel like a little kid afraid of the boogeyman, but at the same time, the rush of adrenaline was exhilarating.

Sam found nothing but air and carpet. She turned to the closet and sighed again. *Fucking slats.* The closet door was comprised of slatted wood placed at a down-and-outward slope. If Masterson were hiding behind it, he would be able to see her, but Sam wouldn't be able to see him.

There's no avoiding it. She reached for the knob with her left hand. Her right hand held her pistol tucked near her breast. She yanked open the door.

In the movies, a cat always jumped out. Sam used to wonder why Hollywood thought cat owners always locked their cats in the closet until one time when a black furball came screeching out at her. It had taken all her willpower not to shoot the fluffy demon.

Masterson's closet contained no cat. No vicious killers were lurking there, either. *Clothes. Just clothes.*

Sam returned to the hallway. Sergeant Rollins came out of the far room, shaking his head. They headed back to the dining room, where Ansari was waiting for them.

"The second floor is clear," he said.

"He's not here? Fuck!" Sam pounded her fist on the table.

There's still the knife. She headed into the kitchen to look for the weapon. When she spotted the knife block, she instantly noticed that one was missing. She didn't need to guess which one.

"Well," she said, walking back into the dining room, "this was exciting. Let's get the word out. Ansari, radio in the suspect's description, and get out an APB on him. Rollins and I will start tossing this place. On your way out, tell Bostick and Cromartie to get in here and help."

Rollins flipped on the dining room light as Sam headed back into the hallway. The light illuminated most of the hall, and Sam noticed something different about the wall, probably nothing, having passed by the peculiarity before it even registered in her brain. About waist high, a black, greasy streak that had no logical reason for being there was smeared across the wall. Given the house's otherwise pristine nature, the mark warranted her investigation. It looked as though a sneaker had scuffed the wall. Sam looked up and saw an attic door above the mark. She knew where her suspect was hiding.

"Wait, you two." She pointed at the hatch with her gun. "Who is this guy, Jackie Chan?"

She didn't see a dangling rope handle for a pull-down staircase like some attics had. She raised her hand, but the door was just out of reach. Rollins jumped up and pushed open the hatch. Above, there was only darkness.

"Give me ten fingers," Sam said.

Officer Ansari interlocked the fingers of both his hands and bent at the waist to lower the makeshift step. She placed her foot inside the cradle, and with the grace of an acrobat, he raised her into the ceiling.

With the blundering of a clown, Sam fell toward the floor. "Fuck!"

As she had started to rise, a sharp pain shot through the back of her head. The blow left her reeling, and she rolled back through the opening. Fortunately, Ansari and Rollins were there to catch her before the hardwood floor could break her fall. Her gun slipped out of the holster she'd forgotten to snap and rattled across the floor like a spinning quarter.

When the officers stood her on her feet, she put her hand to the back of her head. She ran her hands through a mat of bloody hair, trying to gauge the size of the wound. Dizzy, Sam thought she might have a concussion. Her best guess was that Masterson had punted the back of her head.

She picked up her gun but couldn't even see straight enough to aim it. "Get that son of a bitch," she hissed.

Rollins pointed his gun at the ceiling and cocked his head, listening for movement. "We need to get you to a hospital. We can flush him out—"

"No." Sam shook her head then stopped moving when another lance of pain ripped through her skull. "No hospital. It's just a cut."

A crash came from above, the sound of glass breaking. That was followed by thumping footsteps.

"He's on the roof!" Sam yelled. "Go after him."

Rollins boosted Ansari into the attic. A scream came from the direction of the backyard. With the sergeant's help, Sam stumbled toward the sound's origin.

When they went out the back door, Bostick was crouched over Cromartie, who had dark blood gurgling from a wound in his side.

"It was definitely Masterson," Bostick said, his voice fraught with worry and anger. "He took off running that way." He pointed toward their left. "Officer Ansari is chasing him."

"Go," Sam said. Bostick didn't need to be told twice. He sped off to join the chase.

Rollins keyed his radio. "Officer down. I repeat, officer down. Send emergency units to 78 Winchester Street immediately. All available units should be sent to said location. The suspect, Christopher Masterson, is a white male approximately five-ten, one hundred sixty pounds. He's on foot, pursued by Officers Ansari and Bostick. Suspect is armed and dangerous. I repeat: suspect is armed and dangerous." The sergeant returned his radio to his belt and gestured at Cromartie. "How is he?"

"Not good," Sam replied. She was sure he'd already lost more blood than a human could stand to lose, and she was grateful that he was unconscious. "He's not going to make it."

"Christ," Rollins said, stomping the ground. He shook his head and fumed quietly while they waited for the paramedics to arrive.

As she listened to Cromartie breathe his final breaths, Sam blamed herself for the death of the good man they would soon lose. One man armed with only a knife had somehow outsmarted her and the four officers under her command. She wasn't sure what she could have done differently, but death occurred only when she was less than perfect. Whatever her failing had been, she was disgusted by it. And if she couldn't figure it out, Internal Affairs would be sure to fill in the gaps for her.

At least if Ansari and Bostick managed to come back with Masterson, Sam could avenge Cromartie. She hoped they would shoot Masterson or at least rough him up a bit, but not kill him. She wanted a go at him first. Masterson had crossed the final line from killer to cop killer. Like the rest of her blue-blooded friends, Sam took the death of one of her own personally. She doubted Masterson would survive to see a trial, and she didn't care. Justice would be done.

CHAPTER 25

" **M**ICHAEL? THERE'S SOMEONE AT THE door for you."

Helen's voice carried up the staircase like a fart through a colon. Its hoarse smoker's tone made Michael cringe every time he heard it. She sounded as if she had more than just a foot in the grave. At fifty-seven and with her nasty habit, her death probably wasn't far off. If Greg died first, Helen would have no one but Michael to care for her should her health fail.

Maybe that's why they took me in. The Plummers had no children of their own. Michael usually thought Helen and Greg fostered him out of some weird sense of Christian duty, as if they felt they had to give back to the world or something stupid like that. They didn't seem to really enjoy having him around, not that he'd always made it easy for them. At least they never touched him. More than one of his foster friends had been sent away only to return to the orphanage soon after with dirty secrets they would never be able to wipe clean.

Michael rolled his eyes as that raspy voice again hollered for him to answer the door. Happily engrossed in the latest *Assassin's Creed*, he didn't want to be disturbed. He had no friends, except maybe Sam, who would have called before coming over. So he was pretty certain whoever was at the door wasn't there for him. Besides, if fate saw fit to constantly expose him to death and destruction, he would prefer to see it played out in a digital world. And if someone was at the door for him, it couldn't be good.

Reluctantly, Michael paused the game and tromped down the stairs. Maybe it was Willie the mailman with more comic books—Willie, who was still alive and kicking. *Or the DCF investigator.* He wasn't looking forward to that conversation, but if it was the investigator, he was early. Helen had spent most of the day trying to make the house look what she called "presentable." As far as he could see, the place looked exactly the same as it had that morning.

When he pivoted around the banister at the bottom of the stairs, he couldn't believe who was standing in the middle of his living room. Tessa Masterson was chatting with Helen and Greg as if the three of them were good friends or something.

"So nice of you to join us," Helen said. "Jaime was just telling us that you have a few classes together."

"We're happy to finally meet someone like you." Greg cleared his throat. "A girl, I mean. We were starting to wonder if Michael was one of those—"

Michael leaped off the last step. "Thanks for that, Greg." He turned to Tessa. "So, *Jaime*, what brings you here?"

"I thought we could study together for our math midterm," Tessa said coolly. "You know I could use the help."

"I thought you said your midterms were over?" Helen seemed to be studying Michael, waiting to see how he would respond.

"They are," Tessa said, answering before he could blubber a response. "Our teacher allowed those of us who did poorly to retake it. He said he would average our two grades. I didn't do so well the first time around, and Michael offered to help me study. He's so smart, much better at that stuff than I am." She smiled. "I'm sorry to show up unannounced. I live close by, and my phone's not working, so I figured I would just stop by and see if Michael was busy. I hope I didn't catch anyone at a bad time."

"Well, Michael does have... an appointment of sorts in a few hours," Greg said, "but I don't see why you can't hang out until then."

Michael appreciated Greg's discretion. He just knew DCF was going to recommend counseling. Hell, they had recommended it when he got into a fight in middle school, when he set off a chlorine bomb in his neighbor's gazebo—which he still maintained was an accident—and most recently, when he'd had his head swirled around in a toilet. But given his present company, he guessed he wasn't the only one for whom DCF would order counseling.

"Michael's friends are always welcome," Helen chimed in. Her smile was warm, but her face was wrought by worry. She turned to her husband. "Are you sure now's such a good time, though? I mean, Michael's been through a lot, and we're all under—"

"Now's not the time to be turning away friends." Greg put his hand on Michael's shoulder. "That's very Christian of you, Michael, offering to help her like you did." He leaned in close and gave Michael a nudge. "Like she would be coming to you for help in *math,* of all subjects." He chuckled. "There's hope for you yet, son. I do hope she's telling the truth about that extra credit exam, though."

Michael ducked out from under Greg's arm and studied Tessa's face. He wondered what had brought her there and what she expected of him. He thought she was still in that center. He had even considered that she might end up like him, a foster kid.

"Will your lady friend be staying for dinner?" Helen asked.

"I... um..." Michael didn't know how to answer.

Tessa replied cheerfully, "If you'll have me."

For someone as screwed up as she must be, why is she less awkward talking to strangers than I am?

"Great. I'll set an extra spot at the table. I hope you like roast pork."

What just happened? Michael couldn't believe the nerve of Tessa. She had shown up uninvited and unwanted and managed to weasel her way into a free dinner. The verdict on her was still out; Michael couldn't unsee what he had seen in his vision. Yeah, he felt a little sorry for her, but that didn't mean he was okay eating at the same table with her. *As if roast pork night wasn't bad enough.*

Well, he wasn't going to get answers with his foster parents standing there. Michael cleared his throat. "Te—uh, Jaime, we should get some studying done before dinner."

"Okay," Tessa said, smiling as though everything was made of sunshine and rainbows.

If all the world was a stage, Michael preferred her to act her part elsewhere. *Her smile is as phony as the rest of her.* But he couldn't let on right then, so he nodded and led her up the stairs and into his bedroom.

He started to close the door when Helen yelled up, "Leave the door open. I'll call you when it's time for dinner."

Michael grumbled but not loud enough for anyone downstairs to hear. He shut his bedroom door anyway. When he turned around, Tessa was standing by his bookshelf, peering at his comic book collection.

He grabbed her shoulder and shook her. "What the hell are you doing here?" He let go when he realized he was touching her. After waiting a few seconds, he let out a sigh of relief at not having spiraled into another vision.

Instantly, the mask Tessa wore fell away. The scared, fragile girl returned. "I didn't know where else to go. I couldn't stay at that halfway house. Father would have found me there. Once he finds out that your detective friend is going after him, he'll know I told. He'll come after me. I broke his number one rule: don't tell."

"So you thought coming *here* was a good idea? Look, I don't know what kind of sick family games you two like to play, but I don't want any part of it. I did what I could. I got you out of that house."

"But Father's still out there. What if that detective can't stop him?"

"Then you're putting everyone in this house in danger by being here. Who asked you to come here anyway? You can't just show up at my house uninvited."

"Why not? You did at mine, and look at all the trouble that caused."

"You came to me for help. I did you a favor."

"You did? I'm not so sure. Right now, it's a coin flip."

"Geez! You're so—"

"Stop." The word came out more like a plea than a command. She sank down onto Michael's bed and started to cry. She hid her face behind her hands. "I'm scared, Michael. I didn't know where else to go. I'm sorry."

"No, I'm sorry." Michael tentatively perched beside her, not knowing what he should do. He'd never had to comfort someone before. For as long as he could remember, he'd been alone. People didn't share their feelings with him, and he didn't really talk to anyone but Sam. He gingerly stretched out his arm and draped it across her shoulders, being careful not to make skin-to-skin contact. "You're right. You're going to be okay. You're safe here."

She leaned back against his arm, and his forearm touched the skin on the back of her neck. His breathing hitched, but no vision came, so he relaxed a little. He had no idea why he wasn't getting another vision, but he was truly happy for it. Equally surprising, Tessa didn't pull away. Instead, she rested her head in the crook between his shoulder and chest.

Now what? Michael stayed frozen in that pose, with a million thoughts running through his head, until she finished crying. *Why are you helping her? Comforting a killer? The whole situation is absolutely crazy.* Yet he couldn't deny that he wanted to help her. He wanted to hold her, to keep holding her for as long as she would let him.

She sniffled a little then hiccupped. "Will you keep me safe?"

"I'll... I'll try. No, I will. I promise." *What are you doing promising something like that? If her father comes looking for her, would you really be able to stand between them?* "Anyway, from what I've seen, you can take care of yourself," he said, trying to lighten the mood.

"What do you mean?"

"When we first touched, that day at school, I had a vision."

"I know." She looked away. "Whatever you saw, I'm sure it was horrible. He makes me do things, things most people can't even imagine."

"You stabbed him." *Repeatedly.* He decided to keep that last thought to himself.

She raised her head and gaped at him. "I did *what*?"

"I saw you kill your father."

"*I* killed *him*?" She stared at him for a full minute, then she started to laugh. At first, it was a hesitant, stifled giggle, but that soon blossomed into full-blown laughter.

Michael chuckled. He couldn't figure out what was so funny, but her laughing was way better than her crying.

After she calmed a bit, she asked, "Are you sure? I'm too scared to even speak around him. Maybe that brain of yours is broken?"

"Or maybe you're stronger than you think?"

His cellphone rang, and Sam's name and number appeared on the screen. Michael answered it. "Hello?"

"Michael," Sam said. "Are you home?"

"Yes."

"Good. Masterson got away. The girl confessed to everything. Making matters worse, she's missing, too."

"She's here," he said.

Tessa gasped and jumped to her feet. As she started toward the door, Michael grabbed her arm with his free hand.

"It's okay," he whispered. "It's Sam. Detective Reilly."

Tessa still looked ready to make a break for it, but after a moment, she nodded and sat back down beside him.

"What's she doing there?" Sam asked.

"She didn't feel safe at the halfway house." Michael knew he hadn't truly answered Sam's question. He'd only explained why she had left, not why she was at his house.

Sam seemed too frazzled to delve deeper. She spoke quickly, as if every second mattered. "Keep her there, but be safe. Warn your foster parents. Lock your doors, and don't open them for anyone other than me."

"Why? You don't think he would actually come here, do you?" Michael hadn't considered the possibility.

Tessa seemed to be holding her breath. Her body was tense, and her leg bounced against his as he pulled her closer. But he remained calm. *Wouldn't her father be more concerned with escaping than with coming after us?*

"He might," Sam said, "if he thinks she's there."

"I knew it," Tessa mumbled. "I knew she couldn't stop him."

Michael stroked her leg, trying to calm her. "How would he even know where I live?"

"I'm not sure. The charges and other legal documents filed in his case shouldn't have included any of your personal information. If the police report did, it should have been redacted before it was given to Masterson's attorney. But there could have been plenty in there—your foster parents' names, school information, whatever—for Masterson to use as a starting point in researching your address. Anyone with even a smidgeon of investigative ability would know half a dozen ways of finding you just from knowing your name."

"That is not a comforting thought."

Sam's silence was even less comforting. Michael had just come to accept Tessa's presence, but Sam had unraveled his false sense of calm faster than a kitten with a ball of yarn. *Do your job, and catch the psycho,* he wanted to tell her.

When Sam spoke again, her voice was quieter. "Michael, I'm sorry, but I have to ask. How much do you trust Tessa? You said you didn't know her very well, so how did she know where you live? Also, her going missing at the same time that her father did is a little suspicious. At first, I was worried that he had gotten her, but the social worker said Tessa snuck out of the center within a half hour after I left. Her father had been released from custody around the same time. We know he went home first, but where he's gone since is still a big question mark. We don't think he's left the area, and we're certain he's armed and dangerous."

A heavy breath whistled through the speaker. "She's done things, Michael, terrible things—things she and I are going to have to have a long talk about. I'm sure we're just beginning to uncover a long list of her father's victims. Who knows how many secrets that girl holds? I'm a little worried that she went to him. And now she's with you, so…"

How did she find me? The question was a good one. Michael glared at Tessa suspiciously. She stared back, looking confused and scared but completely innocent. *She wouldn't. There's no way she would lead him here.* His heart sank. *Would she?*

He had easily found Tessa's address. He just looked up her last name in an Internet phone directory and *voila.* But Michael's last name wasn't the same as his foster parents'. Tessa would have to have known *their* last name to do that kind of search. Michael wasn't even sure if their address was listed.

But looking down at Tessa, sitting next to him and fidgeting, he couldn't bring himself to think badly of her. He whispered into the phone, "I can trust her."

"I would rather you didn't," Sam said. "In fact, I'm telling you not to. I'm sending a car around. It'll be parked outside until Masterson resurfaces. Tell the officers if you notice anything out of the ordinary, and not just outside the house. I've got work to do now. I'll check in on you as soon as I can."

As usual, Sam hung up without saying goodbye. Michael barely noticed, his thoughts upon more important matters. Could the girl who had just cried on his shoulder be leading him into a trap? He'd heard women were nothing but trouble. Michael had never even kissed a girl before, and already he was forced to wonder if this girl would be the death of him.

CHAPTER 26

Officer Nicole McEvoy rubbed her knuckles. The skin over them was red and cracking. She hated New England winters, but she still had another six years before she was eligible for early retirement and could take her cushy cop pension and retire to West Palm Beach. Brown slush covered the floor mat, dripping from her boots. She looked outside the patrol car window at the salted and sanded yet still icy mess of a street and wondered just how long those six years would seem.

"It's so cold out tonight," Officer Ryan Noble said. He had a knack for stating the obvious, another factor that made her patrol years seem long. He crossed his arms over his chest. They couldn't have the car running on a stakeout, which meant no heat. "This is a waste of time. Masterson's not going show his face around here." He unfolded his arms long enough to slap the steering wheel. "Why do we get stuck babysitting some brat while everyone else is out looking for that cop-killing fuck?"

Nicole nodded. "I know. I'm freezing my ass off. Maybe we should let the car run a bit." She looked across the street at the Plummer residence. "Still, he's out there somewhere."

"If he has any brains, he'll be halfway to Mexico by now. Screw it. I'm just gonna run it long enough to get us a little warm." Ryan turned the key. The engine started, and the automatic headlights sprang to life, illuminating the road in front of them. "Shit! I forgot the lights." He reached for the knob.

Nicole squinted through the fogged-up windshield. A man was standing directly in the beam of the left headlight.

"Where the hell did he come from?" She moved her hand toward her service pistol, keeping her eyes locked on the stranger.

The guy was dressed in a heavy winter jacket with the hood hanging almost completely over his eyes. He puffed out a steam cloud each time he exhaled. As he stepped closer to the patrol car, Nicole saw a bag in one of his hands and some kind of tray in the other. He kind of matched the description of Masterson, but so did a good portion of the male population. They had a picture, but his facial features were obscured by his hood and the night. She could tell that he wasn't wearing glasses like Masterson, but she didn't let down her guard, just in case. Holding up his hands, along with the bag and tray, the man walked around to the driver's side.

Ryan lowered his window. "What can I do for you?" He obviously wasn't feeling comfortable with the situation, either, since his hand lay on his open holster.

"Hello, Officers." The guy bent a little to look inside the car and grinned at them. "I hope I didn't startle you. My name is Greg Plummer. I live at the address you've been assigned to watch, and I'm a friend of Detective Reilly's. I wanted to thank you both personally for helping to protect my son, Michael. He's had a rough week, and we're all worried about this sicko who's on the loose."

"Why aren't you in the house?" Nicole asked. "We never saw you come out."

"My car's right there in the driveway." The man pointed at a silver Nissan Altima parallel parked among the row of cars that lined the street.

Hadn't it always been there? Nicole couldn't remember. Not wanting to look like an idiot, she didn't question it aloud, but her suspicions of the man remained.

"Anyway, I wanted to get you guys a quick pick-me-up to show my appreciation." The man held up the bag, which had a local doughnut shop's logo. The tray contained two cups that most likely held hot coffee. "These are for you."

Ryan's eyes lit up. He played right into the cop stereotype. On a cold December night like that, a hot coffee would have enticed almost anybody.

Anybody except Nicole. "No, thank you," she said.

"Relax, Nicole," Ryan said. "It's just coffee." He turned to the man. "Don't mind if I do. Thank you, sir." He took the bag of doughnuts and set it on the console. Then he grabbed the tray of coffee.

Nicole whispered, "At least ask to see his ID first."

"Oh, give it a rest, will you?" Ryan popped the lid off one cup. "Mmm, it smells so good." He passed it to Nicole then opened the second one.

Nicole set the cup on the seat between her legs. She wanted her hands free while their visitor was standing so close.

"How much do we owe you?" Ryan asked. Nicole knew it was an empty offer.

"Oh, no. It's my treat." The man crouched beside the car door, blocking Nicole's view of the side mirror.

She watched him cautiously. Something seemed slightly off about him, but she couldn't put her finger on what it was. She slipped her hand down and unsnapped her holster. "Thank you, Mr. Plummer. But what I could really use is a bathroom. Would you mind if I follow you back to your house? I'll only be a minute." *All the time I'll need to see if you are who you say you are.*

The man smiled. "No problem."

Nicole watched for any hint of uneasiness, but the man remained comfortable and carefree. *Too carefree. Particularly for a man whose son might be targeted by a killer.*

Ryan chuckled. "Women and their bladders." He raised his cup and took a hearty gulp.

He started coughing. Coffee splashed onto his hands and lap.

"What?" Nicole slid her pistol three-quarters of the way out of the holster. "Ryan, are you okay?"

"It's fucking hot!" Ryan sputtered. "The coffee is good, though." He looked up at the man. "Thanks again, Mr. Plummer."

"Please, call me Greg."

"You're an idiot, Ryan." Nicole relaxed a little and let her gun slip back into place.

Ryan blew on the coffee then took another gulp. "So, what do you do for a living, Greg?"

"I'm retired. I was in the army for a while. After that, I kind of bounced around a bit."

"Army man, huh? I was in the Navy myself. I've got fam—" Ryan reached for his neck as though he were trying to strangle himself. The cup fell from his hands, and coffee spilled across his lap. His eyes appeared as if they might pop out of his head. His face turned red and continued to darken with each passing moment.

Nicole smirked and shook her head. "Burned yourself again? Real swift, Ryan."

Ryan started convulsing. White foamy saliva bubbled from his mouth.

Nicole looked down at her cup. She picked it up and threw it onto the floor. "What did you do to him?" She reached for the radio to signal for backup with one hand, at the same time moving her other toward her gun.

The man lunged through the window, simultaneously splaying over Ryan and slashing out with a knife. By the time Nicole saw the blade, its point was already heading toward her left eye. She had no time to react before it made contact and plunged into her eyeball. Her sight in that eye went dark, and something with the consistency of egg yolk oozed down her cheek.

Then came the pain.

She screamed. She raised her hand to grasp the knife. Her mind screamed for her to get it out, over and over again. Her eye felt as though someone had stuck a bunch of lit firecrackers directly into her pupil, each miniexplosion tearing deep into her brain. It made her thoughts wild and her actions purposeless. The flaring pain was unlike anything she'd ever felt. Her nerve endings were on fire.

She tugged at the knife handle with both hands. She knew the man was somewhere nearby, probably preparing for another strike, but the thought came second to getting that awful thing out of her face. Blind in both eyes, the uninjured one blurring with tears, she yanked hard on the handle. The knife stuck at first, then it slid free with a popping sound that echoed through her mind.

A hand wrapped around hers and pried her fingers loose. Her attacker's zealous grin made Nicole's heart sink. Pain and fear immobilized her completely. Aside from some uncontrollable twitches, her body would not move.

"I'll take that," he said, pulling the knife from her grip.

He used the blade to cut the cord to the radio. She willed her trembling, bloodied hand to move toward her service pistol.

"Uh-uh," the man said in the same tone as one would scold a small child reaching for off-limits candy. He shifted and jabbed the blade deep into her stomach.

Nicole coughed, and blood sprayed from her mouth. Her hands went to the fresh wound. The seat beneath her moistened, and she didn't know if she sat in poisoned coffee or urine. The man withdrew the blade, and Nicole was surprised to feel nothing more than a tugging sensation.

Vomit rose in her throat. She tried to scream, but all that came out was a gurgling sound.

He wiped the knife on Ryan's uniform as he crawled back out the window. "Hey, are you going to eat those?" he asked, pointing at the bag of doughnuts.

Nicole tried to shrink back as he reached into the car again, but she couldn't move. The man picked up the bag he had given Ryan.

Bent over in front of the window, he pulled a chocolate glazed doughnut from the bag and took a bite. "See? These were fine. You could have had one. In my house, we don't waste."

He tossed the bag back onto her lap, chuckling when she flinched again. Then, he straightened, wiped his hands on his thighs, and walked away.

Nicole couldn't move. *Help will come. Someone had to have heard something.* She couldn't look at her partner.

Her mouth dropped as her car door opened. She tried to find her voice but only managed a whimper.

"Will you shut up?" The man sounded angry, no longer the jovial doughnut eater from a moment earlier.

He grabbed the back of her head and slammed her face into the dashboard. Nicole felt the nauseating motion, but she no longer felt pain. As he repeated the act again and again, her mind and vision retreated into the darkness. Every now and then, she caught a glimpse of a pulpy dashboard or her own matted hair flashing in the waning light. Her face began to feel less solid, and she wondered if what she was feeling was what dying felt like.

Finally, he stopped. The motion of her body didn't, and she fell forward into the dashboard one more time. She was barely conscious, gazing out the window through a fluttering eyelid. She saw the man walking away, toward the quiet house across the street.

CHAPTER 27

"So..." Tessa stared past Michael at a poster of a comic character she didn't recognize. The wicked-looking biker dude had a flaming skull for a head, and his broad grin bared skeletal teeth. For some reason, the poster reminded her of Father. She shook her head and looked at Michael. Something in his eyes made her smile. "What do you like to do for fun? I mean, when you're not having visions, hanging around with cops, or stabbing people?"

He shrugged. "What else is there?" His goofy smile made him look like a little kid.

"Well, I know you like comics." She picked up a controller from the floor. "And video games, like most boys, I guess. I've never played them. Father thinks they're everything that's wrong with the world. He doesn't even let me listen to the music I like half the time. He thinks *American Idol* is a bunch of spoiled brats looking for a handout."

"Sounds about right." Michael chuckled. "He probably wouldn't like my music."

"What kind of music do you like?"

"Rock. The heavier, the better."

Tessa bobbed her head, letting her hair thrash around wildly. "Is this how you dance?" She laughed.

Michael said, "I have to ask you something."

A sudden wave of anxiety made her nauseated. "Yeah?"

"How did you know where I live?"

"Huh?" When she realized he was serious, she started to laugh. Soon, she was laughing so hard her sides were splitting. Blood rushed to her head, and she felt dizzy. She hadn't laughed that hard since—

Michael was frowning at her. "What's so funny?"

Tessa tried to talk, but after she took a few deep breaths, a second fit of laughter erupted. "Michael," she wheezed, "we've been on the same school bus all year."

His nose crinkled. "No way."

She nodded, finally getting her giggles under control. "Yep. I get on way before you, and I always sit in the very back. You're like second-to-last to get on, and you always sit in the second seat on the left. You never talk to anyone. I don't think you even look at anyone. It's no wonder you never noticed me."

Michael grinned sheepishly. "I notice you."

"Yeah, now maybe."

Michael looked away, his face turning red. She felt warmth in her own cheeks, so she lowered her head and doodled on the bedspread with her fingernail.

"So why the fake name?" he asked. "Who's Jaime?"

"What's wrong with Jaime? Besides, I just thought it would be easier—"

"We have to tell Greg and Helen who you are. Your father might be looking for you. Sam has some cops out on the street outside our house, and my foster parents have been told all about him, which is great 'cause now they don't think I'm going around stabbing people for the heck of it. If he somehow makes it past the police, they need to know not to unlock the door for anyone. They're nice people and all, but they can be a little gullible."

"Maybe they just choose to see the good in people."

Michael laughed, but there was no humor in it. "You and I both know there's no good in people... or at least not most people."

"They see the good in you. That has to mean something, right?"

"Yeah... I guess." He shrugged. "Anyway, they do seem to want to keep me. This social worker will be coming over soon to talk about what I went through at the school and, you know, at your house. Poor

Greg and Helen are kinda stuck in the middle of it all. They didn't have nothing to do with it, but they're sticking by me." Michael straightened, his mouth curving into something close to a smile.

His foster mother called from downstairs, "Michael!"

"Dinner must be ready," he said. "Come on. But I warn you, Helen's roast pork tastes like used cat litter."

"You eat a lot of cat litter, do you?"

"Ha, ha," he said sarcastically, but the laugh that followed seemed sincere. She liked his laugh.

Michael opened the door, and she got up and followed him out of the room. For some weird reason, she even liked the back of his head. She wanted to reach out and touch his hair. When he froze midway down the stairs, she nearly bumped into him.

"Hey, I almost—"

Michael whipped around and put a hand over her mouth. Tessa stared at him in shock, then she realized there was a new voice drifting up the stairs, one she knew all too well. She crept back up a step. She could see only the back of the man's head, but that was enough. She had seen it so many times before, envisioned bashing it with a rock or other blunt object over and over again. She knew its every contour. But killing him had never been more than a fantasy. Father had always done the killing in their family.

He's found me. Her heart thumped so loudly that it echoed through her skull. Trembling, she felt faint. *Oh God, he's here!* Every cell in her body yelled at her to run, but her feet seemed frozen to the floor. *The front door! I can reach it. Just ten steps, a turn of the knob, and I'm gone. Run, damn it!*

Her mind commanded, but her legs disobeyed. They even moved in the opposite direction, and she shuffled back to the top of the stairs. *Father would catch me. He's faster than I am. And when he catches me, he'll make me bleed.*

Michael, standing just behind the spot where the wall ended and the railing began, whispered, "What the fuck is he doing here? Why would they let him in?"

"Michael, I—"

"Shhh." He crouched and leaned forward a little.

Tessa carefully took one step down and stood on the step above Michael.

"He has company at the moment," Mrs. Plummer said. "We weren't expecting you until after dinner."

"I have to admit that I often show up unannounced," Father said. "We at DCF like to view the child in his normal setting, see how he's really coping with things, particularly in situations as grave as his. I can only imagine what the boy has gone through."

"Well, we would appreciate it if you didn't let his girlfriend know why you're here," Mr. Plummer said. "Michael doesn't have many friends, and it's nice to see him finally opening up to someone besides that detective."

Girlfriend? Tessa almost giggled, but fear stifled the impulse.

"A girlfriend, you say?" Father asked. "Well, that *is* progress."

"They think he's the investigator from DCF," Michael whispered. "I have to warn them." He handed her his cellphone. "You run outside and get the cops. They're parked across the street."

Tessa heard his instructions, and she wished she could do that. She wished that, just once, she could be brave. Father stood in the center of the living room, talking with Michael's foster parents as if he were only a neighbor stopping in for a friendly chat. He wore a thick ski jacket, and Tessa knew he could be hiding anything beneath it. Not that it mattered. He was dangerous enough with just his hands.

"What are you waiting for?" Michael asked, waving his arm. "Run. It's him. You need to run."

Tessa realized that if she fled, she would at least have a chance of surviving the night. If she stayed where she was, she was good as dead. She headed down the stairs, hoping Michael would be right behind her. But as she went for the door, Michael turned the corner and headed straight for Father. Out of the corner of her eye, she saw Michael dive into a man who would likely kill him.

"Michael!" Mrs. Plummer blurted. "What are you doing?"

The attack had caught Father off guard, but he never lost his footing, even as Michael drove him into the side of a chair.

Father straightened and pantomimed dusting himself off. "These teenagers today, huh, Greg? They don't know how good they have it."

Michael's foster parents stared, mouths agape, clearly not understanding the danger.

"It's him!" Michael shouted, jabbing a finger at Father. "It's Masterson, the killer!"

With lightning-fast speed, Father pulled a knife from his jacket, and before anyone could react, he was behind Mr. Plummer with the blade buried beneath the man's Adam's apple. Mr. Plummer's eyes were wide as he stood frozen.

Mrs. Plummer gasped. "Let him go!"

Michael ran to his foster mother's side, and she shoved him behind her. Tessa had opened the front door. Only a glass storm door stood between her and escape. But she couldn't leave Michael. She turned away from the night and hurried over to him, taking two of his fingers into her hand.

Father tsked. "Children. They do whatever they want." He smiled like a predator who had cornered his prey. "They stay out to all hours of the night, making noise, causing all sorts of ruckus. They don't listen. They don't obey. They certainly don't respect their elders." He laughed, but it was cold, empty. "You try and you try to raise them right, yet they constantly disappoint. So you set some ground rules, enforce them with an iron fist, and hope that doing so will guide your children toward purposeful futures, but even the best-made gauntlet is weak at its joints. Without constant supervision, our children find ways to displease us, to spit in the face of all we champion. Before you know it, one of the little brats is trying to stab you with your own kitchen knife. Isn't that right, Michael?"

Mr. Plummer mouthed "Run" while staring at Michael and Tessa.

"And now your little brat thinks he can get away with fucking my daughter," Father stated in a flat tone that didn't match his nasty words. "I'll kill him first. I'll kill all—"

Mr. Plummer slammed his head back into Father's face. Tessa heard something crunch.

Staggering against Father, Mr. Plummer tried to wave a hand at his wife. "Get them out of here. Get the children—" With a sharp intake of breath, he fell to his knees, still reaching out for his wife.

Father pulled the blade from Mr. Plummer's back. He grabbed a tuft of the man's hair and tilted the head back. With one swift motion, Father ran the blade across Mr. Plummer's neck. Mr. Plummer raised his hands to his neck as blood began to flow.

Mrs. Plummer shrieked, then she shoved Michael and Tessa toward the door. "Run!"

Tessa grabbed Michael's hand tighter and tugged him along. He didn't struggle, but he couldn't seem to take his eyes off his foster father. Tessa got him out onto the front steps, then she was shocked when Mrs. Plummer, instead of following, closed the door between them.

Michael pounded on the storm door, rattling the glass. Inside, Mrs. Plummer screamed.

"The cops! We need to get the cops!" Tessa shouted, yanking Michael away from the door.

Michael finally quit resisting. He pointed at a police cruiser across and a little way down the street. "There!"

As they approached the car, Tessa realized something wasn't right. The headlights were on, and the engine was running, warm steam rising from the back of the car. But the inside was dark and still. They ran over to the passenger side.

Michael got there first and reached for the handle. He stopped with his hand outstretched. "Oh my God!"

Tessa skidded to a stop beside him. Blood was streaked down the window, thick as maple syrup and looking a lot like it in the dark. Michael stepped away, bent over, and vomited.

Tessa stared back at the house, expecting Father to burst out the door at any moment. She grabbed Michael's hand. "C'mon! We have to go."

"But—"

She pulled harder. "We can't help them. We need to go. He'll come after us."

CHAPTER 28

MICHAEL RAN. HIS HARRIED MIND told him repeatedly that it was what he needed to do. They had to go somewhere safe, someplace he could get Sam to meet them. The only place he could think of was the school.

He felt Tessa's hand, warm and sweaty, in his. His mind kept flashing back to that empty black hole in the officer's face where an eye had once been. Maybe Tessa was no stranger to blood and guts, but Michael doubted he would ever get used to it, visions or not.

After a few blocks, they had to stop. Tessa bent over, panting. While she worked on catching her breath, Michael plucked his phone out of her back pocket. He scanned the street and houses for danger, as if it could pop out of anywhere.

He called Sam but got her voicemail. "Sam, it's Michael. I'm with Tessa. Masterson came to my house. I think he"—his voice cracked—"killed Greg, and he's gonna hurt Helen. We ran. We're heading to the school. I'll call you when we get there."

As soon as he hung up, they started running again. Both kept checking over their shoulders, and they ducked behind bushes and cars every time they saw headlights. That slowed them down considerably, but they finally made it to the school.

They made their way around the building, testing window after window for one that was unlocked. Michael found one in the east wing and shimmied it open. After sliding through, he took Tessa's hand and helped her inside.

The classroom was dark, but the setup was familiar. Five orderly rows of chairs, the kind with fold-out desks attached to them, lined the floor. A teacher's desk would be at the front of the room, centered in front of a giant whiteboard. All classrooms at Carnegie were set up the same way. Michael hurried over and pulled the door open. Right then left, he searched the hallway, but he saw no one. As far as he could tell, he and Tessa were alone.

He entered the hall. Placing his index finger over his lips, he beckoned Tessa to follow. Michael spotted a janitor's closet and decided that would be the best place to hide. There, he and Tessa huddled together among sponges and bottles of bleach.

Michael pulled out his phone and called 9-1-1.

"Nine-One-One. What is your emergency?"

"My name is Michael Turcotte." He hesitated, trying to think how best to say what needed to be said without falling apart. "I think my foster parents have been murdered."

"Please hold."

"What? Wait!"

"What's happening?" Tessa asked.

"She put me on hold."

A few seconds later, a new voice came on the line. "Michael?"

"Sam?" His eyes filled with tears, the good kind. Her voice alone was enough to make him feel stronger. "Is that really you?"

"Yes. I had the operators on alert for your call. Where are you? Are you safe?"

"I'm alive, if that's what you mean. We didn't know where else to go, so we headed to the high school. Didn't you get my message? Ah, never mind. Tessa's here with me, too."

"Michael..." Sam let out a heavy sigh. "Your foster parents are—"

"I know."

"You know? God, I was hoping you didn't have to see that. I'm so sorry."

"I didn't see it, not all of it, but I... I just know. Jesus Christ, Sam! The officers out front... what happened?"

"They're dead, too."

"I know. I don't get it. He's just one guy. Please tell me that you've caught him."

"Not yet. We got a call about fifteen minutes ago from a DCF caseworker who went to your house. By the time we got there, Masterson was long gone. He's running, but he'll get picked up sooner or later, probably several states away. By now, his picture is plastered all over the news and has been given to every law enforcement agency in the region. His freedom will be coming to an end shortly. You can count on that. I just wish I could be the one to catch him, for your and his victims' sakes."

Michael wasn't satisfied with her answer, but he had faith that Sam knew what she was doing. She'd pulled him out of a dozen shitty situations before. She wouldn't let him down, not when he needed her most. "What should we do?"

"For now, stay put. I'll come and get you."

"I mean, neither of us has any place to go."

"Yeah... I have some ideas on that. It's going to take some figuring out, but... we can talk about that some more later."

"What about Tessa? Her father is still out there. We have to help her, hide her someplace safe."

"Tessa is going to need proper care, the kind I'm not qualified to give her."

Michael placed his hand over the mouthpiece and turned to Tessa. "Sam says we can stay with her for the time being," he lied, faking a smile. "Would that be okay with you?"

Tessa frowned. Michael couldn't understand her reluctance. Or did she know he was lying? She didn't exactly have a bunch of options. Tessa apparently reached the same conclusion because she finally nodded.

Michael grinned. "We'll be okay," he whispered, then removed his hand from the mouthpiece. "How soon can you get here?"

"Can you hold up there a little while longer? We got a hit on Masterson's credit card from a Gas and Go. It's actually only a few blocks from Carnegie. But don't worry. He can't possibly know you're there. But just in case, stay hidden and stay quiet. I'm going to check it out, see if the employees can tell me anything useful, and after I'm done there, I'll swing by and pick you two up. I'll meet you at the same place where you get on the bus. But again, just to be safe, stay hidden until you see my car. I'll call you when I get there."

"Sounds like a plan."

"Great. I'll see you as soon as I can."

"Yep." Michael slid his phone into his pocket.

"What are we going to do now?" Tessa asked.

"Sam wants us to wait here." He put his arm around her, drawing her closer.

Michael didn't know if they had been followed or if anybody, friend or enemy, was looking for them. None of that would change what he needed to do. He had made a promise, and he intended to keep it. He had promised to keep Tessa safe. For the time being, the janitor's closet seemed like the only safe place on the planet. He sat on the grimy floor, slouching against a wall. Tessa rested her head on his chest and wrapped her arm around his waist, tucking her hand beneath his armpit. Michael didn't mind it. In fact, he sort of liked it.

Tessa almost seemed at peace. The only signs of distress were her scrunched-up forehead and occasional shiver, which could be from the cold or fear. Michael stroked her hair. She responded by holding him tighter. He liked that, too. He watched her head rise and fall on his chest in time with his own breathing.

"You protected me," she said so softly Michael almost didn't catch it. "Just like you said you would."

"We're not out of trouble yet."

The reality of their situation was hard to face. They couldn't stay in that closet forever. Gently, Michael lifted Tessa's arm from across his chest. He sat up, still holding her, trying to shake out the pins and needles. His back was stiff from lying in the same awkward position with her weight against him. Not that he was complaining.

Like an elderly man stricken with arthritis, Michael slowly rose to his feet. He turned and offered her his hand. He let her hand linger in his a bit after she was already standing, then he let go and put his ear against the closet door. All quiet. He doubted anyone was in the school. Still, he hesitated before opening the door.

"I don't want to go out there," Tessa said. "Not just yet anyway. What will we do? Where will we go?"

"Sam will take care of us." He believed it. He hoped she would, too.

All Tessa's fear once again showed on her face as soon as they stepped out of the closet. She started pacing and chewing on her nails. Her hair was kinked and poofy, her clothes wrinkled. Eyes shimmering, Michael looked at her as if she were a hurt puppy. He felt as if a solid mass had formed in his throat.

He thought of his foster parents. "Greg... Helen." His eyes burned. "It's my fault..."

Tessa wrapped her arms around his waist and squeezed him tightly. "No. It's not your fault."

"They didn't deserve it," he said, fighting back his tears. "I shouldn't have left them. I just ran, and now..."

Tessa looked up at him. "What you did back there took courage. I need you to stay brave for me a little while longer."

Courage? Michael didn't remember courage. He remembered being terrified. Christopher Masterson had entered his home and killed his foster parents. *What did I do? I ran.* "I'm so sorry," he said, no longer able to hold back his tears.

She hugged him again. "You don't need to be sorry." She kissed his cheek. "You're a hero. You attacked Father to save your foster parents... to save *me*. It's more than I ever did." She kissed the corner of his mouth. The warmth of her breath against his cheek caused the hairs on the back of his neck to rise. "No one has ever done anything like that for me before."

Embarrassed, Michael broke away. "Come on," he said, pulling her back toward the classroom where they had broken in. "Sam should be here any minute. She just has to stop by a gas station fir—" He froze. "Wait! Where's the Gas and Go around here?"

She gave him a confused look. "Do you mean the one near the liquor store at the bottom of President Avenue?"

Michael pictured the gas station in his mind. On the side of the building were two large ice bins. Over them hung a giant blue tarp with the word "ICE" printed on it. The lights over the pumps were always so bright at night, and the parking lot looked exactly like the one he had seen in his vision, the one where he had seen Sam violently murdered.

He grabbed Tessa's shoulders. "I have to go. Sam's in trouble."

"What's wrong?"

"Your father set a trap for her. He's waiting for her to show up at that convenience store. I can't explain right now. There's no time. You stay here. Keep calling 9-1-1 until someone connects you with Sam. Tell her not to go to that gas station. Tell her that whatever she does, she can't go there."

He had saved one damsel from distress, only to let another fall victim to his oversight. He scrambled through the window and took off at a sprint. He knew he would have to run faster than he had in his vision. In his vision, Michael had been too late to save her.

CHAPTER 29

THE LAST HALF HOUR HAD been hectic. Sam hadn't slept since she'd let Masterson slip away, and she had four more deaths to chalk up to her mistake. Michael's foster parents were among the dead. Greg Plummer had been gutted like a fish. His entrails flowed from a trench dug into his belly and spiraled on the floor like soft-serve ice cream.

Helen's death had been less gruesome but just as horrifying. Her throat had been slit. A gash severing bone and tendon ran across her hand. She must have tried to grab the blade before it could slice through her carotid artery. Blood was splattered everywhere, even on the untouched roast pork sitting on the dining room table.

Sam had been sent to the Plummers' home when neighbors reported a woman's screams. While Sam was on her way over, a DCF employee who had been unfortunate enough to arrive shortly after the carnage called 9-1-1. One neighbor reported seeing two kids, a boy and a girl, running from the house and down the street. Many more had seen a man matching Masterson's description exit the home after the screaming had stopped. If the eyewitness accounts were accurate, and Sam had no reason to think they weren't, Masterson was headed in the same direction as Michael and Tessa.

When she received Michael's call, Sam was relieved, but she still had a psychopath to catch. Masterson's gas station stop spoke volumes. Experience had taught Sam that such errands were always in preparation for flight. He was probably on his way to Mexico or Canada. Unless someone spotted his vehicle, he would be extremely difficult to find, assuming he was smart, and the trail would go cold. Then, when money or supplies dwindled, Masterson would resurface. That was when law enforcement would catch him.

It's only a matter of time before he screws up. When he does, he'll be coming back to us, barring any outstanding warrants in other states. Tessa said he had killed others. Maybe one of them was in a state that not only has the death penalty but also the balls to enforce it.

Masterson had screwed up, not once but twice, and Sam knew it. He'd given the Fall River Police Department multiple chances to catch him, and each time, Sam and her team had squandered them. Secured in their evidence locker was the very weapon used to murder Gloria Jackson. Jackson's DNA was speckled all over the damn thing. After some slick lawyering had foiled that arrest, Masterson's daughter came through with a tell-all biography of her father's crimes. Again, Sam failed to bring Masterson to justice, losing a fellow officer in the attempt.

Still, Masterson hadn't immediately fled. He dawdled in her city, evidently planning to kill the one person who could finger him for his crimes. She scolded herself for taking her eyes off Tessa and wondered if she had been blinded by her closeness to the case, particularly to Michael. Perhaps the threat of her own death was what had made her sloppy.

A quadruple homicide later, Masterson was still in Fall River. It was as if he were mocking her whole damn department. He had even used his credit card down the street at the Gas and Go, and they had still missed him. Her squad's delay, like the rest of its mistakes, was inexcusable. So many chances had been blown.

We have to get him. She couldn't accept the possibility that her murder suspect had slipped away unseen. Masterson would be only the second killer to get away in her long career. The first, though many years prior, never left Sam's mind. He tormented her thoughts every day—the one who had killed her partner. She didn't like leaving things unresolved. Her cases weren't supposed to go cold.

And the current case had become personal. Masterson had threatened the life of someone Sam held dear. She felt she had to catch the man for her three deceased officers, for Gloria Jackson, for the Plummers, and even for Tessa. But most of all, Sam had to make him pay for what he'd done to Michael. She was the one who had put the boy in a killer's crosshairs, so she had to remove all possibility that Michael could be hurt by Masterson.

Just give me one more chance, you son of a bitch. Sam slammed her fist against the steering wheel. *Give me one more chance, and I promise you, I won't waste it.*

Thoughts of vengeance filled Sam's mind as she pulled into the gas station parking lot. She scanned the lot then double-parked her car along a row of spaces at the edge of the lot running parallel to President Avenue.

Inside the store, she flashed her badge at the clerk. "Detective Reilly, Fall River Police Department. I need you to answer a few questions."

The clerk, a biker type with a gray handlebar mustache and a bandana partly covering thinning wiry hair tied back in a ponytail, leaned over the counter. "Uh…"

She slammed Masterson's picture on the counter. "About fifteen minutes ago, this man was a customer here. What can you tell me about him?"

"I've never seen him before, but my shift only started a minute ago. Francine was working before me."

"Francine?"

"Delaney."

"Is she here?"

"No, she left when I came in."

"Did she work with anyone else?"

"She doesn't usually." The clerk shuffled through some papers he pulled from under the counter. "No one else was supposed to be here at that time, but like I said, I wasn't here. So I can't tell you anything for certain."

"Do you know where Ms. Delaney lives?"

"No."

Sam pointed at the papers. "Her address isn't in there?"

He shook his head. "Nah. These are just the schedules. Her phone number is on here, if you want that." He read off a phone number.

Sam pulled a small notebook and a pen from her jacket pocket. She wrote down the number and Francine's name. A video camera in the corner caught her eye. She pointed at it. "How many of those cameras do you have?"

"Four, but they aren't recording."

"You have surveillance cameras, but you don't turn them on?"

"I'm not even sure they work. The boss says he keeps them for their deterrence factor, whatever that means. We haven't been robbed in over a year, so maybe he's right. Of course, we've had the cameras a lot longer than that."

Sam shook her head. She was getting nowhere. She wasn't even sure if there was anywhere to get to. All appropriate authorities had been alerted to Masterson's apparent desire to relocate. Maybe his capture was out of her hands.

After getting Masterson's purchase information from the register— gas only, paid at the pump—Sam left the store. She had a pair of teens to pick up, and they were probably terrified. She smiled. She was looking forward to seeing Michael alive and safe.

She stepped beneath the high-wattage overhead lights, watching her shadow stretch out before her. Her Camry was parked at the far reaches of the bright mirage of protection. Beyond was an unlit field, and to her left, a dumpster sat in darkness, shielded from the lights by the structure between them.

When did it get so dark? The days were short, cold, and the nights colder, typical of New England winters. The streetlights came on around four o'clock.

As she passed the corner of the building, a chilling wind rattled the blue tarp affixed to the wall. Teeth chattering, she hugged herself tightly as she hurried to the passenger side of her vehicle. After opening the car door, she tossed her pad and pen on the passenger seat. Before doing the same with her cellphone, she decided to check it for messages.

"Shit!" Her phone was off. *I must have powered it down after I talked with Michael.* Sam pressed a button, and the screen lit up. She got behind the wheel and placed the phone on the console.

She grabbed the radio handset and keyed it. "Dispatch, this is Reilly. I'm calling it quits for the remainder of the evening."

"Okay, Detective," the dispatcher replied. "See you in the morning."

"Tell the captain I'll bring the girl in tomorrow so we can record her statement. Keep me posted with any updates on Masterson."

"Roger that."

As she returned the handset, she heard someone shouting. She looked through the windshield and saw someone leaping over a drainage ditch in the vacant lot between the convenience store and President Avenue. He was sprinting toward her, screaming the whole way. Instinctively, she put her hand on her gun as she squinted, trying to see if the person was armed.

Is that... Michael? She smiled when she realized it was. She climbed out of the car and rested her arms on the open door, overwhelmed by strong emotions she usually kept subdued. She didn't care. Michael deserved to know how she felt.

"Behind you!" Michael shouted.

The two words registered at the same moment that she became able to make out the fear on Michael's face. Sam spun and jerked sideways just as a large knife was thrust at her. The blade missed her by mere millimeters. Her shirt sleeve wasn't so lucky. The knife tore through then slammed into the car window, creating a fiberglass spider web.

Masterson! Sam hooked her arm around his and held it immobile against her body. She clamped his arm tightly, preventing a second strike. Thrusting her right hand forward, she hit Masterson at the base of his nose with her palm and continued with the upward momentum. The move, if done with enough power, could have killed him. At the least, it was sure to make his eyes water, temporarily blinding him.

Masterson squealed and staggered backward, tearing his arm free of her grasp. The knife grazed Sam's biceps, drawing blood but causing no serious damage. Masterson frantically rubbed his eyes.

I'll give you something that will make you cry. Sam yanked her pepper spray from her belt and blasted him in the face with a generous dose.

Masterson had held onto the knife, and it made small concentric circles in the air as he tried to regain his vision. He was down, but not out. "You fucking bitch," Masterson growled, blinking furiously.

Sam took the opportunity to draw her gun. "It's not so easy when you pick on someone who can defend herself, is it, Masterson?"

"I am going to kill you for that."

She held her gun in front of her. "Drop the knife, and put your hands on your head." Out of the corner of her eye, she caught sight of Michael. He stood a few feet away, looking frightened and confused. "Stay behind me, Michael."

"I should have told you," Michael said. "Oh God, you're bleeding. How could I not have told you? How could I have assumed everything would be okay?"

Sam didn't know what he was talking about, but somehow, Michael had known to be there. He had just saved her life, and it was up to her to keep them both safe.

"It's okay," she said softly. "Just stay behind me."

"Oh, don't worry," Masterson said. "That little shit's time will come soon enough."

Sam extended her arms a little. "I said drop the knife. Don't make me ask you again."

Masterson straightened and flipped the knife in his hand so that its grip was toward Sam. He raised his other hand, empty, as he squatted. "You wouldn't shoot an unarmed man, would you, Ms. Reilly?" The knife, still in his hand, scraped along the cement.

"Not usually, but for you, I could make an exception. Now, for the last time, drop the weapon."

"I think I'll take my chances." Masterson pivoted and extended his legs, springing into a run.

"Freeze!" She fired a warning shot, but Masterson didn't even slow down.

The distance between them was rapidly increasing. Sam lowered her gun to eye level. She had Masterson in her sight, and she was a damn good shot. All she had to do was squeeze the trigger.

But she hesitated, and Masterson was gone. He disappeared into the woods behind the station. The thought of Michael standing beside her like a wounded puppy made her think twice about shooting the man in the back. She'd spent Michael's whole life trying to teach him right from wrong. Shooting a fleeing suspect in the back was wrong, no matter how much he might have deserved it. She couldn't shatter all she had accomplished with Michael for good old-fashioned revenge. The law was supposed to be better than that. In reality, it might not have been, but Sam never stopped trying to make it so.

She leaned into her car and grabbed the radio. "Dispatch, this is Detective Reilly. Masterson was just spotted at my location. He is on foot and running in an east-to-northeast direction. All available units are to set up a perimeter with a three-mile radius from the Gas and Go. No one gets out of it without first having to answer to one of ours. All shifts should be extended, all roads covered. Call in the whole damn department if you have to, but do not let Masterson escape."

Service pistol still in hand, she turned to go after Masterson. "Michael, will you be okay here?"

"Yes," he said sheepishly. "Go get him."

Sam looked at the boy, and her heart sank. Michael wasn't okay. He was terrified. She felt awful for even considering leaving him there alone, defenseless. What if Masterson doubled back? In her festering desire to bring her suspect down, she had nearly lost sight of the "protect and serve" part of her job. Her first priority was to guard two teenagers who had lost their parents, to get them someplace safe and keep them that way.

She holstered her weapon. "Let's go," she said, gesturing at the car. "We'll pick up Tessa and get you guys something to eat. You two must be starving."

Smiling, Michael hopped into the passenger seat. Sam smiled back at him, feeling as though the weight of the world had dropped from her shoulders. Maybe there was more to life than just being a cop.

CHAPTER 30

I *CAN'T STAY HERE. THE COPS* *are everywhere, and they want my head.* *They'll be here any second.*

Christopher's heart was racing. It wasn't the first time he had to disappear, but it was the first time he was cutting it so close. He wondered if he should stick around until his good work was done right. Plenty of people in Fall River needed to be taught lessons, but he couldn't fix the city from the inside of a prison cell. The last time, long before he met Tessa's whore of a mother, he had fled before the bodies could turn cold.

He laid the knife on the kitchen counter and hurried down the hallway to his bedroom. The police had ransacked the place, and he had to hurdle furniture to get there. Each room was in disorder. Not one cabinet, closet, or drawer had been spared. His left eye twitched as he assessed the unruliness of his room, the chaos throwing his mind into disorder. *Nothing is in its place.*

His mattress had been slashed open. The contents of his dresser were strewn all over the floor. He picked up a white tube sock, then another, smoothed them out, and folded them together. The top drawer of his dresser, where he stored his socks and underwear, was pulled out and tilted off its track. Christopher released a breath he hadn't realized he'd been holding as he placed the neatly folded pair of socks against the drawer's back wall.

He crouched to pick up another sock then searched for its mate.

His breaths came shorter. *Ican'tIcan'tIcan't*, he chanted in his mind, then he howled, whipping the sock at the wall. He slammed a palm into his forehead, trying to silence the sound of his own thoughts. Resisting the urge to tidy up the room made him sweat. It put him on edge. He couldn't think straight.

He punched the open drawer hard enough to split the skin over his knuckles. His eye started to twitch faster, until he wanted to pluck out the eyeball. His skin itched as though ants were biting him everywhere. Christopher clawed at his cheeks, his nails digging deep, leaving gashes. He started throwing things at random, adding to the disarray.

Just when he thought he wouldn't be able to take it anymore, not without screaming and breaking, a sense of peace came over him. The warring factions inside his brain called a truce. *The next place will be perfect. A home with rules, enforced without exception. If one wants perfection, he must demand it.*

Christopher looked around his bedroom and chuckled. His laughter grew as he walked back out into the hallway. In the living room, chairs were overturned, a few broken. Stuffing had been ripped out of the pillows and sofa cushions. Pink insulation hung from the opening to the attic, and the hatch door had been removed. The walls, however, remained intact.

They didn't see it. He gnashed his teeth in a feral grin, no longer seeing any reason to tame the predator in him. *Why should they have?* He had plastered the hole as soon as he and Tessa had moved into that house, and he had done the job well. He stared at the wall, admiring his handiwork.

Behind the refrigerator, which was leaning against the counter, the kitchen wallpaper was pressed flat. No bumps or discoloration could be seen through its gray hue. His emergency stash was right where it should have been, right where he needed it to be when he needed it most.

Wasting no more time, Christopher kicked a gaping hole in the wall. He reached into darkness, reaching blindly inside the hole until he felt the package. He withdrew the ziplock bag, which held a hefty wad of cash, approximately a hundred thousand dollars, his rainy-day money. The police presence in his neighborhood, all searching for him, told him it was pouring.

Christopher would need a big chunk of the money to obtain a new identity. The rest, he would need to start over. He knew the drill. After all, he hadn't been born Christopher Masterson. *I never really liked the name anyway.*

Sirens blared nearby. They were getting closer. *Leave it to the police to announce their approach.* Christopher shrugged. *Who cares? They'll be too late, as always.*

He jammed the cash into his jacket pockets, distributing it evenly. With his hands on his hips, Christopher took one final look at his home. *This castle has fallen into ruin. What is a man without his castle? It's time to leave this one behind. A new domicile awaits, and I will rule it with a just and steady hand.*

He headed to the kitchen to retrieve his knife, planning to escape out the back door and into the darkness. The cloak of night, his silent ally, would keep him hidden. It always had. He walked over to the counter, but his knife wasn't there.

"Hello, Father."

Christopher was startled, but only for that split second before he recognized the voice. *Tessa.* He didn't turn to face her right away. He had to hide his excitement first. His daughter, a horse that would not be broken and would thus have to be put down, had gift-wrapped and hand-delivered herself right to him. Her presence was nothing short of miraculous, as if God himself demanded Christopher's brand of justice. He couldn't have hoped for more perfect timing, the opportunity to give her a proper send-off—or himself one, anyway. His only regret was that he would have to do her quickly.

When he spun around to greet her, he was far more surprised than he'd been at hearing her voice. Tessa stood in the kitchen doorway as naked as the day she was born. Her skin glowed white under the moonlight shining in through the living room window. Goose bumps covered her skin. Her expression was cool, but something sparkled behind her eyes, something wild.

But the most shocking thing was that Tessa was holding *his* knife.

"Tessa?" Christopher asked in that wholesome-family-sitcom-dad's voice he had learned from imitating Andy Griffith and Mike Brady.

Tessa didn't scare him. She was nothing but a little whore with a big knife. Little whores needed to be cleansed, but Christopher wanted only to throttle her, to show her how to use the weapon she flaunted before him. Still, he recognized the foolhardiness inherent in a headlong charge. Instead, he kept up appearances, waiting for an opening.

"What are you doing here? Where are your clothes?"

"I took them off so I wouldn't get blood on them." Her voice was low, almost a whisper, but her words came out with a sureness Christopher hadn't heard in them before. "Don't worry, though. I folded them neatly and stacked them on the chair."

She dares to threaten me! The notion sent Christopher into a violent rage. The blaring of the sirens faded into the background, drowned out by the angry heartbeat thumping in his ears. "Give me back my knife, you little cunt." He decided he would stick it in her, in the same place all those boys from school were sticking their tiny little cocks, the same place he might have stuck his own one day if she earned her place beside him. "You need to learn respect."

"I hate you," Tessa said flatly.

He took a step toward her. "Someone needs to remember her place. Your mother was the same way once, until I broke her. I'm going to break you, too, Tessa. I'm going to break you, or I'm going to put you down."

She can't talk to me like that and get away with it. She'll bleed first, then the real fun will begin. He swung a backhand at Tessa's cheek, meaning to slap the teeth from her mouth. Christopher would make sure she never spoke another errant word toward him, even if it meant ripping out her tongue.

But his hand only swooshed through the air. His momentum sent him staggering sideways. He maintained his balance briefly, just long enough to see Tessa's hand retreating from his body, pulling a bloodied blade back with it.

"You little bitch!" Christopher couldn't believe the sniveling brat had actually stabbed him. *Him!* Her *father.* He hadn't even felt the knife go in, but he did feel pain and rage and hate so strong, it needed release. His mind screamed at him to kill her. He had to kill her. She was everything that was wrong with the world. No respect. No gratitude. Not worthy of existence. How dare she stab her own father?

How fucking dare she! He lurched forward to grab her with his right hand, keeping his left on his wound. His movements were too slow and clumsy. Tessa ducked under his arm. She stabbed him again, a little higher on his abdomen.

He wheezed with pain. The fresh wound gurgled. When he coughed, blood sputtered from his lips. Still, he stepped forward, feeling drunk. Feeling afraid.

His life fluid gushed from his stomach. He stopped moving. Tessa stepped back, staring at him. Crimson speckled her white skin. In the dark, it looked as though she had been behind a tire that kicked up mud.

Christopher felt woozy. He wanted to sit down. A chair stood a few feet away. He reached for it, almost fell forward, then did fall onto his butt when he overcompensated. He rested his upper body on one elbow.

Tessa stood over him. She appeared to be smiling. Christopher couldn't believe it. She had always been as he had molded her to be: submissive. He made the rules. She had no right to break them. It was never supposed to be his blood dripping from the blade he'd used to kill so many others.

"What have you done?" Christopher no longer felt powerful or in control. Death had always danced around him, never asking him to be its partner. Yet there it was, the reaper's skeletal face sharing time with Tessa's fleshy one. In her eyes, he saw vengeance and despair. He saw death, and he knew it was his own.

His bowels let go. *What is this suffocating feeling? Is this what it means to be afraid?*

The sparkle behind Tessa's eyes moved to their forefront. Christopher had seen that sparkle many times before, every time he looked into a mirror during a kill and for a long time afterward.

Tessa gripped the knife as if she meant to strike again.

"Tessa, honey, haven't I always taken care of you? Haven't I always been there to provide for you?"

Her face was haunting, demonic. Christopher didn't know what to say to make her fear him again or at least to make her stop.

Tessa shrieked and jumped on top of him, straddling his waist. She raised the knife above her head and plunged it into his chest. She raised the knife again and again and again. He felt a sharp pain each time it entered him, followed by a searing wet heat.

With the fifth stab, he heard a crack, no doubt his rib fracturing. By the eighth, the sirens were blaring outside. He reached out a hand to the police as they entered the kitchen, pleading silently for help. Light from the car headlights shone through the windows, cascading around him as if Heaven had opened its Pearly Gates.

But instead of seeing God's benevolent face, he saw the scornful faces of men and women in blue, brothers and sisters of the officers he had killed. Damning him.

The pain made him delirious. "Please," he muttered, beginning to lose consciousness.

The eleventh strike, Christopher barely felt. His body was numbing to the world. His vision began to fade. The light withdrew. Darkness, lonely and scary, began to creep in around his peripheral vision. The twelfth strike was little more than a thump followed by a gentle tugging.

A familiar woman wrapped Tessa in a gray overcoat and pulled her away. The knife fell from her hand and bounced on the floor next to his body.

Christopher's lungs no longer wanted to breathe. His mind dulled, remembering only panic as it faded into the darkness. As consciousness left him, he thought about the knife and hoped someone would return it to the block.

CHAPTER 31

One month later.

MICHAEL CHEWED HIS NAILS. HE was worried about Tessa. Life had been tough for her, and he wondered when—*if*—that would ever change. She didn't deserve any of it. Her father had made her do it. He'd made her do all of it.

The Fall River Judicial Complex was a resolute, uncompromising structure with lots of sharp corners and hard marble. Michael found no comfort on the wooden bench where he sat outside Courtroom 4, Judge Jeremiah Killoran's session. Sam had told him that Judge Killoran was tough but smart and that she trusted him to do what was fair for Tessa.

When Sam came out of the courtroom, she looked as though her shoulders were weighing down her small frame. But she managed a smile as she approached.

For the first time, he allowed himself to hope for good news. "What's going to happen to her?" It was the only question he wanted answered, and he gave Sam no chance to waste time with less important details.

"The DA has offered a sweet deal, given Tessa's extraordinary circumstances and all the help she's given us in closing some unsolved cases. Remember that home invasion a few months back?"

Michael scratched his head. He nodded because he felt he was supposed to.

"That was him. Tessa says he made her wear a Girl Scout uniform, and... well, never mind that. Tessa's given us half a dozen fact patterns that follow unsolved murders or suspicious accidents tracing all the way back to Denver. And that's just the ones we've been able to pair. Tessa says there are more, including her own mother."

Michael looked away. The idea of one parent killing another made him want to curl up in a corner, though he wasn't sure why.

"Anyway," Sam said, letting out her breath, "the DA says that if Tessa agrees to be remanded to the correctional institution in Framingham for psychological evaluation and treatment, she can be released as soon as they determine that she's no longer a danger to society. No charges will be brought against her."

"How long will that be? Forever? Who'll make sure they're not just keeping her in there for no reason?"

"Michael, it's the best chance she's got. It won't be easy. If all goes well, she'll be out in six months. She just has to show that she won't hurt anyone."

"What then? Where will she go when she gets out?"

"Let's not worry about that just yet. We'll cross that bridge when we get to it. I promise you, I'll be looking out for her best interests every step of the way."

"But—"

"I've been looking out for yours for how many years now?" She sat on the bench beside him. She leaned closer, and for a moment, he thought she might hug him, but she only patted his knee. "It'll all work out. You'll see."

Michael wasn't satisfied with Sam's explanation. There were too many question marks, too many subjective conditions parting Tessa from the freedom she deserved. Yes, she had killed someone, but the world was a better place for it. In killing one, how many others had she spared from her father's evil?

"Is there any way to get her out now? Maybe she could see doctors on the weekends or something."

"I've seen a lot of deals go down in my day, so believe me when I say that Tessa is getting the best deal she can."

"So, basically, she's going to a prison."

"Well, yes, but she'll be in a medium-security ward specifically designed for prisoners with mental health conditions. It's more like a hospital with guards."

"So a prison where they'll keep her drugged all the time?"

"It's for the best. The things she's seen... the things she was forced to do, they won't be easy for her to live with. She's fortunate to have someone like you standing beside her while she heals."

"More like behind her. I'm way back in the peanut gallery. No one listens to me. I'm just a kid."

Fortunately, they *had* listened to Sam. With Masterson's death and his guilt proven far beyond any doubt, Sam's lingering work issues seemed to have been swept under the rug. Michael knew she was already on some new case. He just hoped she would be careful. If the whole ordeal had taught him anything, it was that he didn't ever want to lose her.

Sam didn't like to talk about it, how she had stuck her neck out for them. But Michael wasn't blind. He had seen how she had fought for Tessa, despite her obvious reservations. In the month he'd been with her, Sam had attended every hearing, met with attorneys on both sides of the case, and advocated for Tessa's release into her custody.

"Thank you, Sam... for everything you've done."

Sam smiled and looked away. So did Michael. All that touchy-feely stuff made them both uncomfortable. When he looked back at her, he saw a reddish hue coloring her cheeks.

"Don't mention it," she said.

"Will I be able to visit her?"

"I'll see what I can do. Let's give her some time to settle in first, okay? But, Michael, when you see her, she may not be the same."

"I know."

"The years of abuse she suffered at the hands of that man..." She shook her head. "Masterson wasn't even her biological father, you know? She should never even have been with him."

"I know." Michael had heard it all at the hearings, and it made him angry. The truth brought out a desire for revenge, but Tessa had already taken that, leaving him without an outlet. It turned his stomach.

"Are you ready to go?" Sam asked.

"Sure." Michael stood. He welcomed an escape from the courthouse. He only wished that Tessa would be walking out of there with them.

———————————

Two months later, Michael was granted permission to see Tessa. Her doctors said that she had progressed in her treatment and was allowed visitors at certain prescheduled hours. So far, Michael had been the only one to sign up. He doubted anyone else ever would, since she had no family, so he vowed to visit as often as he could. Sam had done all the paperwork and had signed up to be Michael's chaperone.

He walked into the facility, past several armed guards, and emptied his pockets before going through the metal detectors. After that, he was buzzed through several doors before being led into a recreation room. Michael started having second thoughts. What if Tessa didn't want to see him? Maybe she didn't want to be reminded of the world outside her walls. Maybe she just wanted to be left alone.

But the time to back out had long passed. Willingly or not, Tessa was on her way to see him. Michael tried to prepare for the awkward greeting. Somehow, "hello" didn't seem to cover it.

There was no furniture in the room, just some stained cushions scattered around the floor. Michael grabbed one and leaned it next to the wall then sat on the floor in front of it, facing the door. Sam did the same next to him. The room looked as though it had been childproofed. Besides the walls and floor, nothing in it threatened injury. Some board games were piled in a corner. Magazines and paperbacks filled another. Cartoons played on a television mounted near the ceiling, out of reach. The only other sound came from air blowing through a small heating vent.

Michael picked up a magazine, *Outdoor World*, and thumbed through it, not really interested. He found the publication to be a cruel choice for a place whose inhabitants might never get to experience the outdoors again, except for the occasional walk in the facility's concrete and barbed wire fenced-in garden.

Sam somehow looked proper and powerful while sitting cross-legged on a cushion. She closed her eyes and rested her head against the wall, apparently less wound-up than Michael was. Michael tensed when the door buzzed then opened.

Tessa walked in with a large orderly. Once the door was closed, the orderly moved to a corner and kind of slouched against the wall, but Michael could tell the guy was paying close attention.

Tessa had always been thin, but after three months of incarceration, she seemed to have aged three years. Her face was drawn and pale, with lines that hadn't been there the last time he'd seen her. Her hands shook a lot. Michael was pretty sure she was taking some heavy-duty medication. Still, her hair was neatly brushed, and her clothes looked clean.

She gave him a smile that accentuated her dimples. With that, she looked like Tessa again, and he was really glad to see her.

"Hi," she whispered, holding her hands behind her as she swung her shoulders back and forth.

Michael stood and went over to her. He didn't know what to say. He mouthed the word "hi," and even that was an effort.

Summoning his courage, Michael threw his arms around her. He felt as though he might cry, but he kept his tears inside. Light as feathers, Tessa's arms draped over his shoulders. She leaned in to him, nuzzling her forehead into the curve of his neck.

Feelings for Tessa surged through Michael, almost swallowing him in raw emotion. Picking through his thoughts, trying to make sense of them, Michael realized that no matter what, he didn't want to let go of her. So he didn't. He would have held on to Tessa as long as he could if she would let him, until staff came and tore them apart.

It wasn't fair. None of it. Only God knew what they were doing to Tessa in that awful dungeon. She shouldn't have been there. She should have been with Michael. Tessa deserved a normal life, so much more than all the other kids their age who had done nothing to earn theirs. *Will she ever have one?*

Slower than a crawl, Tessa's nose slid up the side of his neck toward his ear. Her lips, soft as pillows, caressed his cheek. Michael found her touch exciting. He would give anything to keep that sensation going.

But it lasted only a moment more. Michael's eyelids began to flutter. His thoughts scattered like cockroaches under a light. Soon, they were all gone. Something new was coming.

Sam had been trying to give Michael his privacy, but when she saw Tessa moving closer to him, she stood guard. When Michael fell, she was there to catch him.

The orderly held Tessa back.

"It's okay," Sam said. "It wasn't her. He has fainting spells." She caught Tessa staring at her, and when she made eye contact, Tessa gave a slight but knowing nod. She kneeled down beside Michael and cradled his head in her arms.

A few minutes later, Michael returned to reality. He gazed up at Tessa, apprehensive at first, then donning a smile so mixed that Sam couldn't tell if it was genuine or not. She checked his pulse and could feel his heart racing, dangerously fast. His breath came out in short wheezes, as if he had held it too long underwater.

"A vision?" Sam asked from her spot against the wall. Michael nodded.

"My future?" Tessa asked. She frowned and buried her head. "I don't want to know."

Michael sat up and shuffled beside her. He put his arm around her and pulled her close. "It's okay," he said, smiling through tears. "Everything's going to be okay. It will be hard, at first, but eventually your life will be everything you want it to be. You'll see."

Tessa stared into his eyes as though she were looking for signs of deceit. Sam stared, too, but if Michael was bluffing, he had learned to fool even her... and apparently Tessa, too. Her frown disappeared. Her face shone a little brighter. Some of those extra lines, wrought by hardship, seemed less severe. As if by a will of their own, her lips found his.

Sam looked away, smiling wide herself. Maybe Michael was exactly where he needed to be.

Michael and Tessa spent the entire visitation period talking and being together, sometimes even sharing a laugh. Sam didn't even think she or the orderly existed in their eyes. Any barriers between them—any awkward teenage construct, societal restraint, emotional stereotype—crumbled, an awkward psychic and a psychologically damaged killer shooting the shit as if they weren't in a mental hospital but their own private safe haven. When it was time to leave, they separated reluctantly, each being led from the room by their chaperone with only partly complying feet. As soon as Michael exited the prison, he asked when he could visit again.

On the drive home, Sam couldn't keep her curiosity bundled any longer. "Is that what you really saw?" she asked. "Will her life truly turn out fine?"

Michael shook his head. His eyes filled with tears and his nose ran. "No. What I saw... it was horrible. But that's because Tessa already felt like her life was over. I have to believe that. When we got to the prison today, she had no hope left. What I saw was the effects of a life without hope, stuck in that institution. It would end with violence and ugliness and... and death."

Michael paused, letting out a deep breath. "But you and I both know that what I see can be changed. Your life is proof enough of that. So, I thought that maybe, with the hope I gave her today and will continue to give her for as long as she'll let me, Tessa will make her own future into a better, happier one."

Sam was never one for optimism, but she smiled warmly just the same. Maybe Michael was being naive, but she could tell he had to try. He wouldn't give up on Tessa. He wouldn't let her give up on herself. *I only hope it's you lifting her up and not her dragging you down.*

The truth was that Sam didn't know what the future held any more than he did. Michael had caught a glimpse of a possibility only. Make an adjustment here or a modification there, and a whole new timeline could fall into place. After all, he had saved her life. That had to count for something.

The future was what they chose to make of it. Just like life. She wondered if she still had time to make something else of hers.

ACKNOWLEDGMENTS

I would like to thank Angela McRae and the Red Adept Publishing team for their knowledge, skill, and patience with respect to editing and publishing this novel.

I would also like to thank Emma Adams for her editorial contributions pre-submission for publication, Tarrah Parkman for her wealth of knowledge with respect to foster care and social services, Abigail Grace, my family and friends, and all of my wonderful readers, many of whom I've been blessed to have met via Facebook, Twitter, Goodreads, or through my website, for their continued support.

ABOUT THE AUTHOR

In his head, Jason Parent lives in many places, but in the real world, he calls Southeastern Massachusetts his home. The region offers an abundance of settings for his writing and many wonderful places in which to write them. He currently resides with his cuddly corgi, Calypso.

In a prior life, Jason spent most of his time in front of a judge... as a civil litigator. When he tired of Latin phrases no one knew how to pronounce and explaining to people that real lawsuits are not started, tried, and finalized within the 60-minute time-frame they see on TV, he traded in his cheap suits for flip-flops and designer stubble. The flops got repossessed the next day, and he's back in the legal field... sorta. But that's another story.

When he's not working, Jason likes to kayak, catch a movie, travel any place that will let him enter, and play just about any sport (except for the one with that ball tied to the pole thing where you basically just whack the ball until it twists in on knot or takes somebody's head off). And read and write, of course. He does that too sometimes.

CPSIA information can be obtained
at www.ICGtesting.com
Printed in the USA
LVHW032315210821
695820LV00010B/738